MW00607444

About Genesis
An Easy-to-read Commentary on the whole of Genesis
Volume 1
Paul F Taylor, BSc MEd

Published by:
J6D Publications
PO Box 629
Castle Rock, WA 98611
USA

ISBN (printed): 978-1-7337363-3-6
ISBN (ebook): 978-1-7337363-4-3

Printed by Amazon KDP.

Acknowledgments

Many thanks to those who have encourage me, and continue to encourage me, to keep going with this project. It is easy to lose focus on such a big project, but many of you keep me sane!

Thank you to the Board and volunteers at the Mount St Helens Creation Center, without whom I would not have this platform for sharing the truth about God's word.

Special thanks are due to my excellent editorial volunteers, who worked hard to correct my spelling and grammatical errors. They are Chris Bishop, Cris Edens, Tim Constable, Jamie Keipert, and Tom Brown.

Finally, the most special thanks must go to my wife, and fellow believer, Geri. Thank you, Geri, for constantly praying for me and this ministry.

Any errors which still remain are, of course, entirely my fault. It is my prayer that this work will bring glory to God's Name, and help many people to trust in the inerrancy, authority, infallibility, and sufficiency of the Bible.

About the Author

Paul Taylor is the Director of the Mount St Helens Creation Center. He has a long experience in education, having spent nearly 20 years in government schools in the UK teaching science and technology. He has also designed and taught web development courses in the UK. Paul is married to Geri, and they have five children and four grandchildren between them.

Contents

Preface to Volume I

It was in December 2018 that I finally started to type some words, at the very beginning of this book project. This is by far the biggest such project that I have undertaken. Previous books that I have written have contained about 45,000 words. When the word count for this book got to 100,000, I realized that this had to be a multi-volume work.

Back in 2003, I wrote and published my first book, *Just Six Days*. This was a short easy-to-read commentary on Genesis chapters 1 - 11. The book was republished in 2007 by Master Books, under the title *The Six Days of Genesis*. Creationists often feel that they have nothing to say after chapter 11 - that is where their topic ends! One of the unintended consequences of stopping at the end of chapter 11 is that the impression is given that Genesis is really two books. After all, many theistic evolutionists think that real history begins in chapter 12, with the account of Abraham; everything that preceded is just allegory.

Yet my own experience of creation literature was different. I became a Christian in 1977, at the age of 15. I came across creationists at the age of 17, and have been writing and speaking on the subject ever since. So, for my 18th birthday in August 1979, my older sister

Janet bought me a copy of *The Genesis Record* by Henry Morris. This helped to ground my creationist thinking in Scripture, and I read the large book from cover to cover. *The Genesis Record* is a commentary on the whole book of Genesis, and was published in 1976. So it was a comparatively new book at the time. It is a source of great surprise to me that it remains, even today, the most recent easy-to-read commentary on the whole of Genesis, published by a creationist - though there have been several commentaries on the first 11 chapters.

The theistic evolutionists have been more productive, however. Easy-to-read commentaries by such writers as John Walton, Tremper Longman, and Bruce Waltke have become the mainstay of university theology departments and Bible seminaries. Young pastors emerge from such dark places, with a warped and damaged view of the book of Genesis, having been assured that they now have the "conservative evangelical" view, not realising that they have been taught to undermine the truthfulness of Genesis.

It is time for a new commentary on the whole of Genesis. This is my contribution, though, given that there are at least three easy-to-read evolutionary commentaries, if any other creation writers wish to publish another commentary, the field is still wide. Genesis has to be understood as a whole. Genesis 12, for example, depends on the first 11 chapters. I have frequently given a talk about Abraham, from

Genesis 12, showing that we cannot understand his life without accepting the truthfulness of the first 11 chapters.

I think it is likely that this commentary will run to three volumes. Therefore, I wanted to get the first volume published a soon as I could - though, as I have explained, even this first volume has been over a year in the writing. Also, I did not want to split the work at the traditional point, at the end of chapter 11. For that reason, I have chosen to end this volume with the immediate aftermath of the Flood. That means that the material on the Table of Nations (Genesis 10) will form a useful introduction to Volume II. After I have published the separate volumes, one at a time, I intend, DV, to leave a decent period of time to reflect on the volumes, and then will, perhaps, attempt to combine them in one larger volume. But I will have more to say about that in the preface to volume II.

It only remains for me, for the moment, to thank you for buying this volume. I hope it blesses you, and aids you to understand the unity of the Bible's first book, and its foundational nature for all the rest of Scripture.

Paul Taylor

January 2020.

Genesis 1 Part 1 – Approaching Genesis

Bereshit (בראשית)

What are your thoughts, as you open the book of Genesis, and start reading? There are many different ways to read Genesis—though, I would argue that only one actually does justice to the text.

The truth is that the narrative in Genesis is far outside the experience of 21st Century human beings. In our case, we want to understand the text as best we can in a modern, or perhaps post-modern, context—but the text itself will not allow us to do so. Yet, many people do not want to read Genesis, as if it says what it says.

As I will show in these pages, Genesis clearly reports that God created everything in six literal 24-hour periods, followed by one literal 24-hour period of rest. Moreover, it can be calculated from the pages of the Bible that this creation week occurred just over 6,000 years ago. Both these biblical facts are considered contrary to prevailing worldviews, however. Therefore, rather than adjust their worldview to what the Bible says, it is common for many people to re-interpret Genesis, in the light of the prevailing worldview.

Evolutionary Worldview

The prevailing worldview is something that we can call an evolutionary worldview. For convenience, we are going to call it the Evolutionary Worldview. Sometimes, to be even more brief, we will refer to it simply as Evolution.

There will be those who will point out that the word evolution means "change". In the broader meaning of the word, I could indeed say that the creation ministry, which I lead, has evolved over time. This is true, but it is not the standard way of understanding the term today. There will be others who will argue that the term evolution specifically refers to biological processes. However, there are related supposed processes in astronomy (or rather cosmology) and in geology. These can also be placed under the heading of evolution, in the sense that they all attempt to describe how things have got to where they are today, without reference to the creative power of God.

In this book, therefore, our use of the term Evolutionary Worldview is to distinguish a God-free view of origins from a specifically biblical point of view. We will explain how this works out in practice during the course of the book.

Biblical Worldview

The alternative to the above is to hold a specifically Biblical Worldview. This is a worldview in conformity with the words of

Scripture. According to the principles of exegesis and hermeneutics, we will read Genesis as a work of historical narrative, and expect to understand it exactly as it is written.

We find the Bible to be the Word of God—authoritative, sufficient, complete, and inerrant. Therefore, we take the Bible at face value. The Bible states that God created not only the world but the entire universe, physical and spiritual, in just six days and rested on the seventh. I accept these days to be literal 24-hour periods of time. I accept few, if any, gaps in the genealogies, and certainly none in the so-called chrono-genealogies of Genesis 5 and 11. The Bible gives us a timescale for the age of the Earth of a little over 6,000 years.

There are others who own the name of creationist who stretch out this timescale considerably. Some of their ideas will be tackled at the relevant points in this book. For other arguments, I will refer you to other books. Such ideas would include the so-called Old Earth Creationists, who would define each creation day as a long era of time. Some such people would refer to their Day Age Theory, or the idea of Progressive Creation. This latter accepts Cosmological Evolution (i.e. the Big Bang) and Geological Evolution, but maintains that God created different life forms progressively during this long timescale[1]. Still others (the Gap Theory) have suggested a long era of

1 For a refutation of Progressive Creation, see Sarfati, J. (2nd Edition, 2011), *Refuting Compromise*, (Powder Springs, GA: Creation Book Publishers)

time to be inserted into the early part of Genesis. Most such Gap Theorists have their gap between Genesis 1:1 and 1:2, though others have put it between 1:2 and 1:3, while still others have the gap prior to Genesis 1:1.[2]

A much more complicated way of re-interpreting Genesis has arisen among those who would refer to themselves as conservative evangelicals. This group, represented by such theologians as Tim Keller, NT Wright, or Peter Enns, maintain that they believe Genesis to be completely true, but that it doesn't mean what we think it means. They maintain that Genesis is an example of Ancient Near East (ANE) mythology; a polemic against paganism. NT Wright goes so far as to suggest that those of us who accept the six literal 24-hour days are "not reading the text properly". There are a number of names given to the way that these theologians interpret Genesis. Some refer to it as BioLogos, some as theistic evolution, and some as the Framework Hypothesis. There are slight differences between each of these positions, but they are all basically attempting to weld a conservative view of Genesis with an acceptance of evolution[3].

There are others who define themselves as Young Earth Creationists. Such people would suggest that there is scientific evidence, correctly

2 For a refutation of the Gap Theory, see Fields, W. (2005), *Unformed and Unfilled*, (Green Forest, AR: Master Books)

3 For a refutation of these positions, see Gentry, K.L. (2016), *As It Is Written*, (Green Forest, AR: Master Books)

interpreted, that gives an age for the Earth in thousands, rather than billions. Many of these people require an age for the Earth of 10,000 years or less, though there are other Young Earth Creationists, whose model stretches out the age to 30,000 years. I have even heard one such creationist accepting an age of a million years for the Earth.

The previous paragraph underlines a problem within today's creationist community. These ages for the Earth, adopted by Young Earth Creationists, are derived from interpretation of scientific evidence. But, as I shall show, analysis of the biblical text gives an age for the Earth of just over 6,000 years, and certainly less than 7,000 years. So the ages used by many Young Earth Creationists are not biblically derived, though they maintain that they are consistent with a biblical timescale. It is their source of derivation which is at fault, aptly illustrated by their name. If they believe in a Young Earth, what do they mean? "Young" compared to what? The Earth is, in fact, very, very old, according to the Bible. It is ancient. It is over 6,000 years old, which is very old. 6,000 years can only be considered "young", if compared to the deep-time mythology of the evolutionists. We should not define ourselves, by comparison to an evolutionary view. As Christians, we should be starting with two fundamental presuppositions: that God exists, and that the Bible is true. Therefore, our dating is derived from the Bible, and the scientific evidence is shown to be consistent with that, rather than deriving an age from science, and requiring the Bible to be consistent with the age given. For this reason, I am not wont to call myself a Young Earth Creationist. I prefer the term Biblical Creationist.

This commentary will take a Presuppositional approach to Genesis, and will derive its information first and foremost from Scripture itself. This does not mean that science will be ignored. Far from it, but we shall see that the science is led by the biblical exposition, and not the other way around.

Genesis 1 Part 2 – In the Beginning, God

Before the Beginning

If there was a beginning, then what was before that beginning? This might seem an odd sort of question to ask, but it is important, because the Bible speaks of an eternity.

Miriam-Webster defines *eternity* as being infinite time. There are two ways to consider eternity. The first is to consider a period of time with a beginning, but no end. This sort of eternity would apply to humanity. Our acceptance of the biblical teaching of the eternity of the soul, and the New Heaven and New Earth to come, gives us a future eternity to look forward to, yet we had a beginning in time past.

The second way to consider eternity is that way which pertains to God alone. He will not only exist into eternity future, but has always existed from eternity past. Psalm 90:2 states:

> Before the mountains were brought forth, or ever you had formed the earth and the world, from everlasting to everlasting you are God. (Psalm 90:2)

The phrase "from everlasting to everlasting" is used a number of times in Scripture about God, and about the things that He does. This means, therefore, that God was in existence before He created the world, and, indeed, has always been in existence. Not only that, but the entire Trinity was in existence, one God, three persons, from eternity past. We know this because of what is said about the divinity of both Jesus and the Holy Spirit. For example, the beginning of John's Gospel makes clear that:

> In the beginning was the Word, and the Word was with God, and the Word was God. He was in the beginning with God. All things were made through him, and without him was not anything made that was made. (John 1:1-3)

In the Greek, the phrase used for "In the beginning" is *en* archē (εν αρχη). This same phrase is used in Genesis 1:1 in the Septuagint—the Greek translation of the Old Testament.[1] Jesus, the Word, was already in existence at the Creation, and it was He, as the Second Person of the Trinity, who was responsible for that Creation. Therefore, He must have been in existence before Creation, in order to do the creating. The Spirit also was present immediately in the creation, hovering over the waters (Genesis 1:2). The implication is that He,

1 The Old Testament was written in Hebrew (with a couple of sections in Aramaic). The Septuagint is a Greek translation of the Old Testament, probably dating back to the Second Century BC, though parts of it may have been translated even earlier. Citation: Encyclopædia Britannica, < https://www.britannica.com/topic/Septuagint >

also, was present before the creation. In any case, the concept of the Trinity is an essential aspect of the nature of God, so the God who pre-existed from all eternity must have been present as Trinity throughout all eternity.

Moreover, the Bible even talks about certain things that happened before the creation. For example, in John 17:24, Jesus, speaking to the Father, states that the Father loved him "before the foundation of the world". In Ephesians 1:4, we finds that we, also, were chosen before the foundation of the world, while the death of Jesus was also decided upon before Creation (1 Peter 1:20).

Nevertheless, the phrase "In the beginning" suggests that time itself, as we understand it, began when God created the universe. Time is a *thing*. We know that it is inextricably linked with space. So, when God created space, he also created matter and time. So how can refer to time before time?

Schaeffer wrote about this, in his book *Genesis in Space and Time*. He suggested using the word *sequence* to describe the ordering of "events" before creation. Even the word "events" is not a good word to describe what we mean, but it will have to do. Schaeffer describes it thus:

> When we read "in the beginning God created the heavens and the earth" we are not left with something hung in a

> vacuum: something existed before creation and that something was personal and not static; the Father loved the Son; there was a plan; there was communication; and promises were made prior to the creation of the heavens and the earth.[2]

In the Beginning, God...

The first three words in our English Bibles are a translation of just one word in Hebrew – *bereshit* (בְּרֵאשִׁית). The major part of this word – *reshit* – is used without an article, in what is known as an absolute sense; in other words, as a clause, it does not depend on what follows, but what follows depends on it. For that reason, the best interpretation of the phrase is that it refers to the absolute beginning of everything, and that there was no period of time before this beginning.[3]

Genesis begins with the four powerful words, "In the beginning, God...". These four words tells us that:

- God is central to everything
- God was before everything
- Everything had a beginning

2 Schaeffer, F. (1982), *Genesis in Space and Time*, in *The Complete Works of Francis Schaeffer, Volume 2*, (Westchester, IL: Crossway), pp 9-10

3 Phelan, M.W,J. (2005), *The Genesis Gap Theory*, (Waterlooville, UK: Twoedged Sword Publications), p40.

- God was there before that beginning
- God is the key subject matter of the universe

To take just the third of these bullet points for a moment, it should be noted that many modern apologists reverse the logical sequence. They would use this third bullet to argue for the existence of God. Their syllogism is as follows:

Premise 1: Everything that has a beginning has a cause

Premise 2: The universe had a beginning

Conclusion: The universe had a cause.

They then proceed to suggest that the cause of the universe was God. In fact, some even go so far as to suggest that the cause of the universe is a god, without necessarily being the God of the Bible. But Genesis does not work that way around. Genesis is not a high school essay, where a student places all the arguments for and against the existence of God, before giving their considered opinion. Instead, Genesis assumes the existence of God. That is our presupposition. I have written about presuppositional apologetics at length elsewhere.[4] In my book, *Only Believe*, I have shown that there are two presuppositions, on which everything should be pegged.

1. God exists

4 Taylor, P.F. (2016), *Only Believe*, (Toutle, WA: Just Six Days Publications)

2. The Bible is true

In no way does this constitute a statement of faith. I am not accepting the concept of "minimum Christianity". There is a lot more important, primary doctrine to be drawn out of those two presuppositions. But, we should note that the essential, primary doctrines (for example, the Trinity) are believed and accepted, because they are derived from Scripture, accepting that the Bible is true.

Creationists have, in the past, been guilty of a non-presuppositional approach to Genesis. We have frequently provided scientific evidence, which we maintain proves that evolution is wrong, and that creation is true. Therefore, we say, Genesis is true, and the Bible is true. This is a well-meaning position to take, but it is fundamentally flawed. If we believe Genesis, only because of what some evidence currently seems to say, what will we do when the evolutionist provides us with evidence that seems to be counter? Moreover, whatever we use to prove something must have more authority than what we prove with it. Let's say that you want to buy a chemistry text book. You ask me for my recommendation, which I give. You read something in the text book that is contrary to what you have believed before. You question it, and call me to ask my opinion. Once again, I tell you that the text book is to be believed. So you believe it. Which had the most authority – the text book, or my word? In this example, my word had more authority, because you would not believe what the book explained, until I backed it up. In the same way, if we find a piece of evidence that "proves" the Bible to be true, then that evidence has more authority than the Bible. But the Bible is to be our ultimate authority. Therefore, in an attempt to boost the standing of the Bible, we have inadvertently undermined its authority.

For this reason, we do not believe that God exists, **because** everything that has a beginning has a cause. Instead, we believe that there was a beginning to everything, when God created it, because God exists and His Word is true.

One problem that we face today is that the view expressed above is not according to the prevailing paradigm in Western thought—even within the church. Western Christianity has been strongly influenced by Thomas Aquinas. The best way to understand Thomist[5] thought, in my opinion, is to read what Francis Schaeffer writes about him[6]. Schaeffer shows that Thomas Aquinas had divided the world into 2 storeys, or floors, as shown in the diagram.

5 Aquinas is not a surname. He is really Thomas **of** Aquinas. It does not make sense to refer to Aquinianism, therefore, any more than referring to the ideas of Augustine as Hippism.

6 Schaeffer had a great deal to say about Thomas Aquinas, in many of his books. See, for example, chapter 2 of Schaeffer, F. (1968), *Escape from Reason*, in *The Complete Works of Francis Schaeffer Volume 1*, (Wheaton, IL: Crossway, 1982), pp202-216, or chapter 2 of Schaeffer, F. (1976), *How Should We Then Live?*, in *The Complete Works of Francis Schaeffer Volume 5*, (Wheaton, IL: Crossway, 1982), pp91-106

Grace	
Nature	
Grace, the higher	*God the Creator*; heaven and heavenly things; the unseen and its influence on the earth; *unity*, or universals or absolutes which give existence and morals meaning
Nature, the lower	*The created*; earth and earthly things; the visible and what happens normally in the cause-and-effect universe; what man as man does on the earth; *diversity*, or individual things, the particulars, or the individual acts of man.

The result of this Thomist division has been to divorce God from His creation. All Western scientific thought is thereby relegated to the lower storey. In the Academy[7] of today, it might occasionally be possible to refer to spiritual issues, but, generally speaking, the Academy confines itself to the lower storey, and is dismissive of the relevance of the upper storey.

It is not that the Academy does not allow for a god. It is that any god that can be discussed must be a lower storey god—a god who is part of nature, rather than transcendent over it. C.S. Lewis describes this type of god.

> The difference between Naturalism and Supernaturalism is not exactly the same as the difference between belief in

7 The term "The Academy" is being used here, and elsewhere, as a euphemism for modern academic, Western thought.

> a God and disbelief. Naturalism, without ceasing to be itself, could admit a certain kind of God. The great interlocking event called Nature might be such as to produce at some stage a great cosmic consciousness, an indwelling 'God' arising from the whole process as human mind arises (according to the Naturalists) from human organisms. A Naturalist would not object to that sort of God. The reason is this. Such a God would not stand outside Nature or the total system, would not be existing 'on his own'. It would still be 'the whole show' which was the basic Fact, and such a God would merely be one of the things (even if he were the most interesting) which the basic Fact contained. What Naturalism cannot accept is the idea of a God who stands outside Nature and made it.[8]

It is at this point that we note that what people say they believe, and what it is apparent that they actually believe, can be two different things. Few Christians would admit that their god is the sort of naturalist god, defined by Lewis above. The concept of a transcendent God would be written into most statements of faith. In practice, however, those who give a less than literal reading of Genesis tend towards a naturalist god. Only today, as I write this, I was visited by a young pastor, who was upset after a conversation with a fellow pastor friend. This other pastor does not believe in the inerrancy of Scripture, but my young pastor friend did not know how to answer

8 Lewis, C.S. (1947), *Miracles,* (New York: Macmillan Collins), p12

his criticisms, so he was asking me the questions that he had been asked. "How can Science be wrong?"[9] he asked? His fellow pastor has assumed that everything said within the naturalist paradigm, which likes to call itself "science", must be proven. Not only had he not understood the nature of science, he had not understood the nature of God.

The type of god suggested by Lewis's quote above would be acceptable to many modern physicists. For example, Frank Tipler is a senior mathematical physicist at Tulane University, in New Orleans, Louisiana. Tipler developed the so-called *anthropic principle*, in which he described how he believed the universe could only have evolved in one possible way. Any outcome other than the outcome that we now have would, argues Tipler, have been impossible. Therefore, evolution leads inevitably towards the existence of humanity. It is worth noting that this philosophy, though it is not one that I can share, nevertheless puts mankind, and hence the earth, back at the center of the universe, from which it had been so rudely uprooted.

Part of Tipler's anthropic principle is to suggest the existence of something called the *Omega Point*. This is a sort of god. He suggests that evolution can continue onward, until eventually it produces a

9 We can also notice that this question is suggested by a logical fallacy: the fallacy known as *reification*. In this fallacy, an abstract concept – in this case, "science" - is ascribed attributes of personality. Science is neither right nor wrong. Science is a process, by which answers are sought.

vast intelligence, capable of developing time traveling or dilating properties, which enables it to go back and create the universe, which has given it birth! The god that Tipler suggests exists is a part of this universe, has evolved from it, and has now evolved to be outside time. This is reminiscent of the group known as the *eternals*, in Isaac Asimov's novel, *The End of Eternity*.[10] Tipler said "The logically necessary histories collectively comprising the whole of reality can be regarded as 'emanating' from the Omega Point in his/her transcendence".[11]

Just trust in Jesus

Those first four words of the Bible - "In the beginning, God..." - set themselves against the centuries of Thomist teaching. The Bible knows nothing of a two-storey separation. The model is not found in Scripture; instead, it is the application of Greek thought to theology. That sort of practice has allowed such thinking to predominate.

Nevertheless, there is an accusation abroad today that this entire subject is not that important. "It doesn't matter what we believe about Genesis", says a surprisingly large group of people, which includes many pastors and teachers. "All you need to do is trust in Jesus". Yet the truth of the Bible stands or falls on these four words. Either we believe that God was there in the beginning, or we don't.

10 Asimov, I. (1968), *The End of Eternity*, (Lancer)
11 Tipler, F.J. (1994), *The Physics of Immortality*, (New York: Macmillan), p264

Genesis touches on matters germane to real science. As a child was reported to have said to one pastor, who tried to explain the allegorical nature of Genesis, "When did God start telling the truth?" We will see over and over again, in the pages of this book, that the failure to believe the literal truth of what Genesis teaches is an issue of biblical authority. This issue of authority will be addressed at each point relevant in the narrative, rather than taking a bunny trail here to marshal our arguments. We will see that the truth of Genesis is so central to the Gospel itself, that it is clear that teaching this subject is indeed part of teaching people about Jesus. In other words, teaching people about Jesus, while telling them they do not have to believe Genesis, actually undermines the very belief in Jesus which is being sought.

In the beginning, God created...

If we add the fifth English word to our palette of words, we see that we are declaring that God created. In itself, that is a very profound thing to say. It tells us that God was active in creation. He was not a passive bystander. There are those who assume that God could have created by evolution. Of course, in a literal sense, we could indeed say that God could have achieved the creation by any method that He so chose. One fellow creation speaker was accosted by a lady after one of his talks, who said to him "I don't limit God to creating in seven (*sic*) days. He could have created by any method He wanted."

"Madam", said my friend, "I don't limit God either, but I do limit myself to believing that God did things the way He said He did things!"

If the work had come about by long aeons of evolution, in a manner akin to that described by atheistic evolutionists, then we don't really need God. He just set things going, and then was happy to sit back and watch it all unfold.

The Bible speaks against that view, by pointing out that God was active in creation.

However, there is more. The Hebrew word for God is *ĕlōhîm*. This is a plural noun form. The Hebrew word for "created" is *bārā*. But this word is in the singular verbal form. So we have a plural noun for God, together with a singular verb form. This is consistent with God being a Trinity. Of course, the plurality might be consistent with any other multiple number, linked to a singularity, so we do not use this verse to define the Trinity. But, given that we can derive the doctrine of the Trinity from elsewhere in Scripture, we can apply our understanding of the concept at this point. For example, Martin Luther says (commenting on the second verse):

> There is moreover an universal agreement of the Christian Church concerning a revelation of the mystery of the Holy Trinity in this first creative work. The Father through the

> Son, whom Moses here calls the Word, creates "the heavens and the earth" out of nothing. Over these the Holy Spirit broods.[12]

The reason for Luther's confidence at this point is the juxtaposition of the words *ĕlōhîm* and *bārā*.

In the beginning, God created the heavens and the earth.

The purpose of Genesis 1 is to explain that God made everything. There isn't anything around anywhere that was not made by God.

It was always assumed, until recent scientific history, that the best English word to encompass "everything" would be *universe*. Today, however, there are people who speak of multiple universes, and, hence, a multiverse.

If you have not come across the concept of the multiverse before, this is what it means; it is the idea that there are a large number of different universes, all existing parallel to each other. In fact, the number of universes that exist could be infinite. So what is the evidence for these other universes? There isn't any. In fact, by definition, there could not be any evidence for other universes, because that evidence would have to exist in our universe, which

12 Luther, M. (translated by John Niicholas Lemker), (Project Gutenberg: Mobi edition), location 872.

would make it part of our universe, and, therefore by definition, not a part of another universe.

The multiverse is a convenient conceit used in science fiction stories. It enables characters to move easily into different scenarios. But this concept of imagination is all that underpins the "scientific" multiverse also.

The reason why secular scientists like to accept the multiverse is because it is an inevitable consequence of inflation theory, by which deep-time physicists assume that the universe rapidly expanded during the first few millionths of a second after the Big Bang. Because theories of inflation, and other aspects of the Big Bang, are so mathematically sophisticated, it is assumed that the concepts must have been scientifically proven. This is not the case, however. The mathematical sophistication merely provides evidence of the intelligence of those who have framed these theories, not of their truthfulness. Given that there is no direct evidence of other universes, and given the fact that such a postulation is not necessary in a biblical paradigm, it makes sense for the biblical creationist to adhere to the idea that the universe is a word that encompasses all that there is[13].

13 For more creationist discussion on the concept of the multiverse, see Faulkner, D.R. (2016), *Multiverse: Is Our Universe One of Many?*, < https://answersingenesis.org/astronomy/cosmology/multiverse-is-our-universe-one-of-many/ >, accessed 6/13/2018.

Now the Hebrew language does not contain a word for universe. So there must be a different way for the language to refer to everything that exists. To express such an idea, Hebrew uses a type of phrase known as a *merism* – and the merism in question is “the heavens and the earth”.

A merism is a phrase that gives two extremes. The phrase is assumed to include those two extremes and everything in between.

English uses similar constructions. The last house that my family owned in the UK, before we moved to the USA, was in Leicestershire. It was a three storey house. The kitchen and garage were on the first floor, the lounge and master bedroom on the second, and the other bedrooms and master bathroom on the third floor. I have a tendency to lose things. If I lost something, I might tell my wife that I have searched “high and low”. Does this mean that I did not search in the lounge, because it was not “high” or “low”? Of course I searched in the lounge! “High and low” included the middle floor, as well as the top and bottom floor.

So the phrase “the heavens and the earth” refers to everything from the edge of the universe and beyond, and the earth, and everything that is in between. In other words, “the heavens and the earth” refers to the whole of creation; everything that has been created.

Summary

In this section, we have seen how fundamental and foundational the first verse of the Bible is. As a statement, it introduces everything that we will subsequently learn in God's word. It is not an optional extra; acceptance of the truth of this first verse, as with the rest of Genesis, is an issue of the authority of Scripture.

Genesis 1 Part 3 – The Beginning of Day One

Where Does Day One Begin?

Before we launch into a discussion of the events of the first day of the Creation Week, we should pause to ask this question. Where does Day One begin?

The reason for asking this question is because of a number of compromised beliefs, which stretch the age of the Earth well past what biblical creationists accept. One of the most sophisticated of these Genesis compromises is known as the Gap Theory – sometimes known as the Ruin-Reconstruction Theory. According to this theory, the account of the first day of creation does not begin until Genesis 1:2.

The Gap Theory

The Gap Theory is a very sophisticated piece of theology. Its adherents are plentiful, and they are not theistic evolutionists. They are adamant that God created the world, and would not allow a process of random chance to take place. So where, then, do they differ from biblical creationists? The most common label given to their idea suggests the main point. They do not think that the second verse of Genesis 1 follows immediately after the first verse. Therefore, they suggest that there is a gap. There is no consensus on how long this gap might be. Some have suggested a gap of a few days, a few years, or any larger amount, but it is usual for Gap Theorists to suggest a gap of millions of years, during which the Earth could have aged as modern geologists suggest that it has.

Most gap theorists do not think that spiritual matters sat idly by, while this gap between the first two verses carried on. A whole spiritual history has been developed for what happened in this gap, and, because gap theorists, though mistaken, are keen on biblical truth, their arguments come from Scripture – albeit a mistaken interpretation of those Scriptures. And before we are too critical, we must stop and acknowledge that many more orthodox Christians also accept gaps. For example, when did the events of Genesis 3 – the temptation of Eve and the Fall – take place? There was likely a gap between chapters 2 and 3, but we have little indication of how long that gap could be. I suspect, as related later, that the gap was as little as two days.

There is a difference, however. The possibility of a gap between chapters 2 and 3 could be implied by the fact that no timescale is given. However, a clear timescale exists for the first chapter of Genesis, as we shall see shortly.

Ruin – Reconstruction

Two passages used by gap theorists to "prove" their case are Isaiah 14:12-21 and Ezekiel 28:11-19. The former is the well-known passage, referring to the Morning Star. In the Latin Vulgate Bible, originally translated into Latin by Jerome, the Hebrew term for Morning Star (*Helel ben Shahar* - הֵילֵל בֶּן-שָׁחַר), which, in the Greek Septuagint is *phosphoros* – φωσφορος, is rendered as *Lucifer*. It is very possible to suggest that Isaiah 14:19 is referring to the devil, and one does not have to be a gap theorist to take that view. The late Henry Morris thought that Isaiah 14 (and Ezekiel 28) referred to Satan, but he suggested that this "Fall of Lucifer" happened between Genesis 2 and 3[1,2]. I have a lot of sympathy with that view, and it is the view towards which I am inclined. However, we must also recognize that godly scholars, like John Calvin, disagreed that these passages referred to Satan.

> The exposition of this passage, which some have given, as if it referred to Satan, has arisen from ignorance; for the context plainly shows that these statements must be understood in reference to the king of the Babylonians.[3]

1 Morris, H.M. (2012), *The Henry Morris Study Bible*, (Green Forest, AR: Master Books), p1026.
2 Morris, H.M. (2000), *The Long War against God*, (Green Forest, AR: Master Books), p257.
3 Calvin, J. *Commentary on Isaiah Volume 1*, Christian Classics Ethereal Library, < http://www.ccel.org/ccel/calvin/calcom13.xxi.i.html >, accessed 6/14/2018.

Be that as it may, in the gap theorist's cosmogony, the Fall of Lucifer took place some time after God had created the world, but before the events of Genesis 1:2. Their theory has Lucifer as the brightest, shiniest angel, leading the worship in heaven. Then, they say that he became proud, referring to Isaiah 14 and Ezekiel 28, and that he was cast out of heaven. This war in heaven involved great implications for the Earth, which was utterly destroyed and flooded. This flood, known as the Luciferian Flood, left the Earth covered with water. This Luciferian Flood, they tell us, was responsible for producing all the fossils.

So, the world was left chaotic. It had been rendered formless and void. At this point, God re-created it in six literal 24-hour days, following the narrative from Genesis 1:2 onward.

Gap Theory – Scriptural Errors

Became

It is necessary for gap theorists to be able to read a gap into the first two chapters of Genesis. These read:

> 1 In the beginning, God created the heavens and the earth.
>
> 2 The earth was without form and void, and darkness was over the face of the deep. And the Spirit of God was hovering over the face of the waters.

The gap theorists interpret "without form and void" as referring to an imperfection. They do not accept that God could have made the world that way, so they suppose that it *became* that way. They find support for that position, in the Hebrew word *hayah* (הָיָה). They state that it should be translated as "became", instead of "was". In other words, verse 2 should read "The earth *became* without form and void." Now, it needs must be said that there are verses in the Bible where *hayah* clearly does mean "became". However, this is not its primary meaning. It is part of the *semantic range*. One picks the primary meaning from a semantic range, not a more obscure secondary meaning, unless the context demands otherwise. Let me explain.

Sometimes English speakers assume that every language is like a code, and there must be a one-to-one mapping of words from one language to another. This is not the case – even between languages that are closely related. For example, try using Google Translate to change "The woman is very beautiful" into German. It will read "Die Frau ist sehr schön". So the German word Frau means "woman". That is its primary meaning. However, now try translating "My wife is very beautiful". This reads "Meine Frau ist sehr schön". In this case, Frau means "wife". This is because German does not actually have a word that is normally used for wife. But the context clearly shows that the word "wife" is to be used, rather than "woman". Indeed, the English form "My woman is very beautiful" nearly means the same thing.

Therefore, the German word Frau has a semantic range. If there is no context, then it will be translated as "woman", but it can be translated with a secondary meaning - "wife" - if the context demands. In the same way, the word *hayah* needs must be translated "was", unless the context clearly demands otherwise. Since "The earth *was* without form and void" is a completely legitimate meaning, it must be the **only** meaning, because the context does not require the secondary meaning.

Without form and void

This brings us to the phrase "without form and void". There are only two places in the Bible where this phrase appears exactly like this. The other is in Jeremiah 4:23.

> I looked on the earth, and behold, it was without form and void.

In Jeremiah, the phrase does indeed imply a lack of perfection, and a judgment, which brings about this formlessness. However, we should dig a little more deeply into the sort of quotation that is being used. If a phrase is repeated, exactly as stated earlier, then it is a form of quotation. In that event, the meaning of the *second* occurrence depends on the *first*, and not the other way about.

For example, in a rousing speech to stir up the people of Britain, during World War II, Prime Minister Winston Churchill said "We shall fight them on the beaches...". In a pep talk to my high school's soccer team, I remember one teacher saying "you need to fight them on the beaches." The second phrase was a quotation of the first, and is understood in light of Churchill's words, not the other way around. Imagine if Churchill were asked what he had meant. Would he have told people to wait until the 1970s, to listen to a British sports coach? Of course not.

In the same way, there is no reason to read any meanings into the Genesis 1:2 appearance of "without form and void". It is not understood in the light of Jeremiah 4. Instead, the Jeremiah 4 passage is understood in the light of Genesis 1.

Genesis 1:1 part of the Six Days.

In Exodus 20:11, we are told the reason for the fourth commandment.

> For in six days the Lord made heaven and earth, the sea, and all that is in them, and rested on the seventh day.

So, the making of the heavens and the earth was part of the six days. That means that Genesis 1:1 is part of the six days, and therefore there can be no gap between verse 1 and verse 2.

Replenish

God commanded the first man and woman to fill the earth and subdue it (Genesis 1:28). However, in the KJV, this reads "replenish the earth". This would seem to imply that the earth was to be re-filled, following the catastrophe of the Luciferian Flood. However, this is not the case. Nor is it the case that the KJV is wrong. On the contrary; the KJV had it right, but the word *replenish* has changed its meaning since 1611. In the early 17th Century, the word *replenish* had nothing to do with "filling again". There was never a word "plenish"! Instead, the word *replenish* has the same root as the word *replete*. It used to mean "to fill completely", not "to fill again".

More on the Gap Theory

There is a lot more can be said about the Gap Theory, its proponents and its refutation. For more information, see Weston Field's book *Unformed and Unfilled*, or M.W.J. Phelan's *The Genesis Gap Theory*.[4,5]

Pre-Genesis Gap

We have become so used to tackling the erroneous idea of a gap between Genesis 1:1 and 1:2 that it comes as a surprise to find that there are people who believe in a gap elsewhere in Genesis 1. One popular idea today, believed particularly by a number of reformed preachers, is that there is a gap before Genesis 1:1. The principle proponent of such an idea is John Sailhamer, in his book Genesis

4 Fields, W. (2005), *Unformed and Unfilled*, (Green River, AR: Master Books).
5 Phelan, M.W,J. (2005), *The Genesis Gap Theory*, (Waterlooville, UK: Twoedged Sword Publications).

Unbound[6]. Anecdotally, I would suggest that this pre-Genesis gap theory is beginning to get more traction than previously among otherwise conservative evangelicals.

In some ways, this view is more difficult than the traditional gap theory, because Sailhamer believes that the first verse of Genesis is the beginning of the whole of the rest of the Bible, and his version of deep-time all occurs before biblical history. However, we have already discussed the use of the opening phrase *bereshit* and have shown that it best refers to the beginning of all things, including the beginning of time itself. This is emphasized by the only other place in Scripture where *reshit* appears as an absolute, without an article. This is in Isaiah 46:10.

> [I am God] declaring the end from the beginning and from ancient times things not yet done.

The context shows that this is referring to the beginning of everything. And this beginning is even referred to as "from ancient times", indicating that nothing is more ancient than the beginning of the world. This is an important point, because the idea that God is "the Ancient of Days" (Daniel 7:22) is often used to justify deep-time compromises of biblical truth. The assumption is that 6,000 years is "young", while 14.7 billion years is "ancient". Some creationists have

6 Sailhamer, J.H. (2011), *Genesis Unbound*, (Portland, OR: Dawson Media, Second Edition).

even encouraged this, idea, by accepting the use of terms such as "young earth creationist". However, the Bible makes clear that 6,000 years is "ancient". By extension, therefore, 14.7 billion years is simply mistakenly mythological.

Soft Gap

Yet another take on Genesis 1, which seeks to add deep-time to Genesis, while not allowing for evolution, is the Soft Gap Theory, which suggests a gap between Genesis 1:2 and 1:3. The idea behind this theory is that the Spirit must have been hovering over the deep for a very long time, before there was sufficient energy for creation to begin. This idea gained currency in a book by Gorman Gray.[7] The refutation of this idea is exactly the same as the refutation of the traditional Gap Theory. The making of the heavens and the earth must be part of the six days of creation, according to Exodus 20:11, so there cannot be any gap.

Conclusion

In this chapter, we have looked at some of the most common methods people use, to attempt to add millions of years to what the Bible teaches, without disturbing the obvious Scriptural truth of the literal 24-hour days of creation. It follows that our next task, in our studies

7 Gorman Gray (1997), *The Age of the Universe: What Are the Biblical Limits?*, (Washougal, WA: Morningstar Publications).

in Genesis, must be to make clear that the days of the creation week were real days.

Genesis 1 Part 4 – The Length of the Genesis Days

The deep-time compromises of the previous chapter all accepted that the days of the creation week were real days. But there are a lot more compromises that refuse to accept that timescale. In order to "harmonize" the millions of years of deep-time geology and astrophysics, they have required that the days of creation might not be actual 24-hour days and that they might refer to long ages of time. There are a number of theories about Genesis 1, which require such an allegorical use of the word day – old-earth or day-age creationists, progressive creationists, and theistic evolutionists.

In the latter camp, however, are some who do not necessarily think that the days of Genesis 1 are long periods. Rather, they believe that the whole structure and substance of Genesis 1 has nothing to do with timescale at all. For example, Walton relies on the concept of seven being a mystical number throughout Scripture, and suggests, therefore, that the seven days of the Creation Week are allegories of the preparation of the Cosmos as a temple.

> The day-age theory and others that attempt to mitigate the force of the seven days do so because they see no way to reconcile seven twenty-four-hour days of material creation with the evidence from science that the earth

> and the universe are very old. They seek a solution in trying to stretch the meaning of *yôm*, whereas we propose that once we understand the nature of the creation account, there is no longer any need to stretch *yôm*.[1]

It seems, therefore, that our defense of the use of the word *day* (*yôm*) in Scripture needs to be twofold. We need to examine why it matters that the Creation Week consisted of six literal days of creation, and one literal day of rest, and also why the word *yôm*, as used in Genesis 1, has to refer to a 24-hour day, and only that time period.

When Is a Day a Day?

It is often pointed out by old earth creationists, that *yôm* can, like the English word *day*, have a number of different meanings. This is true. It can mean an indeterminate period for time, it can mean the hours of daylight, or it can mean an ordinary 24-hour day. So, what does the word mean in Genesis 1?

It is the context of a word like *yôm* which determines its meaning. Consider the following:

> In my grandfather's day, it took five days to ride to London, during the day.

1 Walton, J.H. (2009), *The Lost World of Genesis 1*, (Downers Grove, IL: InterVarsity Press), p92.

That sentence uses the word day(s) three times, but I doubt that you have any trouble understanding the meaning.

"In my grandfather's day": this is an indeterminate period of time, in the past, when my grandfather was alive.

"During the day": this use of the word "day" suggests the hours of daylight.

"It took five days": this suggests the use of "day" as an ordinary period of time. So, if the ride began on Monday, it would end on Friday – 5 x 24-hours later.

None of this is particularly difficult, and nor should it be difficult, when applied to the Hebrew word *yôm*. So what internal evidence do we have in Genesis 1 about how the word day should be used?

It should be seen immediately that the other two uses of the word "day" are both seen in the early chapters of Genesis. These occur in Genesis 1:5, and in Genesis 2:4.

In Genesis 1:5, we read "God called the light Day". In this phrase, the word is clearly referring to the hours of daylight.

In Genesis 2:4, we read "In the day that the Lord God made the earth and the heavens." This seems to imply an indeterminate period of time in the past. It is the equivalent of saying "*when* the Lord God made the earth and the heavens".

In all the other cases, in Genesis 1, the word "day" is accompanied by a number. Outside of Genesis 1, there are no other places where the word "day" appears with a number, either cardinal or ordinal, where it does not mean an ordinary 24-hour day. Just to add to this, there are no places outside Genesis 1, where the words evening and morning appear together, where they refer to anything other than an ordinary 24-hour day.

Despite the obvious meaning of Genesis 1, there are still those who wish to raise objections to the literal reading of it.

Objection 1: A Day Is Like a Thousand Years

This is a common objection to the plain reading of Genesis 1. If a day with the Lord is like a thousand years, then surely this means that the word "day" can be interpreted as a long period of time.

When you are presented with this objection, it is usually by well-meaning Christians, so it is useful to challenge them as to where they can find this statement in the Bible. I have often found that people have no idea where this is to be found.

In fact, it is found in 2 Peter 3:8.

> But do not overlook this one fact, beloved, that with the Lord one day is as a thousand years, and a thousand years as one day.

It will be noticed that the portion usually quoted is in the middle of this verse. Reading the context makes it more obvious what is actually meant. For example, the final portion of the verse reads "a thousand years as one day". That cancels out the concept of a day being a long period of time. Then, the verse starts with "but", and instructs us not to overlook something. The previous verses and the following verses all make it clear that the topic under discussion is the timing of the Lord's return, not the creation. Peter's followers were beginning to wonder why Jesus had not returned yet. And it is that question, which 2 Peter 3:8 is answering.

Moreover, the application of "one day is as a thousand years" does not make much sense, if applied to other passages with numerical days. For example, Joshua marched the Israelites around Jericho for seven days. Does this mean that the march could really have been 7,000 years? Of course not! The idea is absurd. The context clearly demands that we read it as seven literal days.

Or how about Jonah? He was in the belly of the big fish for three days. Does that mean that he was really stuck in the fish for 3,000 years? No one in their right mind will interpret the passage that way.

Consider Numbers 7. Just in case you are not fully familiar with the story, it is the account of the twelve tribes of Israel bringing their offerings before Moses, for the building of the Tabernacle. In Numbers 7:12, we read:

> He who offered his offering the first day was Nahshon the son of Amminadab, of the tribe of Judah.

Subsequent verses tell us about the other tribes.

> 18. He who offered his offering the first day was Nahshon the son of Amminadab, of the tribe of Judah.
>
> 24. On the third day Eliab the son of Helon, the chief of the people of Zebulun.
>
> 30. On the fourth day Elizur the son of Shedeur, the chief of the people of Reuben.

This continues, every six verses, twelve days in all. Poor old Moses had to remain sat there for 12,000 years!

Of course, the context is clear that this event took twelve literal 24-hour days. Yet the grammar in Numbers 7 is identical to that in Genesis 1. So, if Genesis 1 is to be interpreted figuratively, surely Numbers 7 should also be figurative. Better yet, since Numbers 7 is obviously literal, then Genesis 1 must be six literal 24-hour days.

Objection 2: Hosea 6 Shows that Days May Not Be Literal

Hosea 6:2 reads as follows.

> After two days he will revive us; on the third day he will raise us up, that we may live before him.

Old Earth apologist Alan Hayward suggested that this verse undermines the sort of creationist arguments about literal days that I have expressed above.

> [Hosea 6] is at least one exception that shatters the so-called rule.[2]

In order to understand what is happening in Hosea 2, let's read a few similar passages. This is what we read in Amos 1:

> Thus says the Lord: "For three transgressions of Damascus, and for four, I will not revoke the punishment, because they have threshed Gilead with threshing sledges of iron. (Amos 1:3)

This is a form of numerical construction peculiar to Hebrew. But there is a similar use of language in English. Suppose God had said "I will not revoke the punishment on Damascus for three or four

2 Hayward, A. (1985), *Creation and Evolution, The Facts and the Fallacies*, (London: Triangle, SPCK), 164.

transgressions". Although this is not identical in meaning, it is similar. Compare that with the following:

> He will deliver you from six troubles; in seven no evil shall touch you. (Job 5:19)

This is pretty similar to saying six or seven troubles. You will find similar constructions in Psalm 62:11 and Proverbs 6:16-17. The construction in Psalm 90:10 is significant.

> The years of our life are seventy, or even by reason of strength eighty.

It is clear that this is saying that we live 70 or 80 years.

Now consider how similar constructions would be used in English. We might say that Simon is 7 or 8 years old, while Roy is 70 or 80 years old. Who is older? The answer is Roy, who is perhaps 10 times older than Simon. So the phrase is not as inexact as you might think. The value of the phrase comes from the fact that the actual numbers are used exactly, while the phrase as a whole is vague. In other words, the idea of 70 years is an exact concept, and the idea of 80 years is an exact concept, but the whole phrase 70 or 80 is inexact - but not fully inexact, because we know it is a bigger amount than 7 or 8.

So, we return to Hosea 6. Let's quote it again.

> After two days he will revive us; on the third day he will raise us up, that we may live before him.

In fact, the phrase is not using the concept of "day" in a vague, inexact manner. Two days is a literal period of time, and so is three days, or third day. But the phrase as a whole is inexact – yet not fully. The phrase could mean 2 days or three days. It could perhaps be stretched either way, to include 1 day, or maybe even 4 or 5 days. But it does not, surely, mean 10 days. Hayward is therefore incorrect. Even the in-exactitude of the phrase as a whole is only possible because of the certainty of the individual numbers quoted.

Objection 3: The Six Days Form a Literary Device

A more sophisticated objection is the idea that the days of Genesis fit neatly into a literary framework. This framework consists of two groups of three days. The idea is often labeled as "The Framework Hypothesis", but is often used without the label, and often simply assumed to be true. The Framework looks something like this.[3]

3 Willem VanGemeren, *The Progress of Redemption: The Story of Salvation from Creation to the New Jerusalem* (Grand Rapids: Baker, 1988), 47.

Day	Formation of the World (Items Created)	Day	Filling of the World (Items Created)
1	darkness, light	4	heavenly light-bearers
2	Heavens, water	5	birds of the air, water animals
3	Seas, land, vegetation	6	land animals, man, provision of food

The six days of the creation week are thus divided into three days of formation, followed by three days of filling. Then, there is meant to be a correspondence between the days of formation and days of filling, thus:

On Day 1, God made the universe, while on Day 4, He filled it.

On Day 2, God made the firmament, while on Day 5, He filled it.

On Day 3, God made the dry land, while on Day 6, He filled it.

The parallels look a little too good to be true, and, as is usually the case, if they look too good to be true, they most likely are too good to be true. In fact, McCabe and Chaffey have discussed a number of problems with this neat table. The implication of the framework table is that Genesis 1 is poetic in nature. However, McCabe and Chaffey show that the word order and general use of Hebrew in Genesis 1 is inconsistent with that of a poem, and more in keeping with the style of Hebrew narrative.[4] In addition, the correspondence shown is not actually borne out by the text of Genesis 1. For example, the table states that water is created on Day Two, but, in fact, it was created on Day One. The firmament described in the verses about Day Two is, in fact, the stretching of the universe, so this parallels with Day Four, yet the hypothesis expects Day One to parallel with Day Four. McCabe and Chaffey pick apart a large number of discrepancies found in this Framework Hypothesis, but these two should suffice to show that it is an impossible idea.

When there are such difficulties with the concept, one might wonder why it was ever developed. The answer can be clearly seen. One of the original architects of the idea was Meredith Kline. He stated "The conclusion is that as far as the time frame is concerned, with respect to both the duration and sequence of events, the scientist is left free of biblical constraints in hypothesizing about cosmic origins."[5] Why would he want scientists left "free of biblical constraints"? The very idea suggests that biblical authority was not the primary concern in Kline's mind.

4 McCabe, R.V. and Chaffey, T. (2011), *What's Wrong with the Framework Hypothesis?*, < https://answersingenesis.org/creationism/old-earth/whats-wrong-with-the-framework-hypothesis/ >, accessed 9/20/2018.

5 Meredith G. Kline, "Space and Time in the Genesis Cosmogony," Perspectives on Science and Christian Faith 48 (March 1996): 2.

It should also be mentioned that many ideas, that involve resistance to the concept of 24-hour days, require the seventh day to be unlimited. It is a popular idea to suppose that God's Sabbath Day of rest started at the end of the Creation Week, and has continued for eternity from there. However, it is an idea without any Scriptural warrant. The context in no way suggests an eternal Sabbath, so one should not read it into the text. In other words, Day Seven is a 24-hour day, like any other day, and completes the Creation Week. Therefore, there would be an eighth day, a ninth day, and so on. The insistence by some, without Scriptural warrant, that this first Sabbath did not end after 24-hours, is but one example among many, on how those committed to unbiblical deep-time ideas insist on clinging to those ideas.

For a more thorough refutation of the Framework Hypothesis, please read Kenneth Gentry's book, *As It Is Written.*[6]

Conclusion

The purpose of this section has been to emphasize that the days of the Creation Week are literal 24-hour days. We have seen that this is the most natural, most obvious reading of the text, and that those who choose to interpret the creation days as anything other than 24-hour

6 Gentry, K.L. (2016), *As It Is Written*, (Green Forest, AR: Master Books).

days do so, because of an insistence on interpreting Genesis, by using ideas and categories external to the Bible.

It might be helpful to end with some words from Martin Luther. In his commentary on Genesis, he notes that "Hilary and Augustine, two great lights in the church, believed that the world was made on a sudden and all at once, not successively during the space of six days. Augustine plays upon these six days in a marvelous manner in explaining them. He considers them to be mystical days of knowledge in the angels, and not natural days." While expressing his normal admiration for Augustine, Luther has to refute this idea by writing "With respect therefore to this opinion of Augustine, we conclude that Moses spoke literally and plainly and neither allegorically nor figuratively; that is, he means that the world with all creatures was created in six days as he himself expresses it. If we cannot attain unto a comprehension of the reason why it was so, let us still remain scholars and leave all the preceptorship to the Holy Spirit!"[7] Or, as someone has paraphrased this elsewhere – if you can't understand how God could create in six literal days, at least grant the Holy Spirit is more learned than you are!

7 Luther, M. (1910 English edition), *Commentary on Genesis*, Archive.org, Kindle edition, location 803. O

Genesis 1 Part 5 – The First Day of Creation

(Genesis 1:1-5)

Having already established previously that Genesis 1:1 is part of the First Day of the Creation Week, and that the days of the Creation Week are literal 24-hour days, we can now launch into the events of Day One.

A Universe from Nothing

A Universe from Nothing was the title of a book published in 2012 by atheist astrophysicist Dr. Lawrence M. Krauss. In the book, Krauss argues that everything there is in the Universe came about by itself, without any creative force from without. His arguments are standard Big Bang arguments, but are informed by the latest research into that theory, much of which is his.

The Big Bang theory is basically a worldview, in which God does not appear. This may surprise some people. There are a good many Christian apologists around who make use of the Big Bang theory. The theory basically states that the universe had a beginning, when a quantum event came into existence in a point, known as a singularity. This singularity expanded, so all of space and time was originally concentrated into this singularity, as well as matter. The popular conception of the Big Bang is of a primordial atom expanding into an already infinite universe of empty space. This is not what Big Bangists believe.

The confusion has arisen, because the term Big Bang was not chosen by advocates of the theory. Instead, it was a pejorative term, applied to the theory by the late physicist Dr. Sir Fred Hoyle. Hoyle's view was that there was no God, so the Universe must simply exist in a Steady State. Hoyle said:

> The reason why scientists like the "big bang" is because they are overshadowed by the Book of Genesis. It is deep within the psyche of most scientists to believe in the first page of Genesis.[1]

Apologist William Lane Craig makes much use of the Big Bang theory in his alleged proof of God, known as the *Kalam Cosmological Argument*. The argument is stated in a syllogism, as follows:

Whatever begins to exist has a cause.

The Universe began to exist.

Therefore the Universe has a cause.[2]

1 "BBC, Adam Curtis, "A MILE OR TWO OFF YARMOUTH"". 24 February 2012.
< http://www.bbc.co.uk/blogs/adamcurtis/posts/a_mile_or_two_off_yarmouth >, Retrieved 8/6/2018.

2 Craig, W.L. (2008, 3rd edn), *Reasonable Faith*, (Wheaton, IL: Crossway), p111.

These sort of errors arise, when a theologian or philosopher has not attempted fully to understand physics.[3] In 1927, the Belgian priest and mathematician Georges Lemaître had solved a number of Einstein's relativity equations. He appreciated that, under Einsteinian physics, as well as under Newtonian physics, there still exists a universe with multiple objects of mass, all exerting gravitational fields. It would not be possible for such a universe to exist in a static state. So Lemaître reasoned that the universe must, in fact, be expanding. This was before Edwin Hubble's famous and eponymous Law, that gave rise to the measurement of the expansion of space – and we will refer more to this point in the next section of this book. Lemaître's insight was that, if the universe is expanding now, then he reasoned it must once have been at a single point. This singularity, therefore, is not a by-product of theistic thinking, but rather the antithesis of it. It is a construct of a universe, developed without reference to God. The fact that, as a worldview, it has a beginning point in time, points not to the existence of God, but to His removal.

There are a large number of scientific problems with the Big Bang theory. A number of non-Christian scientists are listed as skeptical of the Big Bang on one aging website.[4] Sir Fred Hoyle's opposition to the

3 I have a more detailed criticism of the Kalam Cosmological Argument, and its use as a supposed apologetic tool, in Taylor, P.F. (2016), *Only Believe*, (Castle Rock, WA: J6D Publications), pp 101-104.

4 < http://www.bigbangneverhappened.org/ >, accessed 8/6/2018.

Big Bang has also already been mentioned.[5] And, within the creationist community, the Big Bang theory has been thoroughly refuted in the book *Demolishing the Big Bang*, by Alex Williams and John Hartnett.[6]

The Horizon Problem

A number of issues would concern creationists about the Big Bang. The most important of these is that the Big Bang theory suggests a different order to created objects to that found in the Bible. Scientific objections include the novelty of an object appearing by a "quantum fluctuation" all by itself, and the inability of the Big Bang theory successfully to explain the apparent evenness of the Cosmic Microwave Background.

According to Krauss, Cosmic Microwave Background Radiation (CMB) "is nothing less than the afterglow of the Big Bang.[7] It is suggested that an event as big as that primordial bang would leave evidence, in the form of an afterglow.

CMB is a background radiation in the universe, discovered in 1964, by Arno Penzias and Robert Wilson. Space between the stars is not fully empty, and the molecules in that space have a temperature of about

5 The big bang in astronomy, *New Scientist* **92**(1280):527, 19 November 1981.
6 Williams, A. and Hartnett, J. (2005), *Dismantling the Big Bang*, (Green Forest, AR: Master Books).
7 Krauss, L.M. (2012), *A Universe from Nothing*, (New York: Atria), pp 42-43.

2.73K. (K = kelvins; like "degrees Celsius" above absolute zero). The photon energy provided is 6.626×10^{-4} electron-Volts, which corresponds to a frequency of 162.23GHz, which is within the microwave band of frequencies. CMB's temperature and energy appears to be pretty constant across the known universe.

Herein lies a problem. In order for CMB to be even, it follows that CMB hotspots, after the Big Bang, would have to be able to send their energy to balance out with cold spots. The only way heat energy could move through a near vacuum would be by radiation. This radiation would travel at the speed of light. According to the latest thinking, the Big Bang occurred 13.8 billion years ago.[8] That means that the maximum distance the radiation could travel would be 13.8 billion light years. This would suggest a universe, with a maximum radius of 13.8 billion light years – i.e. 27.6 billion light years across. Yet even conservative estimates put the size of the universe at 92 billion light years. This clearly creates a light travel problem, known as the *Horizon* Problem, which has been known about since 1956.

Big Bang Theorists would point to a supposed workaround for the Horizon Problem, called *inflation*. Cosmic Inflation, first formulated by Alan Guth in 1979, allows for a period of rapid expansion, shortly after the universe came into existence, called the *Inflationary Epoch*. This

8 Encyclopaedia Britannica, < https://www.britannica.com/science/big-bang-model >, accessed 8/6/2018.

epoch began at 10^{-36} seconds after the Big Bang, and lasted until about 10^{-32}s after the Big Bang.

Readers will realize the oddity of a Big Bang beginning some 13.8 billion years ago, yet only made explicable by an event which lasted less than 10^{-32} seconds. This juxtaposition of incredibly long ages, with infinitesimally short time-spans does not sit well logically. Nevertheless, this is the model, which, mathematically speaking, is used to explain the even temperatures of CMB, which cannot be explained without it. There is, as you would surmise, no hard evidence for this inflationary epoch, and we are bound to say that it would appear to be a *fiddle factor*, designed to make the numbers crunch right, without causing irreparable damage to the evolutionists' worldview.

Ex Nihilo

And this brings us back to the first point, which is that the people who truly believe in a universe from nothing are actually Biblical Creationists – except, of course, that it was God who made everything from nothing. Therefore, the universe did not appear out of nothing. God made it out of nothing, but His own command, at His spoken word.

Ex nihilo is a Latin phrase, meaning "out of nothing". The phrase is usually used in the context of Creation. *Creatio ex nihilo* means "created out of nothing". The use of the phrase implies that there must be a Creator. Moreover, that Creator must specifically be the Second Person of the Trinity.

Do not misunderstand. Everything proceeds from God the Father, so He is ultimately responsible for the whole of Creation coming into being, but in Colossians 1:16-17, we read:

> For by [Jesus] all things were created, in heaven and on earth, visible and invisible, whether thrones or dominions or rulers or authorities—all things were created through him and for him. And he is before all things, and in him all things hold together.

While in John 1:3, we read:

> All things were made through him [the Word; i.e. Jesus], and without him was not anything made that was made.

In summary, everything was made through Jesus. Nothing that exists was made by any means, other than being made through Jesus. John's Gospel is particularly pertinent here, as it starts with the famous passage about the Word, who was with God, and who was God. John makes clear that the Word (in Greek, *Logos* λόγος) is Jesus Christ. This would appear to be in keeping with the manner, in which God created, as He did so by spoken word - "And God said..."

Post-exilic Jews spoke Aramaic in everyday life, rather than Hebrew. Gradually, it became necessary for there to be translations of the Hebrew Scriptures into Aramaic. These translations were known as *Targums*. However, these translations were somewhat free, and were really paraphrases, rather than true translations. Hebrew scholar Malachi Yosef has suggested that these targums were the Living Bibles of their day![9] The reason for mentioning these targums is their inclusion of the Hebrew word *memra*, which means “word”.

Psalm 33:6 is very clear when it says “By the word of the Lord the heavens were made”. In Aramaic, the word memra is used. But memra also occurs in other targums, in significant ways. For example, Genesis 1:27 says “God created man in his own image”, but the Jerusalem Targum of Jonathan ben Uziel renders this as “the Word [Memra] of the Lord created man in His likeness”.[10] Yosef quotes a number of other targum passages, which show the use of the word memra, when a reference to God speaking, or relating with human beings, is being established.

Earth First

It is very significant that God made the Earth on Day One. We will say more about this, when we discuss Day Four, with all the rest of the

9 Yosef, M. *The Teachings of the Targums*, < http://oneinmessiah.net/TargumMemraTheWordOfGod.htm >, accessed 9/6/2018.

10 *Ibid.*

universe being made. It is completely incompatible with any form of evolutionary thought for the Earth to be unique. The whole concept of the Big Bang theory, with its expansion of space-time itself, rather than just the contents of the universe, requires Earth to be in no special place. But the Bible puts the Creation of the Earth fully three days before any other objects of the Universe were made. Earth is indeed unique.

This central importance of the Earth does not imply that the Earth is fixed, flat, or at the center of the universe. God has endowed the Earth with its special significance, and He could easily have brought this about, while causing the Earth to orbit the Sun on the fourth day.

There is nothing unbiblical in accepting that the Earth orbits the Sun. As creationists, we have no issue with the concept of *observational science.* Since our observations lead us to the conclusion that the Earth does indeed move through space, we can accept this, because there is no biblical evidence against it. Some *geocentrists*[11] point to passages like Ecclesiastes 1:4-5.

> A generation goes, and a generation comes, but the earth remains forever. The sun rises, and the sun goes down, and hastens to the place where it rises.

11 People who believe the Earth is fixed in space, at the center of the universe.

The book of Ecclesiastes is well worth studying, and has much to say of relevance to creationists and apologists. Its purpose, however, is deliberately to see the world from a man-centered point of view. The constant repetition throughout the book of the phrase "under the Sun" emphasizes this man-centeredness, and also strongly implies that the abode of God is "over the Sun", which is where our thoughts should be. So when Qohelet – the anonymous writer of Ecclesiastes (but probably Solomon) – talks about the Sun rising and setting, and traveling across the sky, this simply fits with the man-centered nature of the narrative. Indeed, the very inclusion of that description of the Sun, in a passage which is covered by the phrase "under the Sun" is a very strong suggestion that the reality of the relative movements of Earth and Sun are different.

Light

After God had made all the material of the universe, He made light. Genesis 1 tells us that there was light and darkness, because darkness is the absence of light. So, although God created light, there was not going to be light everywhere. God separated the light from the darkness. He called the light *day*, and he called the darkness *night*.

If you are comfortable with accepting what God has written as the truth, then we ought to be able to stop at this point. But, in practice, we have all been evolutionized, so we need to look at the problems that people have with the biblical concept of light.

The first problem that people have is that they believe that there must be a source for the light. In fact, in our Solar System, the main source of light is the Sun. Of course, it is not the only source of light with which we are familiar. We are also familiar with the Moon (which is a secondary source) and the stars – but more on these later. We are also familiar with artificial light sources, such as electric and gas lighting and flashlights, as well as other natural sources, such as lightning, firebugs, or bioluminescence. In truth, the Sun is not necessary as a light source.

Nor does light today even require a light source. For example, in order to measure the speed of light, we shine a laser to the Moon, and make it reflect from one of the mirrors that the Apollo astronauts left there. It takes 1½ seconds for light to reach the Moon and return again. But the laser does not have to be left on for the whole 1½ seconds. After it has been turned on, it can immediately be turned off, but the light it has made continues to travel to the Moon and bounce back. That laser light hitting the Moon no longer has a source. Of course, it needed a source to get it going. But God did not need a source to make the light. Light is a transfer of energy by wave motion through the electromagnetic field. It occurs by alternate compressions and expansions of that field. In order for there to be days, it was not necessary for the Sun to be there immediately. It was simply necessary for there to be unidirectional light. The rotation of the Earth within that light measures for us the periods of light and darkness, or day and night.

High school students are usually taught that there are nine types of energy – heat, light, kinetic (movement), potential (elastic), gravitational (a form of potential), chemical, sound, electrical, and nuclear. In practice, there are only really two forms – kinetic and potential. Light incorporates both kinetic and potential energy. The electromagnetic fields oscillate by simple harmonic motion. The movement begins against the forces of the electromagnetic field, so the motion is converted to potential energy. Eventually, this reverses, as the field forces the motion back again. When the potential is greatest, the movement is momentarily at rest, at the crest or the trough of the wave. This rippling motion of the universe's electromagnetic waves seems to be the sort of energy that might be provided by the Spirit "hovering". Perhaps the Spirit was Himself the localized source of light, which, shining on a rotating Earth sphere, caused the day and the night. Whether or not that is so, it seems that there must have been some point source of light, until this was replaced by the Sun on Day Four.

Summary

In summary, this is what happened on the first day of Creation. On the first day, the Creator, showing many of the attributes and characteristics of the Second Person of the Trinity, made all the material of the universe, including, and especially, the Earth. He spoke light into existence, as an electromagnetic wave form, and set the Earth rotating within those rays of light. Then came the first evening, and the first morning - the end of the first day.

Genesis 1 Part 6 – The Second Day of Creation

(Genesis 1:6-8)

I have often wondered why the quantities of creative activity in each day of the Creation Week differ so much. Day Six seems to be so busy, with the creation of land animals and human beings, with, we surmise, the Garden of Eden created, and the naming of the animals, all during that day. Yet, on Day Two, God does not seem to do much. It is simply the Day of the Firmament.

Was It Good?

One of the marks of the brevity of Day Two is the absence of God stating that He "saw that it was good". Much has been made of this. The absence of this key phrase has been used by some to suggest that Satan fell during this day. The argument proceeds as follows:

> On Day Two, God made the atmosphere, which is what divided the waters above from the waters below. Satan is described as "the prince of the power of the air" in Ephesians 2:2. Therefore, this is when Satan fell.

However, the argument in the above paragraph does not work. If Satan had already fallen, then God could not have described other creations later in the week as "good", nor could He have described the finished creation as "very good".

When we reach the end of the Creation Week, we will see how the use of the phrases "good" and "very good" in Genesis 1 actually represents completeness, so it is not implied that the creation remaining after Day Two was in any way bad, but that it was incomplete. Indeed, all of creation was incomplete until the end of Day Six. However, each daily task was completed by God, which is why He described it as good - except that on Day Two. For a reason only known to the Sovereign Lord, He decided to begin the work of making the universe on Day Two, but did not complete it until Day Four. We do not know why this is the case. Indeed, we do not know the reason for any of the choices God made concerning the order of creation. I suspect that the creation of objects in the universe was spread between Days Two and Four precisely to undermine the foolish arguments that people use today, to suggest that Day Two is simply a poetic parallel of Day Five. We have already critiqued this view, which is known as the Framework Hypothesis.

The Expanse

Genesis 1:6 tells us about the creation of an expanse in the waters of creation, separating waters from waters. This leads us to two questions: first, what was the expanse, and second, what were the waters above and waters below the expanse?

The word *expanse* is the one used in the ESV, NASB, CSB, NET, WEB, and many others. However, the NLT uses the phrase “a space” and the NIV uses “vault”, while the NRSV uses “dome”. NLT, NIV, and NRSV are dynamic equivalence translations, so the translators are trying to find a word that explains the meaning. The earlier mentioned translations are formal equivalence translations – the so-called word-for-word versions. *Expanse* is the nearest word in meaning to the Hebrew word, which is *rāqîya* (רָקִיעַ), as we shall see.

In passing, we must note that the KJV and NKJV, which are both formal equivalence translations, both use the word *firmament* – a choice which is accurate enough, but has led to some confusion. We will see where that confusion has arisen shortly.

Today, there are a number of scholars, who self-identify as conservative evangelicals, who see the Genesis Creation account as being an example of Ancient Near Eastern mythology. They therefore argue that the original author of Genesis did not intend Genesis 1 to be interpreted according to modern science. To understand how this relates to the interpretation of *rāqîya*, we will need to quote an extended passage from the work of one such theologian – Dr. John H. Walton, from his book *The Lost World of Genesis 1.*

> Day two has been problematic at a number of different levels. In antiquity people routinely believed that the sky was solid.[1] As history progressed through the periods of scholasticism, the Renaissance, the Copernican revolution and the Enlightenment, verse 2 became more difficult to handle. For if the Hebrew term is to be taken in its normal contextual sense, it indicates that God made a solid dome to hold up waters above the earth. The choice of saying the Bible was wrong was deemed unacceptable, but the idea of rendering the word in a way that could tolerate modern scientific thinking could not be considered preferable in that it manipulated the text to say something that it had never said. We cannot think that we can interpret the word "expanse/firmament" as simply the sky or the atmosphere if that is not what the author meant by it when he used it and not what the audience would have understood by the word.[2]

The basis of Walton's textual criticism is that people in the ancient world – Babylon and Greece – would have understood *rāqîya* to be a solid dome, and that the word cannot mean anything other than that. As biblical creationists, we would deny both these presuppositions.

1 At this point, Walton references Paul Seely. Seely, P., *The Firmament and the Waters Above*, Westminster Theological Journal, **54** (1992): 31-46.

2 Walton, J.H. (2009), *The Lost World of Genesis 1*, (Downers Grove, IL: IVP), pp 56-57.

As we have stated, the Hebrew word in question is *rāqîya*. The Septuagint (LXX), the Greek translation of the Old Testament, translates *rāqîya* as *stereōma* (στερέωμα). The word means expanse, or spread out, and we are familiar with its inclusion in English prefixes, such as *stereophonic* – referring to older hi-fi systems, that spread out sound, by using two or more speakers. When the Latin translation of the Bible, known as the Vulgate, was produced, they used the word *firmamentum*, and the KJV has transliterated that as *firmament*. However, both *firmamentum* and *stereōma* have a much smaller semantic range than *rāqîya*. The word *firmamentum* even seems to imply something solid and firm. But *rāqîya* is much broader than that.

The root of the word *rāqîya* is *raqa*. This can be found, for example, in Isaiah 40:19.

> An idol! A craftsman casts it, and a goldsmith overlays it with gold and casts for it silver chains.

In this version, the word *raqa* has been translated as "overlays". In fact, *raqa* speaks of how the gold is hammered, until it is very thin. No metal can be hammered more effectively that gold, and in the process of hammering it, it spreads out. Artists and model makers are probably familiar with using ultrathin gold leaf, in decorating pictures, furniture, and other artwork. Another verse where *raqa* occurs is Numbers 16:39:

> So Eleazar the priest took the bronze censers, which those who were burned had offered, and they were hammered out as a covering for the altar.

It would seem, then, that *rāqîya* – the expanse – implies expansion, due to being worked on, and spread out, by God. This would appear to be the action carried out by God on Day Two.

Before we can examine this point further, we had better tackle Walton's opinion that ancient people would always have understood *rāqîya* as a solid dome.

We must first acknowledge that many ancient people did view cosmology in terms of solid domes. Early Greek cosmology viewed the Earth as a flat disk, surrounded by a circular ocean. Above this disk was a solid hemispherical dome, which enclosed the atmosphere, and on which the Sun, Moon, and planets were situated. Aristotle refined this to a central spherical Earth, surrounded by planets, fixed into solid spheres of differing radii. The Aristotelian view was very influential through the Middle Ages and beyond, and had influenced the church of Rome so much, that it led to the persecution of Galileo, and others, who attacked geocentrism.

We are now well used to the fact that there is considerable evidence suggesting that there were other ancients who did not hold to either the early Greek - or later Greek - cosmologies. Therefore, it should not surprise us that there were also ancients, who did not accept the idea of solid domes. For example, Jonathan Sarfati, in his commentary on Genesis, has quoted a correspondence from Nicholas Peterson, which shows that the Greek *chaos* (χαος), used in the LXX to describe the formless and void state of the universe, is related to *chasma* (χασμα), suggesting that a gap must have been opened by God, between waters above and below.[3]

With the primary meaning, within the semantic range of *rāqîya*, implying a stretching, and the fact that the ancients did not necessarily have to restrict their understanding of *rāqîya* to the meanings of *stereōma* or *firmamentum*, we are now in a position to understand what God actually did on the Second Day. The formless Earth consisted mostly, if not entirely, of water by the end of Day One. On Day Two, God made a gap in the waters, with a central sphere of water which was to be shaped into the Earth, and a higher sphere of water, above the gap, or expanse. This would have comprised all the universe there was, at the beginning of Day Two. Therefore, the waters above formed the outer edge of the universe, outside of which there was literally nothing – not empty space, just nothing. So all the space that existed was to be found between the levels of water. Then we must assume that God expanded that space, to form the entire size of the universe. This expansion of space itself is still going on,

3 Sarfati, J. (2015), *The Genesis Account*, (Powder Springs, GA: Creation Book Publishers), p153.

according to Hubble Red Shift measurements, but at a much slower rate. God clearly made this expansion to be greater than the speed of light, which, as Almighty Sovereign Lord, He could do. This is a much better explanation than the similarly rapid expansion of space proposed by the Inflation Hypothesis, discussed earlier.

The Waters Above

This brings us to a discussion about what the waters above could have been.

I hope that no one will consider that this Author does not recognize his enormous debt, along with every other creationist writer and speaker, to the pioneering work achieved by Dr. Henry Morris and Dr. John Whitcomb.[4] In May 1961, they published their seminal joint work "The Creation Flood". This was just a few months before I was born. In the book, Morris and Whitcomb explained the reality of the Genesis Flood from both a biblically theological and scientific standpoint. For decades, there was nothing else like it.

4 In 2005, when I still lived in my home country, I had just been appointed as a speaker for Answers in Genesis (UK). So, the parent ministry invited me to their "MegaConference" in Lynchburg, VA. Dr. Whitcomb was giving a talk at the conference, entitled "The History and Impact of the Genesis Flood". After the talk, despite the fact I already had a copy of the book, I wanted to buy a signed copy. So I bought my copy, and took it to the table, where Dr. Whitcomb was signing. He looked up, as I handed him the book, and read my name badge. "Ah, Paul Taylor!", he exclaimed. "You have just been appointed to work with Answers in Genesis in England!". The fact that my hero in the faith actually recognized my name, and already knew what I was doing, was a special moment for me, which I will never forget.

So, when Morris and Whitcomb introduced the concept of the "Vapor Canopy" in their book, that is what we all believed, because no one had ever written a similar work at the time. There was no other creationist writing with which to compare the text. The idea was that the "waters above" referred to a canopy of water vapor high up in the atmosphere. This vapor canopy created higher pressures on the Earth below, which, they argued, would cause greater longevity of people and animals. It would also shield the Earth from harmful radiation from the Sun. At the time of the Flood, the canopy would have collapsed, and would have been the principle source of rain.

It has to be said that the Vapor Canopy model was abandoned by most serious creationists decades ago, but many ordinary Christians have not yet caught up. The hyperbaric pressure assumed to be produced by this canopy might have helped people with lung complaints, but such high pressure would actually shorten, not lengthen the lifespan of someone with healthy lungs. As for shielding from harmful solar radiation, in fact water vapor does very little shielding.

In Psalm 148:4, we read "Praise Him, you highest heavens, and you waters above the heavens." Psalm 148 was written after the Flood, yet the waters above are still there. And, as we have already discussed, the *rāqîya* separating waters from waters does not refer to the atmosphere, but rather to the whole of space.

We will discuss the source of the Floodwaters at the appropriate time, but for now we note that the main source of the Floodwaters must have been the "fountains of the great deep" (Genesis 7:11).

Conclusion

On the second day, God put a gap into the waters of the great deep, separating waters above from waters below. The waters above are just beyond the edge of the universe, defining its boundary. They did not form an atmospheric vapor canopy. God stretched out the universe, at great speed, in a manner reflected in other verses of Scripture: "Stretching out the heavens like a tent" (Psalm 102:4). "He... stretches out the heavens like a curtain" (Isaiah 40:22).

At the close of Day Two, God had not completed His work on the waters below, so this is probably why God did not make a declaration that everything "was good". That would happen, after the completion of His work on the waters below, during the creation week.

Genesis 1 Part 7 – The Third Day of Creation

(Genesis 1:9-13)

Each day of the Creation Week is unique. Although there are certain patterns that can be discerned, these patterns are often pressed too hard by some commentators – especially those wedded to the Framework Hypothesis. Day Three, in particular, is quite different from the two previous days. The first difference that we note is that God did two main acts of creation during this day; that is, He gathered the waters into one place, while making dry land, and then He made plants. The first of these acts appears to be a continuation of the work He carried out on all the waters, and hence this work is concluded by God calling it good. The second work on Day Three was therefore a separate act of creation, and had its own declaration of being good. Therefore, the first of the two declarations of goodness encompasses the acts of Day Two, and so commentators should not suppose that there was something less than good, or even wicked, about what happened on Day Two.

Creative Acts

Walton is concerned that "at this point some interpreters are troubled by their observation that God doesn't make anything on day three."[1] Walton has made a distinction in his book between what he calls material origins, and what he calls functional origins. He reasons "If [day three] is understood as an account of functional origins, there is no need for God to make something."[2]

However, both his question and his answer are predicated on his prior rejection of the concept of six literal 24-hour days of creation. Therefore, given his presupposition that the views of deep-time scientists are true (regarding geologic ages and evolution), he sees only a symbolic description of the creation of land and plants, which does not conform to reality. This is a good example of why our presuppositions matter. When we approach Genesis 1 with humility, in order to exegete the text, rather than force our framework on to it, we find that there were indeed direct acts of creation on Day Three. These are the creation of land, and the creation of plants.

Creation of Land

It is often important to remember that not everything the Bible has to say about creation is contained in Genesis 1. We find some other information elsewhere in the inspired text. So, in Genesis 1:9, the creation of land is simply stated as God saying "Let the dry land appear." There is, of course, a hint in the text that God was making

1 Walton, J. H. (2009), *The Lost World of Genesis One*, (Downers Grove, IL: IVP) p58.
2 *ibid*

this dry land out of water. However, this fact is explained further in 2 Peter 3:5-6, when the apostle identifies the error of the "scoffers", by stating:

> For they deliberately overlook this fact, that the heavens existed long ago, and the earth was formed out of water and through water by the word of God, and that by means of these the world that then existed was deluged with water and perished.

Peter shows that there are two great events, which undermine a uniformitarian worldview, namely that God created the world and God flooded the world. We will return to the implications of these events later. For now, we should note that Peter states that "the earth was formed out of water". At first sight, one might suppose that this contradicts what Genesis 1 says, when it tells us that the Earth was among the first things that God made. However, in 2 Peter 3:5, the word *earth* is translated from the Greek γῆ (*gē*), from which we get words such as *geology*. As in English, this word can be used to mean the planet Earth, or a bucket of earth (i.e. soil), or the earth as opposed to the sea. Earth can mean soil or land. The context in 2 Peter 3 suggests that the third option (earth vs sea) is the one being used, and strongly implies that God made the materials of the land from the molecules of the water. It is possible that God used some sort of transmutation to make the elements, and their atoms, from the basic building blocks of water molecules, with their hydrogen and oxygen molecules.

Whatever method God used, we note that the land was directly created by God. What materials did it contain? It would need to contain the sort of minerals, that could immediately be used by plants, in order to grow. It is likely that He directly made soils, and loam. Some might argue that this would be deceptive of God, as it would look as if plants had rotted prior to the creation. However, this apparent appearance of age is not a deception, because God is directly telling us what He made, and when. As we will go on to see, God made plants ready to bear seeds, so the land that God made must also have contained the soil required by the plants to grow, as well as the rocks beneath. Note here that, contrary to the accusations made against creationists (and this accusation was repeated in a Facebook thread to me only yesterday!), we do not think that God used this moment to create some fossils in these rocks. Fossils are the clear imprints of organisms that were definitely alive in the past, and it is our supposition that the overwhelming majority of these would have been formed in the Flood. Moreover, fossils are found only in sedimentary rock.

Evolutionary geologists like to divide rocks into three major classifications; *igneous*, *sedimentary*, and *metamorphic*. Igneous rocks are those formed by heat, having cooled from molten rock.

Sedimentary rocks are made from minerals previously eroded from igneous rocks, or other sedimentary rocks, and formed into layers, being deposited by wind or water. Metamorphic rocks used to be sedimentary, but were altered by the action of heat, pressure, or both. Evolutionary geologists will also divide igneous rocks into two sub-groups; *plutonic* and *volcanic* rocks. Volcanic rocks have formed, obviously, in volcanic events. They describe plutonic rocks as those extruded and cooled slowly, over millions of years, crystallizing within the Earth's crust.

These groupings of rocks are easy to identify by appearance, so creationists tend to use them as well, except that the evolutionary definition of plutonic rocks is an impossibility, on a biblical timescale, and that slow extrusion and crystallization is not, in fact, seen in reality. Therefore, creationists would suppose that plutonic rocks are basically those made directly by God, during this creative event on Day Three. As there is a complete difference in the formation of plutonic and volcanic rocks, according to a biblical creationist worldview, it is often convenient for us simply to refer to four major classification groups – plutonic, volcanic, sedimentary, and metamorphic – instead of the three used by evolutionary geologists.

The method that God used to create these rocks is not known. He could have used an accelerated process of extrusion, heating, and cooling, or He could have simply made the rocks in place as they are.

Whatever the case, it would seem to be that that He made a variety of different kinds of rocks. The existence of different minerals is mentioned in Genesis 2:12 (and also in Ezekiel 28:13). Rocks comprise a multitude of small grains, each of which is a piece of mineral. And there is nothing in either list of minerals to suggest that the lists are exhaustive, so we can suppose that a variety of different rocks, minerals, and soils were made.

Waters Gathered Together

Another point, which is easily overlooked, is that God said "Let the waters under the heavens be gathered together into one place." This means that there would only be one ocean before the Flood. In a sense, there is only one ocean today, because all the named oceans are joined together somewhere. But the named oceans are only delineated from each other by the various continental land masses. We can therefore assume that, before the Flood, there was only one major land mass. This does not mean that there were no minor land masses. It is completely possible that there could have been some islands, but the overwhelming majority of the Earth's land would have been joined together in the pre-Flood supercontinent, which we usually refer to as *Rodinia*, from the Russian word for "motherland".

The geologist Dr Andrew Snelling, who is also Director of Research at Answers in Genesis, has done a considerable amount of research on how Rodinia split apart. Rodinia was torn apart by the violent forces of the Flood, in ways that we will describe later. But these pieces of Rodinia are called *cratons*, and it is by analyzing what remains of these cratons in today's continents that we can get some sort of picture of what Rodinia may have looked like. Snelling pictures Rodinia as a giant C-shaped landmass.[3]

Seasons and Axial Tilt

In Genesis 1:14, we read that one of the reasons for astronomical features is that they will mark out seasons. Today, seasons are explicable, because of the Earth's axial tilt. If one charts the plane of the Earth's orbit, and then draws a line perpendicular to that plane, the Earth's axis of rotation is tilted away from that perpendicular at an angle of just over 23°. In the days of the old Canopy model, it was assumed by some that God could have triggered the Flood by sending an asteroid to hit the Earth, and precipitate the vapor canopy. At the same time, this shifted the Earth's axis away from the perpendicular.

This view assumes that there is something wrong with the 23° tilt. In fact, there is not. It would appear that 23° is the ideal angle to cause the cycle of seasons that we have. Therefore, we can assume that the Earth had such a tilt before the Flood, and that there were pre-Flood seasons, albeit not as violent or extreme as today. The angle of the

3 Snelling, A.A. (2014), *Noah's Lost World*, Answers Magazine, April – June 2014: pp80-85.

axial tilt appears to be a design feature, because, without it, there would certainly have been problems in such a world.

The existence of different seasons, and the axial tilt, would also have ensured that different parts of the pre-Flood Earth would have different climates. This will prove important, when we consider the pre-Flood distribution of plants and animals. It should not be assumed that a perfect world had to be a uniform world. Just as there were varieties of animals, plants, and, probably, rocks, so there was probably a variety of weather conditions, and ecosystems.

Creation of Plants

God did not leave this new dry land empty for very long. Before this Third Day was out, He would have filled the dry land with plants.

God said "Let the earth sprout vegetation, plants yielding seed, and fruit trees bearing fruit in which is their seed, each according to its kind, on the earth." And it was so. (Genesis 1:11).

This is the first explicit mention of anything organic in nature. We know that plants can reproduce, by seeds, or by other means. Therefore, evolutionary scientists would class them as living, and would assume that animals and plants share a common ancestor. But Genesis clearly states that plants were formed separately from animals. Therefore, there is no need to link their ancestral biology.

Plants grow, reproduce and die, but there is no reason to suppose that plant growth, or plant death, is in any way related to that of animals.

Indeed, it makes sense for us to suppose that the quality within plants that we call *life* is not the same as that in animals – or, at any rate, that quality of life found in animals which breathe and possess blood.

This topic will be explored in more depth when we refer to the animals of Days Five and Six. But for now we should note that the definition of life, used in the Bible, is - like many other classifications - not the same as that used by secular science. Plants are best understood as biological machines. For example, we are going to read later that death is something that is not good, and was not part of the Creation Week. Indeed, we find that animals and humans were given plants to eat, at the time of creation, and therefore, were not permitted to eat meat. Even in thne immediate aftermath of the Flood, when permission to eat other animals was given, the prohibition on the consumption of blood was still in place, underlining the great importance the Bible places on the sort of life that has blood. More on this later.

The point that needs to be made at this juncture is that something had to be made, which would provide food for animals, giving them the sort of nutrients and compounds that they would need. So, the consumption of a plant is not considered death in the same sense as the consumption of an animal. It is merely the end, and the assimilation, of a biological machine.

Everyone instinctively knows this. If we walk through the forest, and find a dead tree, we might sit on it for rest. We are unlikely to do the same if we come across a dead deer. Likewise, vegans, in their opposition to eating animal products, do not have a similar opposition to eating plants. There must be some sort of delineation in our minds, between the value of the life of a plant and the value of the life of an animal. Evolutionists, by the way, do not have a consistent methodology for drawing these distinctions, whereas biblical creationists do, as we shall see.

We notice that God made an enormous variety of plants. This huge variety of plants - especially of flowering plants - was something that troubled the author of *The Origin of Species*, Charles Darwin. He observed that many, many types of flowering plants "appeared" in the fossil record, in just a few layers, which he assumed to represent a short period of time, according to his deep-time beliefs. In 1879, about 20 years after first publishing *The Origin of Species*, he wrote to Joseph Hooker, director of Kew Gardens, about what he called "an abominable mystery". Yet, when we accept the truth of Genesis 1, there is no mystery.

The main classification or demarcation of plants given in Genesis 1 is the *kind*. The phrase "Each according to its kind" is repeated a number of times. The information required to determine the plant kind is stated in the text to be in the seed, or the seed contained in the fruit. Thus, planting apple seeds will produce apple trees, not fig trees. Yet the apple tree may not be identical to its parent. This is because the concept of a kind – as we shall see when we discuss animals – is broader than that of a species. A number of species of plant may, in fact, be related, and part of the same kind. New species may emerge within those kinds, but this is not evolution, in the Darwinian sense. Selection has taken place only from genetic information, which was already available.

Plants within the same kind could, in some circumstances, be identified by their ability to hybridize. Thus, the wild salmonberries, which I find on trails close to Mount St Helens, are part of the same kind as raspberries and blackberries. However, they would not hybridize with huckleberries, which are not of the same kind as blackberries, but are of a kind with blueberries and wymberries.

The nomenclature of the branch of biology, developed by creation scientists, to help understand the concept of *kind*, will be explained when we discuss animals. Creationists like to refer to these *kinds* as *baramins*, from the Hebrew words for "created kinds".

Marvelous Mechanisms in Plants

Plants include some truly marvelous and mind-blowing mechanisms. Some of these might be unique to the particular kind of plant that is being studied. However, there are also some general traits that can be observed.

This is not a textbook about plants. Therefore, we ought not even to attempt to be exhaustive in our coverage of such traits. Nevertheless, two interesting traits will be identified.

Photosynthesis

It is no exaggeration to state that life on Earth could not exist without plant photosynthesis. This is the process whereby plants begin the manufacture of their own organic compounds. In order to achieve this, the underside of leaves have small holes, called stomata, to facilitate the entrance of carbon dioxide molecules. Molecules of water have been obtained through the roots. The reaction is as follows:

$6CO_2 + 6H_2O \rightarrow C_6H_{12}O_6 + 6O_2$

Carbon dioxide + water → sugars + oxygen

The reaction does not proceed by itself. It requires light energy, and a specific catalyst, called *chlorophyll*. Chlorophyll is the green pigment which gives the characteristic color to leaves.

It is by this means that the beginning of larger organic molecules is made, given that the process produces sugars.

Transpiration

If photosynthesis is a remarkable chemical process, involving leaves, then transpiration appears to me to be an equally remarkable physical process, caused by the same leaves. Trees are, basically, just huge plants. Yet water has to be moved from the roots of the plants up to higher reaches of the trees. The large surface area of the leaves of the trees provides part of the mechanism required. As water evaporates from the leaves, more water is sucked up through the capillaries of the tree's structure to replace it. Therefore, a tree really is working as a machine, lifting water against gravity, so that it is available where it is going to be needed.

The descriptions of photosynthesis and transpiration given are very much over-simplifications. As I said, this is not a textbook about plants. There are a lot of other highly remarkable processes, which plants also use. But these two brief descriptions will at least give the reader to understand that there is a lot of very clever design, that has gone into the making of these remarkable biological machines, the plants.

Sprouting Plants

One factor that we ought to consider is **how** God made these plants. He could very easily have made the plants fully formed, fully grown, in their mature state. However, the account in Genesis 1:11 states: “And God said, Let the earth sprout vegetation, plants yielding seed, and fruit trees bearing fruit in which is their seed, each according to its kind, on the earth. And it was so.” The use of the word *sprout* is important. The Hebrew word is *dasha* (דשא), and it implies that the plants grew. Yet we only have part of one day (possibly the afternoon?) for the plants to grow. So the word *dasha* perhaps suggests that God made the plants grow rapidly, from the ground up.

While there does not appear to be any doctrinal problem caused by believing either that the plants were made fully grown, or made to grow rapidly from the ground up, I like the way this rapid growth was illustrated in the documentary movie *Genesis: Paradise Lost*, produced by my friends at *Creation Today*.[4]

Conclusion

God began Day Three by completing His work with water. He followed the vertical separation of waters on Day Two, with a horizontal work on the waters to produce dry land. For this reason, He declared it as “good”, on completion. Then He filled the dry land that He had just

4 < https://genesismovie.com/ >, accessed 11/26/2018.

made with many kinds of plants. Once again, He declared this work to be “good”. Thus, everything God had made by the end of Day Three can be seen to be good, so the Earth’s rotation continued, with evening and with morning.

Genesis 1 Part 8 – The Fourth Day of Creation

(Genesis 1:14-19)

When I made a series of video lectures on the Creation Week, my talk for Day Four was entitled *The Bible's Astronomy*.[1] That is what the fourth day of Creation is really all about – though perhaps a better title might have been *The Bible's Cosmogony*.

Cosmogony refers to a theory or model of how the universe came to be in its present form. It is therefore a subset of *cosmology* – a study of the universe, and how it fits together. Cosmology and *astronomy* overlap a lot, and writers on astronomy will usually comment on cosmology, though strictly speaking astronomy is more of an observational science, describing our view of the night sky. Hopefully, all readers of this book will be aware that none of the above terms has anything to do with *astrology*, which is a pseudo-religious, occult "art". A case can be made to suggest that astronomy is supported in the Bible (Psalm 19:1). Astrology, on the other hand, is forbidden in the Bible. For example, in Deuteronomy 18:9-12, God says:

> When you come into the land that the Lord your God is giving you, you shall not learn to follow the abominable

1 *The Six Days of Genesis – DVD Series*, Creation Today, produced by Kent Andrew Hovind, 2013.

> practices of those nations. There shall not be found among you anyone who burns his son or his daughter as an offering, anyone who practices divination or tells fortunes or interprets omens, or a sorcerer or a charmer or a medium or a necromancer or one who inquires of the dead, for whoever does these things is an abomination to the Lord. And because of these abominations the Lord your God is driving them out before you.

The telling of fortunes or the interpretation of omens certainly covers astrology, and a strong case is made that these verses forbid astrology, among other occult practices.

The Big Bang

Most people seem to make a start with this subject, by assuming that the Big Bang theory is a scientific fact, and that we must therefore interpret Genesis accordingly. Indeed, belief in the Big Bang theory seems to be more widespread that belief in Darwinian Evolution. There are biblical scholars who refuse to compromise with Darwinism, but think that they have no choice but to add the Big Bang to their biblical accounts. We need to state at the outset that this is not the case. In many ways, the Big Bang can be considered as a form of cosmic evolution, because, like its biological counterpart, its provisions are contrary to Scripture, and it suggests that ordered systems could spontaneously develop out of chaos. We need to state from the outset that not only is it not necessary to accept the Big Bang theory, the biblical account is positively opposed to it.

What Is the Big Bang Theory?

In order to be able to criticize the Big Bang theory, we need to understand what it really is. Now, a commentary on Genesis like this cannot discuss every aspect of the Big Bang theory, so readers need to be referred, for further information, to some of the most important books on creationist cosmogony of the last couple of decades. These would include *Taking Back Astronomy*[2] by Jason Lisle, *Dismantling the Big Bang*[3] by Alex Williams and John Hartnett, *Starlight, Time, and the New Physics*[4] by John Hartnett, *The Created Cosmos*[5] by Danny Faulkner, and *The Physics of Einstein*[6] by Jason Lisle.

It is often mistakenly thought that secular cosmologists assume that every piece of matter in the universe was once in one small point, and that this somehow exploded, sending everything out to expand into space. This is not what they believe. They believe that not only all matter, but also all of space and time was also in that small point, known as a *singularity*, before it burst open. The Big Bang is inferred,

2 Lisle, J. (2006), *Taking Back Astronomy*, (Green Forest, AR: Master Books).
3 Williams, A. and Hartnett, J. (2005), *Dismantling the Big Bang*, (Green Forest, AR: Master Books).
4 Hartnett, J. (2007), *Starlight, Time, and the New Physics*, (Atlanta, GA: Creation Book Publishers).
5 Faulkner, D. (2016), *The Created Cosmos*, (Green Forest, AR: Master Books).
6 Lisle, J. (2018), *The Physics of Einstein*, (Aledo, TX: Biblical Science Institute).

because of the expansion of the universe. Galaxies are moving away from each other, so this movement is extrapolated backwards, to determine at what point that singularity existed. One high school physics textbook in the UK put it thus:

> If we imagine travelling back in time, then galaxies would all be speeding towards each other, making the Universe a denser place in the past. If we continue going backwards, then we should reach a moment in time when the Universe was crammed together into a state of almost infinite density. This reasoning suggests that the Universe began in a sort of explosion.[7]

The Big Bang theory, as stated above, does not suggest that everything has expanded into an infinite cosmos of space. This would imply that one part of the universe would be the center, and that, therefore, observations taken in different parts of the universe would, themselves, be different. However, it is a principle of the Big Bang theory that there is no special place anywhere in the universe, and that all observations from all parts of the universe are essentially the same. The only way to satisfy this principle – known as the *Cosmological Principle* – is to imagine a universe that is not really possible for our heads to get around. It is suggested that our three-dimensional universe is expanding into a fourth dimension. This

7 *Salters Horner Advanced Physics* (2001), (Oxford: Heinemann Educational Publishers).

fourth dimension is not time, as in Einstein's ideas of relativity, but a fourth dimension of space perpendicular to the other three.

To get at least a modicum of understanding on this matter, let us imagine a universe with one dimension less. Let us say that the visible universe has two dimensions instead of three. This universe could be on a flat two-dimensional plane. But let us suppose that it is, in fact, drawn on the outside of a very large balloon. Although the surface of the balloon is curved, it would appear to small occupants of this universe that it is, in fact, a planar surface. Then we can imagine that this balloon is being inflated, so that its surface expands through a third dimension. An ant on the balloon's surface, while thinking that it is on a flat surface, could walk in one direction, and eventually end up back where it started. No point on the surface of this balloon would be the "center" of this two-dimensional universe, because this universe has no boundary – just a curve back on itself. Big Bang theorists take this two- and three- dimensional analogy and apply it to a three and four dimensional scenario.

It needs to be emphasized that this highly unusual cosmological model is not a statement of fact. It is a model. It is for this reason that Dr. Lisle describes it as "a secular **speculation** about the origin of the universe."[8]

8 Lisle, J. (2006), p. 43, emphasis added.

The Biblical Account

Now that we have stated what the secular alternative to the biblical account is, we can more fully examine the biblical account. In doing so, we will see that it is incompatible with the secular Big Bang model.

> 14. And God said, Let there be lights in the expanse of the heavens to separate the day from the night. And let them be for signs and for seasons, and for days and years, 15. and let them be lights in the expanse of the heavens to give light upon the earth. And it was so. 16. And God made the two great lights—the greater light to rule the day and the lesser light to rule the night—and the stars. 17. And God set them in the expanse of the heavens to give light on the earth, 18. to rule over the day and over the night, and to separate the light from the darkness. And God saw that it was good. 19. And there was evening and there was morning, the fourth day. (Genesis 1:14-19)

In verse 14, we see that all the lights of the universe were created by God and therefore He knows where they all are, and how they all work. In no way does this take away from our awe at the vastness of the universe; quite the contrary.

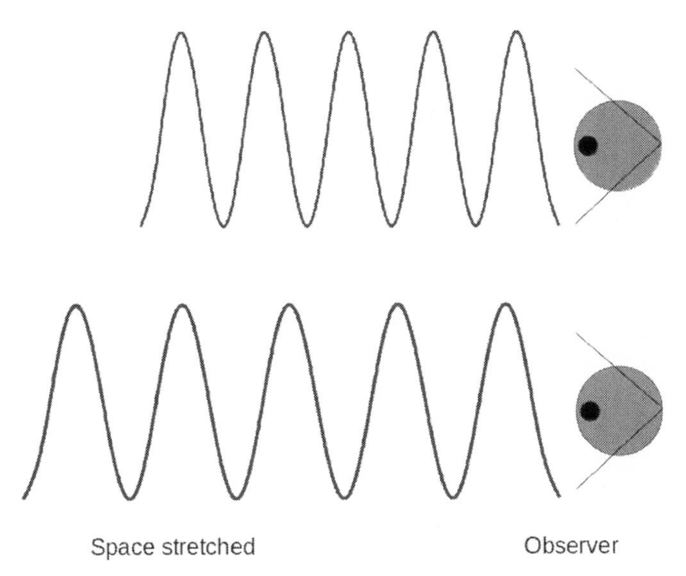

However, it is possible that this also means that however vast the universe is, it is finite. Of course, God could create an infinite universe if He wished, but we have already discussed that the universe is bounded by the waters above the expanse. In verse 14, we have read that God made these lights **in** the expanse. Therefore, the lights are contained within a finite, though hugely vast, volume. It makes sense to suppose, then, that the number of lights is finite. These lights include stars, the Sun, the Moon, planets, asteroids, and, indeed, all astronomical objects. We have already discussed that this expanse is stretching. In the Creation Week, it stretched rapidly, but that stretching continues today. This stretching of what we might call the fabric of space is what gives us our red shift measurements today.

The lights are there to separate the day from the night. This may seem obvious at first, but it is not. In fact, the amount of light from stars presents a paradox, which Big Bang cosmology is unable to explain. The paradox is called Olber's Paradox, and is named for Heinrich Wilhelm Olbers (1758–1840), who formulated it. Also called the Dark Night Paradox, it surmises what might happen if there are an infinite number of stars. Although these stars are not an equal distance away, some are brighter than others, and they could appear at all points of the night sky. With such a scenario, why is there any dark sky at night at all? If there is an equal chance of a star being at any point in the sky, and there are an infinite number of stars, the entire night sky should be covered with stars. Clearly, this is not the case, so Olber concluded that the number of stars is finite.[9]

Genesis 1:14 also tells us that the lights in the sky are for signs and seasons. This fact applies to the Sun and Moon, but equally applies to the stars. Because stars are so far away, they appear fixed. Of course, they are not. Over the centuries, there have been imperceptible changes of the position of the stars relative to each other. In the time of Noah, for example, the star that we now know as Polaris – the Pole Star – was not the one directly above the North Pole. Instead, that position was held by a fainter star, called Thuban.

9 *Olber's Paradox*, < https://www.britannica.com/science/Olbers-paradox >, accessed 11/21/2018.

Thuban is seen in the constellation Draco (the Dragon). The current pole star is Polaris, at the tail of the constellation Ursa Minor (Little

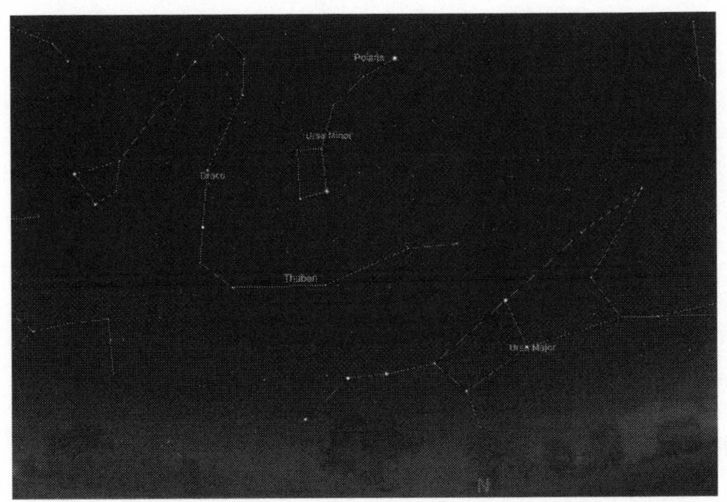

Bear). This apparent movement of these stars over centuries is due to axial regression.

As the stars appear more or less fixed in place in the sky, many people have imagined pictures, by joining lines to the stars, as if they were dots on a page. It takes a lot of imagination to see these rather fanciful pictures in the sky, yet the images are pretty well established, and some of them are even mentioned in the Bible. These constellations act as signs in the sky. Different constellations appear at different times of year, so these signs do indeed mark out the seasons. For example, in many northern hemisphere lands, the appearance of Orion lets us know that Winter is upon us. However, any attempt to see spiritual suggestions in the sky constitutes astrology, which is forbidden in Scripture.

The Earth's axis is tilted at an angle of 23° to where it might be expected. If one imagines a flat surface, or plane, through the Earth's orbit, then a line perpendicular to this would be referred to as the *normal*. The Earth's axis is 23° to that normal. It has been suggested that this axial tilt is abnormal, and must have been caused by the catastrophic events of the Worldwide Flood. This seems unlikely. It is the axial tilt, which is responsible for the seasons, so I would surmise that the axial tilt before the Flood was the same as that today.

The Sun and the Moon are also timekeepers. The Earth's rotation on its axis once every 24 hours is what defines our day, and the rhythm of day and night occurs also because of this rotation. This rotation also causes the apparent motion of the Sun across our daytime sky, and the apparent motion of the constellations during the night. As we have suggested, from Day One there must have been a uni-directional form of light, in order to define these features. On Day Four, however, the Sun was made the focal point of this light. Why did God make the Sun on Day Four, and not on Day One? Many ancient pagan societies worshiped the Sun and / or the Moon, because of their astronomical significance. It seems likely, therefore, that God was emphasizing that the Sun and the Moon are only created objects, and so they are not to be worshiped. This suggestion is somewhat supported by the fact that the Sun and Moon are not named in this account, but simply designated as greater and lesser lights.

The Earth and Sun also define our year. The Earth orbits the Sun once every 365.24 days. The Earth's orbit is nearly, but not quite, circular. It is, in fact, an ellipse, with the Sun at one of the two foci of the ellipse.

In fact, all the major timescales, except one, appear to be astronomical in nature. The year is the period of one orbit of the Earth around the Sun, and the day is the period of rotation of the Earth around its axis. The month is closely related to the orbital period of the Moon around the Earth. This period is 28 days, though appears to be longer, when one observes the phases of the Moon, because, by the time the Moon has completed an orbit, the Earth's position has shifted relative to its own orbit around the Sun. The more irregular months can also be defined by the rising of the zodiacal constellations. These are the twelve constellations, which are close in the sky to the ecliptic – the apparent path of the Sun during the year, which actually represents the orbit of the Earth. These twelve constellations are mostly named after animals – hence the zodiacal constellations. However, no mystical significance is to be given to these constellations, which are only apparent images, seen with the eye of imagination.

The ecliptic (that apparent path of the Sun) is of great significance in looking for other astronomical objects. All the eight planets of the Solar System orbit in more or less the same plane, so they can all be found in the sky close to the ecliptic. The word *planet* means wanderer. The planets appear like stars in the sky, but they generate no light of their own; like the Moon, they reflect sunlight back to us. Ancient people named them wanderers, because they are not "fixed" in the sky, like proper stars, but move across the sky. Their apparent movement is mostly in one direction, but at the point when the Earth nears its closest point to a planet further away from the Sun, that planet can appear to go backwards in the sky, due to the effect known as *retrograde* motion, as shown in the diagram.

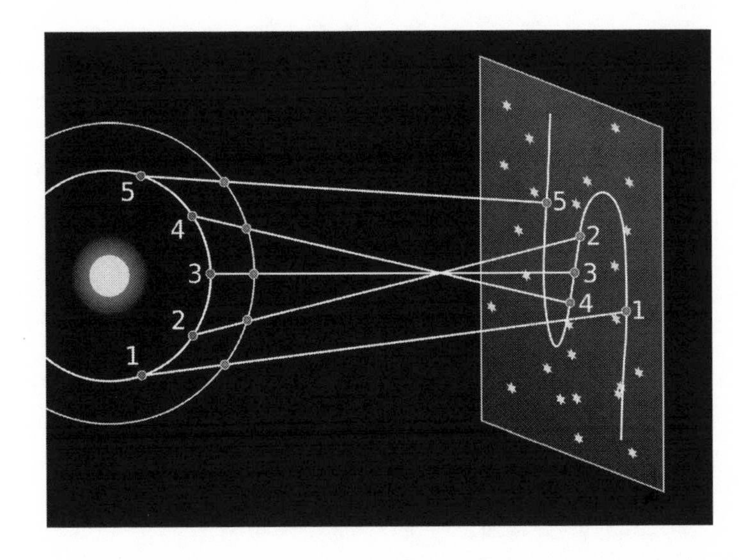

It should be noted that the Sun and the Moon are not actually named in Genesis 1. The theistic evolutionary commentator John Walton suggests that this is because the cosmos is actually a Temple, and that the lack of names for these lights – and, indeed, the fact that they are not mentioned until Day Four – suggests that the purpose of Genesis 1 is simply to speak against the polytheism of "other" Ancient Near Eastern myths. I am sure that God made these lights on the fourth day, to emphasize that the Sun and Moon were not creation gods, as indeed many other cultures suggest. But this fact in no way detracts from the truthfulness, integrity, and historicity of Genesis 1. Therefore, for Walton to suggest that the historicity of Genesis 1 does not matter, compared to its symbolic "truths" is an entirely unbiblical way of approaching the text. The text is more *typical* than *metaphorical*. Remember that, in a biblical context, a *type* is something which is both real and metaphorical at the same time. For example, the Passover Lamb was a real lamb, and the Passover a real event – but it is also symbolic of the death of Jesus, and the salvation of those for whom He shed His blood. It is in the same manner that we say that the deliberate non-naming of the Sun and Moon, and the deliberate creation of them three days later than the Earth is both symbolic of their relative importance, as well as historically true.

The Sun is the Greater Light, which rules the day. The Sun is – after Day Four – the source of our light, that we get during the daylight hours. It is the Sun which sets up the daily rhythms of night and day, evening and morning. It also sets up the rhythm of the seasons throughout the year. The Moon, meanwhile, not only governs the night sky (more on this in a moment), but also governs the passage of months, and its gravitational pull on the Earth governs the almost twice-daily rhythm of the ocean tides. It is no wonder, then, that early Celtic Christians, for example, used these rhythms to influence their times of prayer:

> The first Christians naturally adopted a rhythm of daily prayer and of weekly celebration of the Lord's Supper.... Their Scriptures revealed that God expressed rhythm in

> his universe; in the seven days of Creation, in the seasons and in the cycle of each day.[10]

The Moon, like the planets, does not generate its own light. Instead, it reflects the light of the Sun. While the Moon is sometimes visible during the day, and not always visible at night, there is no doubt that when it is visible during the hours of darkness, its brilliance mitigates against the darkness quite a lot. There are many nocturnal animals that would not be able to find food, if it were not for the limited visibility enabled by moonlight.

When we consider the multiplicity and complexity of the universe, it is startling to find that the creation of the stars is summed up in one phrase – almost a throwaway comment at the end of verse 16.

> And God made the two great lights—the greater light to rule the day and the lesser light to rule the night—and the stars. (Genesis 1:16).

Psalm 8:3 refers to the stars as "the work of your fingers", yet Psalm 19:1 gives us another reason for the existence of the universe; "The heavens declare the glory of God, and the sky above proclaims his handiwork." We can assume that the term *stars* is much broader than our current use of the word, and includes all astronomical objects –

10 Simpson, R. (2014), *Celtic Christianity*, (Vestal, NY: Anamchara Books), Kindle edition, location 848.

planets, comets, galaxies and so on. There are so many objects of so many different kinds. Our Solar System (objects that orbit the Sun) consists of eight planets – Mercury, Venus, Earth, Mars, Jupiter, Saturn, Uranus, and Neptune. There are also a number of dwarf planets. There could be a hundred of these, but five have been given names – Ceres, Pluto, Eris, Makemake, and Haumea. The Solar System also contains comets, which seem to be basically balls of dirty ice, orbiting the Sun, often in highly elongated elliptical orbits, whereas most planetary orbits, though also elliptical, are closer to being circles.

Comets give us an interesting upper bound for the age of the Solar System. As the comet passes close to the Sun, some of its material is thrown into space, by the action of the Sun. This material can often be seen, for larger comets, as a comet tail, which points away from the Sun, not, as is sometimes thought, opposite to the direction of motion. It is possible to calculate the rate at which comets lose this material, and, if we do so, we find that no comet should exist for more than 100,000 years. This does not mean that I think the Solar System is 100,000 years old. I think it is about 6,000 years old, because that is what the Bible says. Nevertheless, this fact shows us that the Solar System cannot be more than 100,000 years old. However, evolutionary astrophysicists have developed a coping mechanism for this. They refer to a nursery of comets, far beyond the orbit of Neptune, which they call the Oort Cloud. This contains a lot of comets, and, every so often, a passing star can nudge a new comet out of here, so that it can orbit closer to the Sun. There is, however, no evidence for such a cloud, and, if we accept the Genesis account, there is no need even to postulate such a cloud.

Remember that I am not trying to blind you with science with comments such as these. I am simply showing that genuine scientific evidence is consistent with the biblical account, rather than with the concept of deep time. When we start by accepting the account of creation in Genesis 1 as historically accurate, we find that everything else falls into place.

There is a great deal more to say about biblical astronomy. However, if you want more detail on the subject, you need to read a book which is solely concerned with such a subject. Dr. Danny Faulkner's "The Created Cosmos" and Dr. Jason Lisle's "Taking Back Astronomy" would be two such books, and both are footnoted earlier.

The Horizon Problem

Having examined the biblical astronomy, we now need to address a serious problem that applies to a number of cosmogonies – namely the starlight problem. We should first note that the Big Bang Theory has an inherent, yet under publicized, starlight problem of its own, to which there seems to be no observable scientific solution.

The problem, called *The Horizon Problem*, concerns a phenomenon known as *Cosmic Microwave Background Radiation.*

Space is not completely a vacuum. It is the nearest thing we know to a perfect vacuum, but it does actually contain some particles, atoms, and molecules. These particles are in motion – and motion of particles implies a temperature. In fact, throughout the universe, there is a background temperature of about 2.75K.[11] Although this is a very, very low temperature, it is still a bit above absolute zero. The energy required for this temperature is supplied by radiation which has a frequency of 160.23 GHz, which places it in the microwave range of the electromagnetic spectrum, corresponding to a photon energy of 6.626×10^{-4} eV. This energy is surprisingly homogeneous. That is to say it is found to be the same in every direction in every part of the universe. Yet, the "Big Bang" must have been a randomized event, that would suggest there should initially have been hot spots and cold spots throughout the universe. To get the current homogeneity, there

11 K stands for Kelvin, which is a unit of temperature. There are two better known temperature scales; degrees Fahrenheit has the freezing point of water at 32°F and the boiling point of water at 212°F – a difference of 180 degrees. Celsius places the same two references – more logically – at 0 and 100°C respectively. Therefore, there are 100 degrees difference between these two. Absolute zero is defined as the coldest temperature possible – when all particles cease moving. This occurs at -273.15°C. In the Kelvin temperature scale, this absolute zero is set at 0K, and then each subsequent Kelvin unit is the same amount of temperature rise as degrees Celsius. Therefore the freezing point of water is 273.15K, and water's boiling point is 373.15K.

must have been a transfer of energy by radiation. This radiation could have traveled at a maximum speed of the speed of light.

According to Big Bang theorists, the universe is about 13.7 billion years old. Therefore, the maximum distance that could have been traveled by the Cosmic Microwave Background radiation is 13.7 billion light years. For this to be achievable, the universe would have to be less than 27.4 billion light years across (twice the maximum energy difference, to represent energy radiating in all directions). However, the universe is known to be much bigger than 27.4 billion light years. Therefore, CMB is associated with a light problem, specific to the Big Bang theory, which is not soluble by observational science.

The Big Bang coping mechanism for this is a concept known as *inflation*. Now, the expansion of the universe appears to be governed by a constant known as the *Cosmological Constant*, and this is a "fiddle factor" introduced by Einstein, which he later considered to be a blunder. However, if there is such a constant, then the inflation model suggests a temporary increase of this constant by a factor of 10^{100} (1 with a hundred zeros after it), during a period from about 10^{-36} to 10^{-32} seconds after the Big Bang singularity.

Dr. Faulkner has suggested an alternative - and better - explanation for CMB. He relies on the previously discussed concept that the universe must be bounded by the "waters above". As this water is at the edge of the universe, it follows that it must have a red shift of the water spectrum greater than any other observed red shift. The radiation from this water, Faulkner shows, would have to be about that of a cool blackbody, which is precisely what it is! So the events described in Genesis 1:6-8 provide a better explanation for the existence of the CMB than does the Big Bang / Inflation Theory.

Creationist Cosmogonies

This brings us to one of the most frequent accusations made against the belief in a historical Genesis. How can you believe the universe is only 6,000 years old, when light has to have traveled from stars for many millions of years? As creationists, we refer to this question as the Starlight and Time Problem. It is often stated as follows:

> "How could light have traveled for millions of years across the universe, yet reached us after only 6,000 years?"

Yet Dr. Faulkner has shown that the question is even more tricky than this! It is a little lengthy to explain this important point, so it is best to pose the problem in Faulkner's own words.

> Most treatments of the light travel time problem concentrate upon the question of how we can see objects more than 6,000 lys away. Because most objects clearly visible to the naked eye are well within 6,000 lys, they aren't a problem in a recent creation. But while it is

possible for us to see most of the naked eye stars and today, some millennia after the Creation Week, it would not have been possible for Adam to have seen any stars (other than the sun) for at least four years after his creation. The stars were made on Day Four, and Adam was made on Day Six. The nearest star after the sun is 4.3 lys away, so Adam could not have seen even the closest star for more than four years, and then stars would have slowly winked in over the succeeding years. However, the stars could not have fulfilled their God ordained functions when Adam first saw them after Day Six. These functions include being used to mark seasons and the passage of time (we still do this today with the day, month, and year). The passage of the year and the seasons are reckoned by how the sun appears to move against the background stars as the earth orbits the sun. Absent these background stars, it would not be possible to determine the passage of the year and of the seasons. Therefore, to truly solve the light travel time problem, light from stars even a few light years away must have been visible only days after their creation (and it is likely that the light of all the astronomical objects reaching the earth today also reached the earth at this early time). Any realistic solution to the light travel time problem must explain how Adam

> could have seen any stars on the evening following Day Six.[12]

It must be pointed out immediately that the Bible does not always give us a direct answer to questions of this nature. Such questions do not concern issues of human or even Christian behavior. However, our presupposition that the Bible is true is not problematic, because it is possible to build an explanation, which is scientifically coherent, which acknowledges our biblical presupposition.

We should also mention at this point that there are a number of variations of the Big Bang theory, and there are other non-biblical cosmogonies. Although it is the majority view, there are many astrophysicists who do not accept the Big Bang Theory. Sir Fred Hoyle's Steady State Theory is not generally accepted today, but it is still out there. Also, there is a five-dimensional cosmogony called Cosmological Relativity, devised principally by the Israeli cosmologist Dr. Moshe Carmeli.

With this diversity of secular cosmogonies, it should not be an embarrassment to creationists to discover that there is not one creationist cosmogony, but several. This is because, although the Bible is inspired, our creationist models are not. They are scientific

12 Faulkner, D., *A Proposal for a New Solution to the Light Travel Time Problem*, Answers Research Journal
6 (2013):279–284, < www.answersingenesis.org/arj/v6/light-travel-time-problem.pdf >.

explanations, that attempt to help us understand what has been happening. As some have said – we hold tight to Scripture, but loosely to our scientific models.

The existence of even one scientific model that starts from Scripture, and consistently explains the scientific phenomena, is sufficient to show that the Bible's science can be taken seriously. The fact that different creation scientists have developed different, but scientifically valid models simply underlines that true science is consistent with Scripture.

Coupled with the above comments, we need to add that, although I currently favor one of the models mentioned below, I cannot tell you that it is definitely true, nor that it will ever, in this life, be "proved" true, because scientific models do not work like that. I will explain, after relating the models, which one I prefer, and show that it is a helpful explanation, but it must be remembered that it is Scripture that is inerrantly true, not our scientific models.

A. Mature Creation

This explanation takes, as its analogy, the appearance of Adam and Eve in the Garden. Suppose one had a time machine, and could see Adam and Eve in the Garden of Eden, before the events of Genesis 3 had happened. No sin had yet occurred, so no aging processes had begun. How old would the first man and woman have appeared? They would certainly not have been babies, or even children. It is likely that they would be approximately similar in appearance to young adults in their early twenties. They were certainly created physically mature, as God had commissioned them to "Be fruitful and multiply and fill the earth and subdue it" (Genesis 1:28) Yet, the two of them, in reality, were probably no more than about 10 days old.[13]

In the same way, it is reasoned, God could have created a mature universe. Therefore, a star which is a million light years away, could have been created as if it were a million years old. The light shining from it could also have been created, in a stream stretching most of the way across that million light years. So what we see is not the star itself, but its apparent age, in the already created stream of light.

Many serious creationists of the past have adhered to this view. For example, this is the explanation used by the late Dr. Henry Morris in his commentary, *The Genesis Record*:

> The light trail from the star was created in transit, as it were, all the way from the star to the earth, three days before the star itself was created!... The universe was created "full-grown" from the beginning.[14]

13 It is my opinion – not set in stone – that the events of Genesis 3 occurred on the tenth day after the beginning. My reasons for this are detailed later in the relevant chapter.

14 Morris, H.M. (1976), *The Genesis Record*, (Grand Rapids, MI), pp. 55-56.

Most of us in the creationist community owe far more to Dr. Morris than we can ever say, so who am I to criticize this particular viewpoint? However, I believe I can do so, without undermining respect for the man. In the modern era, Dr. Morris was a pioneer. He was the first modern creationist to write a one-volume commentary on the book of Genesis. He paved the way for others to research further, and therefore develop new ideas, while adhering to Scripture.

The principle problem with this mature creation model is that we are comparing apples with oranges. In the example of the apparent age of Adam and Eve, there is no deception involved in this apparent age, because God has clearly told us that they were created on Day Six of the Creation Week. The apparent age of starlight is different. Take, for example, the case of a supernova. A nova is an exploding star, so a supernova is a very brightly exploding star – possibly exploding by means of "core collapse". Supernova 1987A is so called, because it was the first supernova recorded in 1987. It was in the dwarf galaxy known as the Large Magellanic Cloud, which is 168,000 light years away. So, if we explain this phenomenon by the mature creation model, we have to say that the light stream created from that galaxy to the Earth includes elements that, in 1987, would be interpreted as an explosion hundreds of thousands of years ago that never happened. This does not appear to be a satisfactory explanation. Dr.

Jonathan Sarfati, explaining how the mature creation model fails to explain "core collapse" supernovae in general, writes this:

> In "core collapse" supernovae, [the] explosion is preceded by a collapse of the outer layers. This results in huge amounts of fusion reactions that produce enormous numbers of neutrinos. These are ghostly particles that interact only by the "nuclear weak force", so mostly pass straight through matter. Then this *im*plosion "bounces" off the star's core, creating the *ex*plosion that we see. But because neutrinos pass almost unimpeded through matter, while light doesn't, we detect the neutrinos from a supernova several hours before the light. But the "light-created-in-transit" model would entail that a neutrino stream was created followed by a light stream, and just *appear* as if a supernova had exploded according to the laws of physics.[15]

15 Sarfati, J. (2015), *The Genesis Account*, (Powder Springs, GA: Creation Book Publishers), pp. 217-218.

B. Decay in the Speed of Light

This concept was first suggested in 1981 by Australian creationist Barry Setterfield. He examined measured values for the speed of light taken over a period of 300 years, and discovered that there seemed to be a downward trend in this speed. Therefore, he proposed that, over time, the speed of light must have changed. He even proposed a formula for this change in speed over time.

$$\Lambda = a + e^{kt}(b + dt)$$

a, b, k, and d are constants, t is time, Λ is the cosmological constant, proportional to c^2.

The claim was that the increased speed in the past would have made short work of light traveling from distant stars. However, it fails because of the nature of c, the speed of light. There are many values in physics which depend upon the value of c. For example, Planck's constant determines the size of the packets (or *quanta*) of energy emitted by electrons as they decay from an excited state. Planck's constant depends on c, so it, too, would have changed over time. But this would have caused abnormal and unsustainable amounts of radioactivity in the past, if the value of c had changed. For this, and other reasons, this model – often referred to as CDK – is not generally accepted by creationists today.

For a much more detailed analysis of this model, please see Danny Faulkner's book, *The Created Cosmos.*[16]

C. Time Dilation

Since c represents a speed (or, more correctly, a velocity), we can take a look at the basic equation of motion.

$$v=\frac{s}{t}$$

where v is velocity, s is distance, and t is time.

Mature creation implies that the distance of the light is not constant. CDK implies that the velocity of light is not constant. If we have rejected both of these options, perhaps it is time that is not constant.

For this reason, there have been some very successful attempts to address the starlight and time problem by what is known as time dilation.

In 1994, Dr. Russell Humphreys suggested a solution, which he called *White Hole Cosmology*[17]. In my previous commentary on Genesis, this was the model that I favored, and we should note that this model, unlike the first two, successfully explains the starlight and time problem. Humphreys noted that gravity dilates time. Although this

16 Faulkner, D. (2016), *The Created Cosmos*, (Green Forest, AR: Master Books), pp. 208-213.

17 Humphreys published a popular-style version of his theory in his book, Humphreys, R. (1996), *Starlight and Time*, (Green Forest, AR: Master Books).

seems counter-intuitive, we know that time runs slower in a stronger gravitational field. This can be seen even here on Earth, by synchronizing accurate atomic clocks at sea level and high in mountains, where a measurable difference in time can be observed, caused by the time-slowing effects of the greater gravity at sea level (being closer to the center of the Earth).

The Big Bang model of the universe suggests an infinite, 4D universe, in which no point is favored. This would result in the gravitational field everywhere being the same. However, we have already stated that a creationist view of the universe is as a finite bounded entity. Therefore, there must be a net gravitational field towards the center of the universe. If we assume that our galaxy is somewhere near the center of the universe, then we see that time at the Earth would run slower than time at the edge of the universe. We have already discussed the expansion of space. So at its creation, the universe would be a lot smaller than it is today, and the effect of gravitational time dilation would be much greater, meaning that, while the 24-hours of Day Four happened on Earth, there could be the equivalent of millions of years of star formation at the event horizon.

Dr. John Hartnett also proposed a time dilation model, which also works well. In his book, *Starlight, Time, and the New Physics*[18], Hartnett notes that time dilation is also caused by the stretching of space.

18 See reference 4.

Hartnett worked on a creationist version of Moshe Carmeli's *Cosmic Special Relativity*, which postulates a five-dimensional structure to the universe.

It should be noted that Hartnett has, more recently, seemingly abandoned time dilation[19] in favor of a version of the Anisotropic Synchrony Convention, discussed below.

D. Anisotropic Synchrony Convention

Dr. Jason Lisle is an astrophysicist, and quite probably the most brilliant man I know. He had mentioned solutions to the starlight and time problem, even during the days when he was a student. In 2010, he published his first version of his elegant solution, which he called Anisotropic Synchrony Convention[20], or ASC. This relies on the fact that, whenever anyone talks about the measurement of the speed of light, they unwittingly have to adopt a time convention. Einstein assumed that the speed of light was the same in all directions. This might seem self-evident at first, but it does lead to some anomalies. One of these is the famous thought experiment, which Einstein himself proposed, which is to ask what would the universe look like, if we were traveling along a beam of light? Or how about if one's speed

19 Hartnett, J.G., *A Biblical Creationist Cosmogony*, Answers Research Journal 8 (2015):13–20, < www.answersingenesis.org/arj/v8/creationist-cosmogony.pdf >.

20 Lisle, J., *Anisotropic Synchrony Convention—A Solution to the Distant Starlight Problem*, Answers Research Journal
3 (2010):191–207, < www.answersingenesis.org/arj/v3/anisotropic-synchrony-convention.pdf >.

was 99% the speed of light? It was these thought experiments that led Einstein to realize that time would dilate in certain circumstances, such as gravity.

A word to describe something which is the same in all directions is *isotropic.* So, Einstein was proposing an Isotropic Synchrony Convention.

Lisle's conjecture is that light could, in fact, follow an anisotropic synchrony convention. The speed of light might be different in different directions.

Lisle shows that it is not possible to measure the one-way speed of light. The speed of light is only measured as an average – "there and back". But if this speed is anisotropic, then the average speed tells us nothing about how fast light is traveling in either direction.

The "simplest" way to measure the speed of light today would be to fire a laser at the Moon, and catch its reflection. The start and stop of the laser beam would be measured by the same clock, so no synchronization of clocks is necessary. However, this is only measuring the average speed of light.

How could we measure the one-way speed of light from Earth to Moon? To do so, we would need two clocks – one on Earth and one on the Moon. These clocks would have to be synchronized. But to synchronize the clocks would require sending a signal from one to the other. This signal – possibly by radio – would itself travel at the speed of light; the very value that the experiment is actually trying to measure!

Perhaps an alternative would be to synchronize both clocks on Earth, then take one of them to the Moon. But the acceleration of the rocket traveling to the Moon sets up its own time dilation.

From these problems, it can be seen that we cannot know the speed of light in one direction. Therefore, we could assume that the speed of light away from the Earth could be ½c, while the speed of light coming back towards Earth could be nearly instant.

An objection to ASC might be that just because something is possible, does not make it probable. However, this explanation now seems to me to be the best explanation, as it fits with Einstein's ideas, as well as staying true to the Scriptural account. Time dilation methods require us to assume that the Earth is close to the center of the universe, whereas ASC does not. For a fuller, more detailed explanation of ASC, and other relativistic corollaries, derived from Genesis 1, see Dr. Jason Lisle's book *The Physics of Einstein.*[21]

E. Dasha Solution

As you might have guessed, the first word in this section's title is not English. It is a Hebrew word, and was addressed under Day Three. In

21 Lisle, J. (2018), *The Physics of Einstein*, (Aledo, TX: Biblical Science Institute).

Genesis 1:11, we read "And God said, Let the earth sprout vegetation, plants yielding seed, and fruit trees bearing fruit in which is their seed, each according to its kind, on the earth. And it was so." The word "sprout" is the Hebrew word *dasha.* As mentioned in the previous chapter, the word implies that God did not make plants fully grown. Of course, he could have done, but the word *dasha* implies that He actually grew the plants from the ground up at a very, very accelerated pace, so that it happened almost instantaneously, but not quite.

In his book *The Created Cosmos*, Dr. Danny Faulkner suggests that the word *dasha* might enable us to understand a solution to the starlight and time problem. Faulkner appeals to the fact that there is no necessity to propose that events in the Creation Week followed post-Creation laws of physics. So, just as God could have made the plants by sprouting them upwards, so He could have made the stars, and their starlight, by rapidly maturing that light, causing it to travel from the star to the Earth in miraculously short timescales.

In many ways, this solution is like a return to the mature creation model – albeit with rapid, rather than instantaneous, production of the light trails. Of course, much of what God did in the Creation Week is not susceptible to scientific analysis, and yet there are established physical phenomena, to which creationist astronomers point when discussing the universe, such as red shifts. It is not clear how the

Dasha Model gets to grips with this. Nevertheless, we see that this does appear to be a viable creationist cosmogony, so I would suggest that we now have three major creationist models that help explain the universe.

Conclusion

In this section, we have examined what Scripture says about the creation of the universe, and what secular Big Bang theory says. We have found the latter to be wanting, both scientifically and biblically.

We have seen that creationists have developed a number of biblical models to explain cosmogony, three of which seem to hold water scientifically.

At this point of writing, my personal preference (given that I do not have a high level of expertise in science; my expertise is in science education) is for the Anisotropic Synchrony Convention. Although this seems to answer my own questions most effectively, the Time Dilation models also work, and I used to teach those in my presentations for many years.

Genesis 1 Part 9 – The Fifth Day of Creation

(Genesis 1:20-23)

“And on Day Five, God made fish and birds”, said my Religious Education[1] teacher. He probably didn’t believe that this was literally true; I clearly remember him casting doubt on the authenticity of the Virgin Birth – despite the fact he was an ordained priest in the Church of England. But even if he had believed what he said, he would not have been correct. There was a great deal more to Day Five than just fish and birds.

The Creatures of the Waters

The account of Day Five begins with Genesis 1:20:

> And God said, Let the waters swarm with swarms of living creatures, and let birds fly above the earth across the expanse of the heavens. (Genesis 1:20)

This quotation is from the ESV, which appears to have the best translation. My reason for saying this, with very little knowledge of

1 Religious Education is a compulsory subject for children in schools in England and Wales. The 1944 Education Act laid down that RE should be mostly Christian in character. However, this aspect of the regulations has not always been followed, and, even if it is, the definition of Christianity is not normally that of Bible-believing evangelicals.

Hebrew, is the repetition of the word *swarm*. The BibleHub website has a table, which illustrates the fact that this word is repeated in the Hebrew[2].

[Table 1.9.1 – Hebrew Analysis of Genesis 1:20]

Strong's	Hebrew	English
559	וַיֹּ֣אמֶר way-yō-mer	And said
430	אֱלֹהִ֔ים ’ĕ-lō-hîm,	God
8317	יִשְׁרְצ֣וּ yiš-rə-ṣū	let abound
4325	הַמַּ֔יִם ham-ma-yim,	the waters
8318	שֶׁ֖רֶץ še-reṣ	with an abundance
5315	נֶ֣פֶשׁ ne-p̄eš	of creatures
2416	חַיָּ֑ה ḥay-yāh;	living
5775	וְעוֹף֙ wə-‘ō-wp̄	and birds
5774	יְעוֹפֵ֣ף yə-‘ō-w-p̄êp̄	let fly

2 The table is taken from the BibleHub website, < https://biblehub.com/text/genesis/1-20.htm >, accessed 12/4/2018.

5921	עַל־ 'al-	above
776	הָאָרֶץ hā-'ā-reṣ,	the earth
5921	עַל־ 'al-	across
6440	פְּנֵי pə-nê	the face
7549	רְקִיעַ rə-qî-a'	of the firmament
8064	הַשָּׁמָיִם׃ haš-šā-mā-yim.	of the sky

As is often the case, Strong is very helpful to those of us without Hebrew. Strong's numbers 8317 and 8318 have the same root, the former being the verb form, and the latter being the noun. It is usual for such a repetition to indicate an emphasis, so some versions quite properly use words that indicate an emphasis, rather than using word repetition. The result of the word repetition is to focus our thoughts on the "abundant" number of sea creatures, which is why the word *swarm* is appropriate. God didn't make just a few fish and other sea creatures. He created a great deal of them, and also a great variety of them. On Day Four, these oceans were lifeless. By the end of Day Five, the oceans were filled with swarms of creatures.

The creatures are described as "living" - *hayyah* (חַיָּה). We can assume that this also applies to the flying creatures. We should note that, on Day Three, plants were not described as *hayyah*. This underlines the point that we made there. Plants are not living creatures in a biblical sense.

We also see that these water-borne animals are described as "creatures", for which the important word *nephesh* (פֶּשׁ) is used. We will have a lot more to say about *nephesh* later on. For now, we will note that the "living creatures" of the water must include fish, but is not exclusive to fish. All types of water creatures must be included, as we will observe in the next verse. We also need to say more about the term "fish" later in this chapter.

Although we need to return to verse 20 to talk about flying creatures, we should note that verse 21 goes on:

> So God created the great sea creatures and every living creature that moves, with which the waters swarm, according to their kinds, and every winged bird according to its kind. And God saw that it was good. (Genesis 1:21)

BibleHub has the following analysis of verse 21.

[Table 1.9.2 – Hebrew Analysis of Genesis 1:21]

Strong's	Hebrew	English
1254	וַיִּבְרָא way-yiḇ-rā	So created
430	אֱלֹהִים 'ĕ-lō-hîm,	God
853	אֶת־ 'eṯ-	-
8577	הַתַּנִּינִם hat-tan-nî-nim	sea creatures
1419	הַגְּדֹלִים hag-gə-ḏō-lîm;	great
853	וְאֵת wə-'êṯ	and
3605	כָּל־ kāl-	every
5315	נֶפֶשׁ ne-p̄eš	thing
2416	הַחַיָּה ׀ ha-ḥay-yāh	living
7430	הָרֹמֶשֶׂת hā-rō-me-śeṯ	that moves
834	אֲשֶׁר 'ă-šer	with which
8317	שָׁרְצוּ šā-rə-ṣū	abounded
4325	הַמַּיִם	the waters

	ham-ma-yim	
4327	לְמִינֵהֶם lə-mî-nê-hem,	according to their kinds
853	וְאֵת wə-'êṯ	and
3605	כָּל־ kāl-	every
5775	עוֹף 'ō-wp̄	bird
3671	כָּנָף kā-nāp̄	winged
4327	לְמִינֵהוּ lə-mî-nê-hū,	according to its kind
7200	וַיַּרְא way-yar	And saw
430	אֱלֹהִים 'ĕ-lō-hîm	God
3588	כִּי־ kî-	that
2896	טוֹב׃ ṭō-wḇ.	[it was] good

In this verse, we find that a distinction has been made between the "great sea creatures" and the living [creatures] that move. The word *nephesh* is not repeated, but must be implied. It has probably not been attached to the *hayyah* for "living", as this might have implied that the great sea creatures did not have *nephesh.* The importance of the use of the term *nephesh* to cover both the sea creatures and the other creatures in the ocean cannot be underestimated, as we will see.

When we refer to the "great sea creatures", the word being translated as "creatures" is *tannin.* This is translated in many places in the KJV as *dragons,* and I think that is the correct translation. When referring to land dragons, we are probably referring to dinosaurs, or similar creatures. However, these "sea dragons" probably include a large number of kinds of large sea creatures. The LXX uses the term *kete* (κητη), which we can recognize as the origin of the word *cetacean* or whales and dolphins. However, the term probably includes other large sea creatures, which we would not today class as cetaceans, such as plesiosaurs and ichthyosaurs.

If we assume that both the great sea creatures and the living creatures of the sea are *nephesh*, then this tells us a great deal. The word *nephesh* gets some extra context, when we look at Leviticus 17:11. - "the life of the flesh is in the blood". The word translated "life" in this verse is not *hayyah*, but *nephesh.* The *nephesh* of the flesh is in the blood. This implies a relationship between *nephesh* and blood. It suggests that the sort of animals, to which we refer, have blood. All vertebrates have blood. Some invertebrates, also, seem to have blood, but the majority do not have what we would call blood. Therefore, the great sea creatures, and the swimming creatures (that move in the water) are probably mostly, if not wholly, vertebrates.

It is noteworthy that the sea creatures, other than the great sea dragons, are not referred to as "fish". They definitely include fish, but may include other animals, such as some of those invertebrates that have blood, and perhaps including some animals, where it is difficult to define them as land or sea creatures, such as seals. Personally, I cannot say whether seals class as Day Five or Day Six animals. There is a Hebrew word for fish. It is *dagim* (דָּגָה). I think that the fact that the word *dagim* is not used in Genesis 1:21 underlines that a broader class of animals is being referred to, which includes, but is not restricted to, fish.

When I was a high school teacher, we taught the children that the subphylum *vertebrata* (vertebrates) was divided into five classes – mammals, birds, reptiles, amphibians, and fish. Following the work of the late evolutionary biologist Stephen J Gould, eight classes of vertebrates are now recognized[3]. Gould recognized that the term *fish* is largely useless, as there is no closer relationship between any two fish species than there is between species of fish and mammals. Of course, this should have caused Gould to reject evolution, but,

3 As creationists do not accept a common ancestor for animals within these classes, there is no intrinsic problem for creationists also to adopt the splitting of the old fish class into three new classes.

instead, his work led to the splitting of the old fish class into three new classes, which are:

Agnatha (jawless fish)

Chondrichthyese (cartilaginous fish)

Osteichthyese (bony fish)

Most people are probably already aware of the differences between the last two classes. Cartilaginous fish include sharks and rays. Seafood fans will know that these sorts of fish do not have bones, as such. Bony fish are more familiar, such as salmon or cod – again picking those that I like to eat! The jawless fish class includes lampreys and hagfish. The classification of hagfish in this class is controversial, as hagfish do not contain bones, so it is a moot point as to whether or not they should be classed as vertebrates at all. Evolutionists believe that their ancestors had bones, but evolved to lose them. As creationists do not accept that there was any evolutionary development before or after hagfish – given that a hagfish kind, or kinds within the hagfish subclass, would have been separately created – the arguments over where to place these in an evolutionary taxonomy are relatively irrelevant.

The Creatures of the Air

God made the creatures of the air at the same time as the creatures of the water. I have separated them only for my convenience. God made no separation between them, of any importance.

If you refer back to Table 1.9.1, we see that the word translated "birds" is the Hebrew *oph* (עוֹף). In a similar manner to our discussion about fish, we find that *oph* does not mean just birds. In fact, there is another Hebrew word usually used for birds. It is *tsippor* (צִפּוֹר). *Tsippor* appears in Leviticus 14:4, for example.

> The priest shall command them to take for him who is to be cleansed two live clean birds (*tsipporim)* and cedarwood and scarlet yarn and hyssop.

We can also note that there is a similar Hebrew word repetition, as there was in the case of the swarming fish. The Hebrew word for "flying" is *uwph* (עוּף), and for those of us without Hebrew (which, remember, includes me), the Strong's numbers for *oph* and *uwph* are 5775 and 5774 respectively. These words have the same root. So *oph* does not mean "birds", although it clearly includes them. It means "flying creatures". The phrase could therefore be interpreted as "let flying things fly above the Earth". The Hebrew repetition again underlines the importance of what is being said.

So, if *oph* means "flying creatures", what can this include? It certainly includes birds. But I would suggest it must include bats, and, probably, pterosaurs as well. In Leviticus 11:13-20, a list of animals designated as *oph* includes bats. It is possible that *oph* includes some flying insects as well, but this might not be the case.

God caused the flying creatures to fly across the expanse or firmament. This is an important phrase. It does not in any way work against the concept of the astronomical features of Day Four being created *in* the expanse. This is also the sense of the wording in the KJV, if one reads the KJV text as an early 17th Century person would have read it. Some have tried to set up an opposition on this verse between the KJV and other versions, but that opposition is simply not there in real life.

While on the subject of the KJV, that version translates *oph* as "fowl". In 1611, the word fowl would have meant flying creature. It was actually a broader term than bird in the early 17th Century. However, the word fowl has now become restricted, and refers to a group of domestically farmed birds. We must read this text as the translators would have intended in 1611.

Baraminology

The key phrase used to describe how these waterborne and airborne animals were going to fill the earth, is "according to their kinds". Let's look at verse 21 again, with some added emphasis.

> So God created the great sea creatures and every living creature that moves, with which the waters swarm, *according to their kinds*, and every winged bird *according to its kind.* And God saw that it was good.

Therefore, each *kind* of animal was made able to breed with others of its own kind, producing offspring within that kind. The implication is that there could be diversity within these kinds, but it is clear that breeding would not be possible outside of those kinds. So, there must be a very clear and specific scientific meaning to the concept of *kind.*

Many people assume that the word must be synonymous with the word *species.* Indeed, if one looks up *species* in a dictionary, we will find that a secondary meaning is indeed the same as a sort or kind. Thus, the Oxford Online Dictionary gives the following example sentence for *species*:

> "a species of invective at once tough and suave".[4]

4 *Species*, in Oxford Living Dictionaries, < https://en.oxforddictionaries.com/definition/species >, accessed 12/5/2018.

However, dictionaries will show that it is possible for the word *change* to be synonymous with *evolution*, but the latter term has a more specific meaning, when applied to biology. In the same way, the word *species* has developed a more specific meaning in biology than merely the concept of kind.

When Carl Linnaeus (1707-1778) applied the word *species* to taxonomy, he was under the impression that these species were indeed the biblical kinds, and that they were fixed. We now know that Linnaean species are not the same as kinds, because there can be hybridization between species, which are in the same genus, or even in the same family. Linnaeus's system of nomenclature for living creatures has still remained, largely untouched. Names are Latinized. If a Latin word is not available, it appears to be made up! These Latin names usually consist of two words. The first word is the genus, and the second is the species within that genus. So, for example, the common bottlenose dolphin is labeled as *Tursiops truncatus*, where *Tursiops* refers to the genus of bottlenose dolphins, and *truncatus* is the specific species. Thus, we see that *Tursiops australis* (Burrunan dolphin) is in the same genus, but a different species. We will discuss the terms genus and species, as well as the other layers of taxonomy, at the relevant place in Day Six.

Evolutionists have broadly kept the Linnaean classifications, but have suggested common ancestors, not only within the genus and family, but also for all living things, at whatever taxonomic level.

As creationists, we presumably have to use these nomenclatures, as they have already been applied to flora and fauna, but the labels do not really make sense of the **biology** from a creationist viewpoint. For this reason, creation biologists have developed the term *baramin*. This is a made-up word, constructed from two Hebrew words. *Bara* means create, and *min* means kind. Hence a baramin is a created kind.

Creation biologists have therefore developed a number of technical terms, which help us to understand where animals (and, for that matter, plants) fit into a biblical understanding of how creatures have developed and adapted. Evolutionists see all life forms as having developed from a common ancestor. They refer to the first possible organism as IDA (Initial Darwinian Ancestor). There could have been branches from this, which all died out, they suppose, so they also refer to LUCA – the Last Universal Common Ancestor, which they believe evolved into all the life that we have today. By having an IDA as well as a LUCA, they are allowing themselves the possibility of discovering a lifeform for which they cannot find any connection to any modern lifeform. All this ancestry is then represented as a "Tree of Life". They accuse creationists of believing that life ancestry is a series of sticks, because they accuse us of believing in the fixity of species. But, of course, we don't. God created the kinds or baramin, which then developed into various species – by natural selection from the existing gene pool within that baramin. So the creationist diagram of life is not a series of sticks, nor a single tree, but rather a "creationist orchard", with many branched trees.

So, the following terms were developed by Wayne Frair, who first published information on baraminology.[5]

Holobaramin

This is an entire group believed to be related by common ancestry. The Greek word *holos* means whole, as in holistic. A group of related species could thus be described as holobaraminic.

Monobaramin

From *mono*, or one. This defines a group of organisms belonging to the same baramin. A monobaramin could thus be a holobaramin or a portion thereof.

Apobaramin

An apobaramin contains the entirety of at least one holobaramin. There may accidentally be more than one holobaramin in the apobaramin. To say that an organism is part of an apobaramin is to

5 Frair, W., *Creation Research Society Quarterly*, vol. 37, no. 2 (September 2000): pp. 82-91.

state that the organism is not related to any organism outside of the baramin, but we are not sure that the apobaramin in question cannot later be subdivided.

Polybaramin

A group of organisms to which it is helpful to refer, but which comprises all or part of more than one baramin.

These four terms have been developed to enable researchers to identify and classify organisms. The definitions first appeared in this form in my book, *The Six Days of Genesis*[6] – again, quoting from Frier.

Blessing

> And God blessed them, saying, Be fruitful and multiply and fill the waters in the seas, and let birds multiply on the earth. And there was evening and there was morning, the fifth day. (Genesis 1:22-23)

This is a remarkable verse. Throughout the Old Testament, the Hebrew word for bless is used many times – *barak* (בָּרַךְ). For example:

And I will make of you a great nation, and I will bless you and make your name great, so that you will be a blessing. (Genesis 12:2)

6 Taylor, P.F. (2007), *The Six Days of Genesis*, (Green Forest, AR: Master Books), pp. 66-67.

For those blessed by the LORD shall inherit the land, but those cursed by him shall be cut off. (Psalms 37:22)

Then the mystery was revealed to Daniel in a vision of the night. Then Daniel blessed the God of heaven. (Daniel 2:19)

•

So we have blessings bestowed on people, and on God. But in Genesis 1:22, we have a blessing bestowed on animals. How can this be?

It is probably not possible for us fully to plumb the depths of what this means. However, we have already observed that the animals to which we have been referring all possess blood, and that the life (*nephesh*) of the flesh is in the blood. We will soon discover the importance of blood in the forgiveness of sins, in Genesis chapters 3 and 4. Perhaps it is the fact that we are referring to animals with blood that causes them to be blessed.

An interesting passage in Ephesians shows us the extent of God's purpose in salvation, and the fact that it was planned before the creation.

> Blessed be the God and Father of our Lord Jesus Christ, who has blessed us in Christ with every spiritual blessing in the heavenly places, even as he chose us in him before the foundation of the world, that we should be holy and blameless before him. In love he predestined us for

> adoption as sons through Jesus Christ, according to the purpose of his will, to the praise of his glorious grace, with which he has blessed us in the Beloved (Ephesians 1:3-6)

The plan of salvation was there right from the very beginning – indeed, before the beginning.

Summary

In this section, we have looked at how God made the creatures of the sea and the flying creatures of the air. We have looked at what the extent of these groupings of animals imply. We have introduced the subject of baraminology – the study of the created kind. Finally, we have pondered on the reason why God blessed these animals.

Genesis 1 Part 10 – The Sixth Day of Creation

(Genesis 1:24-31)

There is no doubt in my mind that Day Six was the busiest day of the Creation Week. I often wondered why God did not seem to spread the load differently! There wasn't a lot happened on Day Two, for example, whereas Day Six is just so full. Why did He split the creation of animals between Days Five and Six? Why was Day Six not just reserved for the creation of mankind? Why did He create mankind on the same day as all the land animals? I can attempt to answer some of these questions, but I am sure that many others will remain unanswered.

Creatures of the Land

The first thing that God did on Day Six was to make land animals.

> And God said, 'Let the earth bring forth living creatures according to their kinds—livestock and creeping things and beasts of the earth according to their kinds.' And it was so. And God made the beasts of the earth according to their kinds and the livestock according to their kinds, and everything that creeps on the ground according to its kind. And God saw that it was good. (Genesis 1:24-25)

The order of creation itself is very important. The theory of evolution suggests that whales evolved from land animals, such as *mesonychids* and creatures similar to *andrewsarchus*. Evolution also suggests that birds evolved from land animals – specifically from therapod dinosaurs. But Genesis makes clear that birds and whales were created on Day Five, while land animals were created on Day Six. So it really isn't good enough for Christians to say that Genesis is giving a figurative picture of how evolution proceeded. Even without the problems with the timescale, the order of appearance of these animals is wrong. There isn't a way of harmonizing Genesis 1 with evolution, without effectively rejecting the text. Atheist evolutionists like Richard Dawkins understand this, and use it as an argument against the veracity of Scripture. Their position is wrong, but understandable, and, on this issue, consistent. However, the position of Christians, who wish to continue to believe in evolution, in defiance of what the clear reading of Genesis 1 says, are being, at the very least, inconsistent and disingenuous – and, at worst, disobedient.

Dinosaurs

In these opening comments, I have alluded to dinosaurs being land animals. Of course, ichthyosaurs and plesiosaurs could swim, while we think it highly likely that pterosaurs could fly, so those groups of animals would have been created on Day Five, but most of the animals that we think of as dinosaurs were land animals, and therefore would have been made on Day Six.

Skeptics might want to raise an objection to the idea that dinosaurs were created on Day Six – the same day that humans were made. Evolutionary objections would be as follows:

1. Dinosaurs died out 65 million years ago, whereas people only evolved 3 million years ago. Therefore, they were not on Earth at the same time.
2. Dinosaurs were wiped out in an extinction event, caused by the impact of an asteroid hitting the Earth at Chicxulub, on the Yucatán Peninsula in Mexico.
3. The word *dinosaur* does not appear in the Bible.

All three of these objections, and more, can easily be answered.

The dating of the extinction of dinosaurs is found by estimating the age of the rock, in which the dinosaur fossils were found. However, as we will find out later (in the section on Flood Geology, concerned with Genesis 7), the layers of sedimentary rock do not have anything to do with dates. It is an evolutionary assumption, based on faulty logic, which causes evolutionists to date dinosaur-bearing rock layers at 62 million years - before the appearance of human beings. For now, you can assume that there are at least sound logical alternative explanations of the rock layers, and when we discuss Genesis 7, we will find that these explanations are much more sound than those of the evolutionists.

As for Chicxulub, it will surprise some to find out that not even evolutionists are as convinced about this event as might be thought. If you read the article on Wikipedia, you would assume that the event had been proved beyond all doubt.[1] There are also a number of geologists and paleontologists who dispute the idea of Chicxulub having caused the extinction of dinosaurs. Dr. Gerta Keller of Princeton University wrote about her doubts on the subject in 2006.[2] Dr. Timothy Clarey, a geologist, who takes a biblical creationist view, has also analyzed all the data pertaining to the alleged Chicxulub event, and he shows that the impact was much smaller than many evolutionists suppose. Clarey relates the Chicxulub impact to possible cratering events, either on Day Four in the Creation Week, or at the onset of the Flood.

The third objection was that the word *dinosaur* does not appear in the Bible. This is true. By the way, the word *cat* does not appear in the

1 You should note that Wikipedia pages can change frequently. However, as I was writing this book, the Wikipedia reference was: < https://en.wikipedia.org/wiki/Chicxulub_crater >, accessed 12/8/2018. It is usually possible to "wind back" a Wikipedia article to a particular date.

2 Keller, G. (2006), *Chicxulub: The Impact Controversy*, < https://gkeller.princeton.edu/chicxulub >, accessed 12/8/2018. This is her blog article, and contains links to her research on the subject.

Bible, either, so the absence of a word does not imply that such creatures were unknown. In any case, *dinosaur* is an English word (albeit, invented by putting together two Greek words), and the Bible was not written in English. There is a long tradition of translating the Bible into English, however. There is a word in Hebrew, which we have already met – the word *tanniyn* (תַּנִּין). This word is usually translated in the KJV as *dragon*. This would seem to be a good translation. The KJV was originally translated into English in 1611. The word *dinosaur* was invented in 1841 by Sir Richard Owen, founder of the Natural History Museum, in South Kensington, London, England. So when the KJV translators were at work, they did not have the word *dinosaur* available to use. In fact, in the years before 1841, the scientific literature, regarding the discovery of various dinosaur fossils, referred to them as dragons. And just as there were many different types of dinosaurs, we find that the world's mythologies contains many different descriptions of different dragons, which were clearly different animals. It seems very sensible to suppose, then, that the dragons of mythology were dinosaurs, in which case these magnificent beasts were seen by human beings well into comparatively recent times. Other versions of the Bible often translate *tanniyn* as *serpents*, which is also acceptable, because a serpent did not always mean a snake, but could refer to other reptilian creatures. However, some versions sometimes translate *tanniyn* as *jackals*, which does not seem to fit the descriptions. In my opinion, however, the word *tanniyn* should, today, be translated as dinosaur.

Of course, my comments here open up all sorts of other issues. Why did dinosaurs become extinct? Could there be dinosaurs alive today? And, as we have discussed baramins, how many dinosaur baramins were there?

There is not the space to go into a long bunny trail on these matters. Whole books can, and have, been written about dinosaurs. In my opinion, two of the best are *Dinosaur Challenges and Mysteries* by Michael Oard[3] and JD Mitchell's *Guidebook to North American Dinosaurs According to Created Kinds.*[4] There are also some excellent books on dinosaurs for children. Both the quoted authors here have produced versions for children.

However, brief answers to the three questions posed above are:

1. Lots of animals have become extinct. In any case, the word dinosaur was invented to cover a whole class of extinct animals, so asking why they became extinct is like asking why water is wet. And we cannot even prove that they are extinct.

3 Oard, M. (2011), *Dinosaur Challenges and Mysteries*, (Powder Springs, GA: Creation Book Publishers).

4 Mitchell, J.D. (2014), *Guidebook to North American Dinosaurs According to Created Kinds*, (Portland, OR: CEC Publishing).

2. Which leads to this answer. It is possible that there are still some dinosaurs left. We often hear rumors of them – *mkele mwembe* in Congo, *firebirds* in Papua New Guinea. Personally, I am skeptical. I think they really are extinct. But I can't prove it, and it is always possible that someone will find one someday.
3. How many baramins of dinosaurs were there? We estimate about 50. And only a few of these were very big. Many more were very small. The average size was about that of a sheep.

There seems no doubt to me, however, that dinosaurs were seen and known about in history. Another book, that contains much of this historic information, is *Dragons or Dinosaurs* by Darek Isaacs.[5] Darek also produced an extremely informative and interesting documentary, available on a DVD by the same title.

5 Isaacs, D. (2010), *Dragons or Dinosaurs*, (Aluchua, FL: Bridge-Logos Publications).

Biblical Classification

It is interesting to notice that Genesis 1 uses a very different sort of classification than evolutionary theory does. The biblical classifications of land animals have nothing to do with evolutionary taxonomic classification. Instead, a practical and pragmatic classification is used, relating to how these animals interact with mankind. The three biblical classifications are:

1. Livestock
2. Creeping things
3. Beasts of the Earth

Beasts of the Earth probably refers to large, wild animals. *Livestock* (some versions have *cattle*) suggests domesticated animals, or, at least, animals which are capable of being domesticated. *Creeping things* seems to suggest reptiles and amphibians. This group probably includes dinosaurs, which are still thought of as reptilian in nature. All three classes are subdivisions of the "living creatures" of land. This phrase again includes the term *nephesh*, so we must assume that all three groups are vertebrates, with blood.

This means that the creation of invertebrates, or non-nephesh animals, such as insects, spiders, etc., has not been mentioned. In truth, Genesis 1 does not give an account of everything that God made. However, we are told that everything that God made was made during this Creation Week (Genesis 1:31, Genesis 2:1, Exodus 20:11, Colossians 1:16-17). It is by these passages that we can infer that angels were created during the Creation Week, even though they are not directly mentioned in Genesis 1. As we read Job 38:4-7, we realize that these angels were probably created early on Day One, but, again, Genesis 1 does not directly say so. In the same way, Genesis 1 does not report what day non-nephesh animals were made. They could have been made on Days Five and Six, along with the nephesh equivalents, or they could have been made on Day Three, when the plants were made – because perhaps non-nephesh animals are really just biological machines, like plants, and not really *alive* in the biblical sense of the word.

It might be that some people would want, at this point, to classify animals as carnivores (meat-eaters) and herbivores (plant-eaters). However, Genesis 1 is very clear on this matter.

> And to every beast of the earth and to every bird of the heavens and to everything that creeps on the earth, everything that has the breath of life, I have given every green plant for food. And it was so. (Genesis 1:30).

So all animals were created to eat plants, not meat. Meat eating must have been a result of the Fall – of Adam's sin. People were not permitted to eat meat until after the Flood (Genesis 9:3). Whether or not some humans had started to eat meat before the Flood, in contravention of God's law, we are not told, though I would not doubt it, since man had corrupted their ways (Genesis 6:12).

But what about lions and tigers and bears (oh my!)? Surely these animals eat meat.

In fact, bears are omnivorous – they eat both plant and meat matter. Many types of bears are largely herbivorous – not just giant pandas. All bears are capable of being herbivorous. The most nearly carnivorous bear – the polar bear – lives in an area where meat is really the only food available to them. The sharp teeth of giant pandas seem to be remarkably well designed for tearing bamboo, yet evolutionists tell us that they evolved to eat meat.

Lions and tigers are part of the same baramin – felidae, or "the cat family". God did not create them separately. They developed from a common ancestor – not a single-celled organism, as "popular" evolutionists might teach, but a common original cat ancestor. Lions and tigers are species, which would have developed from the original felidae, by natural selection, within an existing gene pool, in the years after the Flood. The digestive system of the felidae must have been different before the Fall (Adam's sin). In many cases, we cannot tell exactly how the originally benign functions of some animals got turned into attack-defense mechanisms, but, in the light of Genesis 1:30, we have to conclude that there must have been such changes.[6]

Referring again to the way that the Bible classifies the three groups mentioned above; in creationist circles, this has become known as a *cognitum*. A cognitum is a recognition of classification, according to observed characteristics, including traits that are not immediately visible. Thus, it would be for cognitum reasons that we recognize the classes of animals, such as that of mammals. It is completely reasonable to group such animals together, who all suckle their young with milk. It is not scientifically reasonable, however, to assume that, because we can make such a classification, there must be a common ancestor.

A cognitum grouping is very useful for creationists, and it does not have to fit with known baramins, let alone evolutionary taxonomy. For example, we might wish to refer to *grazing animals*. This group would include cattle, and wild cattle, such as water buffalo. But it might also contain completely unrelated animals, such as kangaroos in Australia. It could even include sauropod dinosaurs, because we assume that the Behemoth of Job 40 is a sauropod, and we are told

6 For more information on attack-defense mechanisms, see Hodge, B. and McIntosh, A. (2007),
How Did Defense/Attack Structures Come About?, in Ham, K. (ed.) (2007), *The New Answers Book 1*, (Green Forest, AR: Master Books).

that "he eats grass like an ox". The word translated as ox is *bâqâr* (בקר) which is better translated as *grazing animal.*

Baraminology and Taxonomy

To understand these concepts better, we should return to the subject of baraminology, which we mentioned briefly in parts 7 & 9 (Third and Fifth days of creation).

Baraminology, you will recall, is a biblical taxonomic study. It is a word derived from both Hebrew and Greek. *Bara* means *created*, and *min* means *kind.* The "ology" come from the Greek *logos*, meaning word or law, but we recognize the suffix today as really referring to the science or study of something. Hence: *biology*, the study of life.

In Genesis 1, it does not, in fact, directly state that *min* should be considered as a technical term. It is possible that the word is being used in a general sense, in a similar way to that of the English word *kind.* However, it is clear from the accounts of the creation of plants, sea and air creatures, and land animals, that the term is being used to refer to breeding. We should also note that human beings are not made "after their kinds", so the concept of baraminic boundaries within these biblical classes does not hold true for humans. We will expand on that point shortly, but for now the use of *min* with animals and plants, but its non-use with humans, strongly implies that the term could be used as a technical term, defining the boundaries for breeding.

In addition, we notice the way the word *min* is used in Genesis 6:19-20, and again in Genesis 7:14. The fact that a pair of each kind was taken on to the Ark suggests that each pair was for breeding for that kind, to repopulate the world after the Flood. Again, it is suggested that the word *min* is being used within a technical category.

It is also true that the word *min* appears in other places in Scripture, in ways that do not reflect a technical use. Whether or not *min* is being used technically is easy to ascertain from the context. For that reason, it is easier for us to distinguish the technical kind in English by using this new word baramin.

How to Recognize a Baramin

I have taught creation apologetics at Bible colleges, and the first question that I get asked is this; what is the nearest equivalent to a baramin in Linnaean taxonomy? It is a fair question, but there isn't a direct answer.

Linnaean taxonomy, as used by evolutionists, recognizes a number of taxonomic levels, as follows:

- Kingdom
- Phylum

- Class
- Order
- Family
- Genus
- Species

Modern evolutionists have added considerably to this list, with some intermediate groupings. For example, evolutionists sometimes refer to the suborder, below order, or the super-family, above family. Suborder and super-family may or may not be the same.

It must first be understood that there is no necessity for the concept of baramin to be equal to any one of the Linnaean levels. Although Linnaeus believed the book of Genesis, the taxonomic system that bears his name is based on evolutionist presuppositions. There is no obligation on scientists, working from the presupposition that the Bible is true, to equate their system with that of the world.

As a general rule of thumb, creationists have usually identified the baramin as being the same level as the family.[7] While this is true for the majority of baramins, it is not true for all. For example, here are some notable exceptions.

7 See Purdom, G. (2010), *Variety within Created Kinds*, < https://answersingenesis.org/creation-science/baraminology/variety-within-created-kinds/ >, accessed 12/11/2018.

Evolutionists distinguish between the pig family (*suidae*) and the peccary family (*tayassuidae*). No hybrids have, at the time of writing, been discovered between pigs and peccaries. Yet so much about the animals within the two families is similar, and there is a very strong cognitum, suggesting that the super-family (*suoidea*) is the most suitable level to identify with the family.

An opposite example would be the *bovidae* family. This is split into a number of subfamilies; aepycerotinae (impalas), alcelaphinae (hartebeests), antilopinae (antelopes), bovinae (cattle), caprinae (sheep and goats), cephalophinae (duikers), hippotraginae (hippotragus antelopes), and reduncinae (reedbucks). Many baraminologists would suggest that each of these subfamilies is a separate baramin, as there is no hybridization between them, nor a strong cognitum. This is slightly complicated by other researchers, such as Dr. Jean Lightner, who suggests that cattle, sheep, and goats are all in the same baramin, at a sort-of super-subfamily level.[8]

The actual work required to recognize a baramin is quite difficult, and is open to a lot of study and debate. While baraminologists agree on the terminologies, they will frequently disagree on where those boundaries are to be found. A baraminologist is often attempting to find out what the originally created animals were like, but for land

8 All of this information on mammalian kinds, quoted here, comes from Lightner, J., *Mammalian Ark Kinds*, Answers Research Journal 5 (2012):151-204.

and airborne vertebrates, we have the added problem that the descent of our modern animals has proceeded not from Creation, but only from those pairs rescued on the Ark at the time of the Flood. Therefore, baraminologists will speak of Genesis Kinds (those originally created) and Ark Kinds (the representative pair of the baramin rescued on the Ark). In the latter case, one can envisage a baramin of animals, which branched into a number of species before the Flood. A pair of only one species out of that baramin were on the Ark, so all other species within that baramin perished, and all modern species within that baramin have speciated only from the pair on the Ark – the Ark Kind.

Baraminologists have suggested three levels of evidence required, to place species within a particular baramin. (Frair rightly adds a fourth, coming before the other three – the Scriptural test. However, there is very little taxonomic evidence in the Scripture).[9]

- Hybridization. If two species can hybridize, then this would seem to determine that they are in the same baramin. That hybridization should proceed a fair way – probably beyond the blastocyst stage. By this method, it can be determined that camels and llamas are of the same camelid baramin. However, negative data (that is, that two species will not hybridize) does not necessarily prove that two species are not in the same

9 Frair, W. *ob cit.*

baramin. It might be that species A and species E cannot hybridize. But maybe A can hybridize with B, B with C, C with D, and D with E. That would seem to suggest that A and E are in the same baramin. Even so, hybridization within a baramin might be blocked by other means. It could be that these animals never get together, as they are geographically separated. They may have speciated into vastly different sizes, being physically incapable of interbreeding. Or they may have developed into species, which aggressively compete in the wild, so are unlikely to mate. So, while positive hybridization data might be the best scientific data to determine baraminology, it is not the only one.

- Cognitum. In some cases, the cognitum is so strong, that it can be used to place creatures within the same baramin. While there are some that would argue that cognitum is a very subjective tool for taxonomic classification, I would push back and point out that it is eminently biblical, as it is the main reason for dividing land animals into livestock, creeping things, and beasts of the Earth.
- Statistical baraminology. A lot of traits and factors can be analyzed statistically, to determine the probability of any two species being within the same baramin. This sort of data is not

as strong as the first two, but is often the only data we have, when trying to group fossils into baramins.

Todd Elder's book, *Created Kinds, Baraminology, and the Creation Orchard* gives a lot more information on the process of determining baramins.[10]

Creation Orchard

One final issue at this point on the subject of baraminology is the subject of cladistics and species. It might not be well known, but evolutionists do not always have a clear idea of what is meant by a species. Indeed, evolutionists will use more than one species concept in their definitions. It is worth making this point, because of the way that evolutionists like to criticize creation scientists for their use of the term *species.* Aldebhiani[11] defines several different species concepts, of which I will extract just two, to show the subtle difference in usage.

3. Biological species concept. Groups of actually or potentially interbreeding natural populations which are reproductively isolated from other such groups.

10 Elder, T. (2017), *Created Kinds, Baraminology, and the Creation Orchard,* (Livingston, TX: Scripture Advocate Publishing).

11 Aldebhiani, A.Y., *Species concept and speciation,* Saudi Journal of Biological Sciences
Volume 25, Issue 3, March 2018, Pages 437-440,
< https://doi.org/10.1016/j.sjbs.2017.04.013 >, accessed 12/11/2018.

4. Phylogenetic species concept. A group of organisms that share an ancestor. In other words, species are individuals show a high degree of resemblances in many unique traits which give monophyletic clusters based on discriminative phenotypes.

Considering that within evolutionism, there are so many different species concepts (and Aldebhiani lists eight), Elder has proposed one of his own.[12] He calls it the Katagenous species concept. Elder has developed the word katagenous from the Greek words found in the LXX for the phrase "after their kinds". Elder says this about his Katagenous Species Concept.

> The Katagenous Species Concept treats species like breeds. It defines a species as a breed within a kind with a specific set of reproductively connected characteristics that produce a recognizable pattern. It is able to reproduce with others of the same species and potentially able to hybridize with other breeds / species within a Kind. It focuses on the ability to breed, gives strong attention to form and morphology, and uses habitat and geography only as indicators of where species boundaries may occur.[13]

Although this introduction of a new species concept does not have widespread use among creationist biologists yet, it is still helpful to

12 *Ob cit.*, p. 87.
13 *Ob cit.* p. 87.

mention, as it usefully defines what the definition of a species can and cannot do.

This brings us to the subject of cladistics. This is the study of how species have "evolved", or, in a creationist context, speciated over time. It records lines of descent, which can be represented in diagrams, called cladograms. These cladograms usually show branches of alleged descent, from the most recent common ancestor.

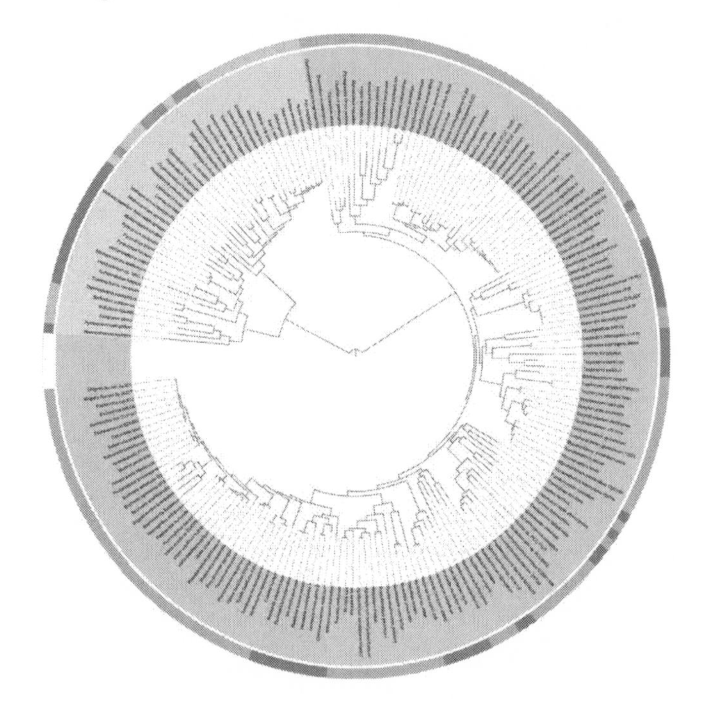

An evolutionist would want to combine all these cladograms into one large "tree of life", showing all organisms of any sort evolving from the Last Universal Common Ancestor (LUCA). Evolutionists have in the past been wont to accuse creationists of believing in a kind of "creationist lawn" where each blade of grass represents an individual, created species, and from which there is no branching. In fact, creationists do not believe in such a model. Instead, we suggest that the Bible teaches a discontinuity systematics, whereby a number of small branched cladograms begin with the original baramin, and branch into the current species. We might refer to this set up as a Creation Orchard of Life. In the Orchard of Life, each tree starts with the originally created kind, and branches from there. In the Orchard of Life, each branch represents a selection from existing data, and hence a re-arrangement or loss of that genetic data. In the evolutionary Tree of Life, each branch represents the spontaneous generation of new genetic data – something which is scientifically impossible.

The Creation Orchard

After the creation of these animals, God declares them to be good. Although Genesis 1 does not repeat the blessing that God bestowed on the animals of water and air, the implication of their goodness is that they are included in this blessing.

Imago Dei

If human beings had evolved from a common ancestor with apes, there would be no need for Genesis 1:26-27. Humans would seem to be land animals, and thereby would be included in the creation of land animals. But God describes His creation of human beings separately, with a number of distinctions, which set humans apart from other animals. I have previously written at length to show that, although the doctrine of the Trinity is derived from the New Testament texts, it can be found reflected in a number of places in the Old, not the least of which is Genesis 1.[14] So the Father, Son, and Holy Spirit confer together and say "Let us make man, in our image, after our likeness".

The Hebrew word translated here as *man* is *adam* (אָדָם). This, we know, is the personal name of the first man. But it is also the name for a man, or for humanity in general. We should not be surprised at this. Hebrew names in the Old Testament actually meant something. It is completely logical, therefore, that the personal name given to the first man should be the word for mankind in general.

There are some who see this as indicative of God making a lot of people, of whom Adam and Eve were just two. Although it could be theoretically possible to read such an idea into the text, it is not the most sensible or natural meaning. The most natural, sensible reading

14 Taylor, P.F. (2014, 3rd edition), *Itching Ears*, (Castle Rock, WA: J6D Publications), chapter 1 "Genesis and the Trinity".

is to see God describing the creation of Adam and Eve in brief on Day Six, and then going on to expand on this information in Genesis 2.

A less certain implication is the suggestion that *adam* might be derived from the Hebrew for red earth. This might suggest that his skin tone would be mid-brown, or reddish. This is very likely genetically, as Adam would have had all the genetic information necessary to produce any and all of the various human skin tones that we see today. Nevertheless, the translation of *adam* as "red earth" is too speculative to be used to derive a doctrine.

How do we know when to translate *adam* as mankind, or as the personal name? Some commentators[15] have suggested that the general rule would be that, if the word has the definite article with it, it means man or mankind. If there is no definite article, it usually means Adam the specific person.

Next, we turn to the fact that God made man "in our image, after our likeness". It might be too much of a stretch to comment that the phrase "after our likeness" appears to be in place instead of the phrase "after their kinds". It seems that it is being emphasized that mankind is **one** species, inside **one** baramin, of which that mankind

15 I note that Sarfati quotes Hamilton to this effect, also commenting that some translations do not follow this. Sarfati, J. (2015), *The Genesis Account*, (Powder Springs, GA: Creation Book Publishers), p. 249, quoting Hamilton, V.P. (1990), *The Book of Genesis, chapters 1-17,* The New International Commentary on the Old Testament, (Grand Rapids, MI: Eerdmans), p. 159.

species is the only member. The use of the word "likeness" shows that we might be similar to God, but we are not identical to Him. We are not, as some modern pastors have suggested, "little gods".

But the key phrase used is that we are created in the image of God - "in our image". In Latin, the phrase "image of God" is *Imago Dei*, and this Latin phrase is very often used to describe this important doctrine, even though Latin is not a biblical language. In Hebrew, only one compound word is used – *basalmênū* (בְּצַלְמֵ֖נוּ). This also lays emphasis on the importance of the concept, because no other animal is said to be in the image of God.

It has been customary in many societies, since ancient times, for gods and idols to be depicted as animals. But these cannot represent the true Deity. Just as the coin that Jesus examined had Caesar's image on it, and hence was symbolic of Caesar, so human beings, with all their frailties and mistakes, nevertheless are the closest thing on Earth to something like God, and therefore what we know about God has, in some measure, to take into account human beings as an analogy. Of course, this analogy must not be pushed too far. God himself reminds us that He is not like us: "These things you have done, and I have been silent; you thought that I was one like yourself. But now I rebuke you and lay the charge before you". (Psalms 50:21)

With the caveat of the previous paragraph in mind, we can state that being made in the image of God – however tarnished that image has become in the millennia following the Fall – confers on human beings a value and a worth, beyond that of the animals. It is on this basis of worth that we should base our systems of human rights. If other human beings are also made in *imago dei* then we should treat them accordingly. Human rights abuses are based on ignoring or opposing the concept of *imago dei*, and this is why systems of human rights based on humanism, or even secular humanitarianism, are either insufficient, or, in some cases, evil. This quality of *imago dei* exists from the moment a new human life is created, at conception, and is one of the fundamental reasons why a biblical worldview is opposed to abortion, which is the destruction and murder of little human beings, all made in the image of God.

Another issue strongly informed by the concept of *imago dei* is racism. The principle reason why Christians should be opposed to racism is because it denies the dignity and worth ascribed to all human beings by the essential declaration that we are created in the image of God. The apostle Paul put it as follows:

> He made from one blood every nation of men to dwell on all the surface of the earth, having determined appointed seasons, and the boundaries of their dwellings, (Acts 17:26 [WEB])

Most evolutionists would be as opposed to racism as I am, while there have, unfortunately, always been some Christians – who don't seem to know these relevant Bible passages – who hold racist opinions. But an anti-racist position is most logical, when seen in the context of a biblical presupposition, whereas there is really no logical evolutionary reason to oppose racism. Well-known creationist writer and speaker Ken Ham has written about this subject at length in his book *One Race, One Blood*[16].

Our sense of right and wrong – our consciences – come directly from the image of God within us. But the image of God within us is a tarnished image. In Genesis 5, we see the progress of this moral deterioration.

> When God created man, he made him in the likeness of God. (Genesis 5:1)

> When Adam had lived 130 years, he fathered a son in his own likeness, after his image, and named him Seth. (Genesis 5:3)

Seth, who Eve rightly prophesied was to be the carrier of the promised seed, was begotten in the image of Adam, whereas Adam

16 Ham, K. and Ware, C. (2010), *One Race, One Blood*, (Green Forest, AR: Master Books).

was created in the image of God. Seth was born in the image of a man, who was in the image of God.

The fullness of *imago dei* was not to be seen again, until the birth of Jesus, the Last Adam. The parallel between Jesus and Adam is of fundamental importance - so much so, that I have written on the subject at length elsewhere.[17] Notice that Jesus could be perfect, and yet still be fully human. This is because there was a model of perfect humanity in Adam. If we don't believe in a literal Adam, created perfectly in the image of God, and our failed representative in the Garden, then how can we accept Jesus as human? He becomes, instead, a sort-of super-human. Yet the basis of our soteriology is that He was, and is, at once both God and man - 100% God and 100% man. As Paul says:

> He is the image of the invisible God, the firstborn of all creation. (Colossians 1:15)

Atheists do, of course, know the difference between right and wrong, but have no logical argument for knowing why. When the Holy Spirit dwells within us, we are, in some ways, restored to a deeper sense of morality. We still fail. We still make great mistakes. But we know the One, from whom all measurement of morality is made.

17 Taylor, P.F. (2010), *Itching Ears*, (Castle Rock, WA: J6D Publications), pp. 69-101.

Male and Female

There are differences between men and women. These differences became more noticeable after the Fall, but some of these differences are creation ordinances – part of the established order that God created. When we study chapter 2, we will see that it is an expansion of this account of the creation of the first man and the first woman. But this short section underscores some of the important similarities and differences that God put into the human race.

There are some who say it is not politically correct to refer to the human race as mankind. Therefore, some propose new translations of the Bible, which render such phrases as "people". But that misses the point. The Bible refers to God with a masculine pronoun. When the plural word *Elohim* is used, the accompanying verb is always in masculine singular. It is because mankind is made in the image of God that mankind is referred to, collectively, as masculine. So references to man, in the sense of mankind, are addressed as male, yet refer to both man and women – humankind. Any promises made to mankind are actually made to all people. As it states in Genesis 1:27:

> So God created man in his own image, in the image of God he created him; male and female he created them.
> (Genesis 1:27)

Firstly, we are reading that God made mankind collectively in His image. Then we note that He made *them* male and female. That means that Jesus is the Savior of all people, men and women. One Lord, one Savior, one God.

It is important to note this divine mandate, in the creation of genders. In today's society we are told two untruths about gender.

1. There are far more than just two genders.
2. Our gender is what we say it is, and does not necessarily have anything to do with biology.

Genesis 1 cuts across both these ideas. Although it is now becoming popular for people to refer to themselves as non-binary, the Bible makes clear that God created a binary humanity. And this was God's creation – it is He who decides what our gender is, not we ourselves.

In a fallen world, where human beings have a great many mutations, there are sometimes people born with genetic defects, where their reproductive organs have formed incorrectly, and they may display attributes of both male and female genitalia, for instance. This is a sad, and real, genetic illness. But when people, today, refer to gender dysphoria, it is not that genetic condition to which they refer. Gender dysphoria refers to how someone, who is biologically male, believes themselves to be female, or vice versa. The word *transgender* has been coined to describe this condition. In dealing with such conditions, we should take the utmost care and sympathy, because there is a very real problem presented. But that fact does not change the fact that they have been made by God either male or female. For many such people, the taking of hormones, and even gender reassignment surgery, has become the norm. But their physical mutation does not change how God has made them. A number of startling statistics are now becoming available, which show that many people who have started the process of gender reassignment – even after surgery – find that they want to return. These gender reversions gain a lot less sympathy from the politically correct establishment, than those who initially declare themselves to be transgender.

Dominion and the Cultural Mandate

In the second half of Genesis 1:26, we read that, in the eternal covenant agreement, God purposed that mankind would have dominion over all animals. Then in verse 28, we notice that:

1. God blessed the man and the women (and hence their offspring).
2. God commissioned them to reproduce and fill the Earth.
3. God gave them dominion over all the animals.

Some have suggested that the blessing at the beginning of verse 28 applies to all land animals. I do not think so, because other animals are not given any form of dominion. In any case, as I have explained above, the blessing of God on the vertebrate land animals can be assumed because of the way that their creation is described. So the blessing in Genesis 1:28 is a special blessing for humanity, and includes the dominion and the cultural mandate.

As an aside, we note that the KJV renders Genesis 1:28 as requiring the man and the woman to "replenish the earth". Some have used this to imply that the Earth was being re-created, rather than created for the first time. This leads to the well-known *Gap Theory*, discussed earlier. In fact, in the early 17th Century, the word "replenish" did not mean to "refill" - it meant simply to fill completely. Therefore, correctly understood, the KJV does not support the Gap Theory. Indeed, translations of the Bible earlier than the KJV – such as the Geneva Bible, or Tyndale's Bible, render the word in Genesis 1:28 as "fill", and not as "replenish".

Genesis 1:28 has often been labeled as the *cultural mandate* or the *dominion mandate*. Once again, the essential differences between humanity and animals are underscored. This dominion mandate has been criticized by some atheist and evolutionary commentators. For example, the broadcaster Sir David Attenborough once blamed the Bible for environmental damage in the world.

> An atheist raised in an academic, non-religious family, Sir David said Genesis peddled untruths about how animals and plants appeared on earth and was also at the root of why there was now serious environmental degradation due to the greedy overexploitation of the earth's natural resources.
>
> "The influence of the Book of Genesis, which says the Lord God said 'go forth and multiply' to Adam and Eve and 'the natural world is there for you to dominate', [is that] you have dominion over the animals and plants of the world," Sir David said.
>
> "That basic notion, that the world is there for us and if it doesn't actually serve our purposes, it's dispensable, that has produced the devastation of vast areas of the land's surface."[18]

Of course, Genesis 1:28 does not say what Attenborough says that it says. The word *dominion* does not mean *dominate*, even though both words have the same root. It is true that the verse tells us that everything in the world is created for our purpose, so it is indeed true

18 This article originally appeared in the UK's Independent Newspaper, but has since disappeared. However, I have rediscovered it, using the web.archive.com website.
< https://web.archive.org/web/20090204023659/http://www.independent.co.uk/news/uk/home-news/attenborough-genesis-it-can-go-forth-and-multiply-1521668.html >, accessed 12/14/2018.

that this philosophy cuts across secular ideas of green and environmental politics. However, this dominion mandate also lays a responsibility on people. The Earth is not actually ours to do what we like with. We are the managers, but not the owners! This responsibility is summed up in the concept of *stewardship*. When we appreciate that the Earth is ours to **manage** on behalf of God, we get a completely different impression of the true meaning of dominion in Genesis 1:28.[19]

The Westminster Shorter Catechism puts it very succinctly.

> Q. 10. How did God create man?
>
> A. God created man male and female, after his own image, in knowledge, righteousness, and holiness, with dominion over the creatures.[20]

It Was Very Good

Six times during the Creation Week, God declared what He had made to be good. We have already suggested that this refers to a form of perfection, rather than a moral use of the word good, so that when

19 The Cornwall Alliance is a Christian ministry dedicated to this point of view. See, for example, the following article on biblicla environmentalism. Jayaraj, V. (2018), *Why Christianity Is the World's Most Eco-friendly Philosophy*, < https://cornwallalliance.org/2018/09/why-christianity-is-the-worlds-most-eco-friendly-philosophy/ >, accessed 12/14/2018.

20 < http://shortercatechism.com/resources/wsc/wsc_010.html >, accessed 12/14/2018.

something is “not good”, as we shall see in Genesis 2, this means that it is not fully perfected, not that it is evil.

With that in mind, God now declares, in Genesis 1:31, that His creation was “very good”. The extra force being used here, indicated by the word “very”, suggests that God’s creation is now fully complete. The beginning of the next chapter shows that God’s creative work was complete. Therefore, the completion of creation implies a perfection that was achieved only at the end of the Six Days.

A study of Genesis 1 reminds us that Earth is indeed the center of the universe, metaphorically and spiritually, despite its many orbits through the universe. This world is here for a purpose. Once again, the Shorter Catechism reminds us of this fact.

> Q. 1. What is the chief end of man?
>
> A. Man’s chief end is to glorify God, and to enjoy him forever.

Genesis 2 Part 1 – Sabbath Rest

(Genesis 2:1-3)

And so to Day Seven.

I was once asked by a student, after a meeting in a university somewhere in the United Kingdom, "Do you believe that God made the world in seven days, like it says in the Bible?" I replied, "No, I don't" - and just as the look of satisfaction was creeping into his face, I continued "I believe that God made the world in six days – like it says in the Bible". This seemed to please the other students no end, who had previously warned me that this student was too clever for his own good.

But, clearly the issue that we must address concerns how many days of creation there were. We see that God made the world during the six days of creation, but then there was a seventh day, to round off the week. During this day, we read that God rested. So what was all this about?

Day Seven – A Real Day

There are many, who use the concept of this seventh day of rest to suggest that this was not a real day. And when they think they have established that Day Seven is not a real day, then they apply this to the other six days.

At the root of this discussion is the phrase, quoted six times in Genesis 1, that "there was evening and there was morning, the first [second, third, etc.] day". Old Earth Creationists, such as Hugh Ross, make much of the fact that the account of Day Seven does not end in this way.

> In Genesis 1, each of the creation days—except the seventh day—is marked off with the same refrain: "There was evening and there was morning." This literary device provides a pattern for the events of the first six creation days. Each "day" was of an unspecified duration, with a starting time and an ending time. But no such boundary is assigned to the seventh day, in Genesis or in any other passage of Scripture, which strongly suggests God's day of rest had, or has, not yet ended.[1]

Theistic Evolutionists, like Denis Alexander, have made the same point.

> It has also often been noted that whereas Days 1-6 are always completed by the phrase 'and there was evening and morning – the [1-6]th day', this phrase is lacking from the seventh day upon which God rested Jesus himself gives us insight into what this means in John 5:17 when he was criticised for healing on the Sabbath day,

1 Ross, H. (2014), *The Continuation of Creation Day Seven*, < https://www.reasons.org/explore/publications/rtb-101/read/rtb-101/2014/04/29/the-continuation-of-creation-day-seven >, accessed 12/15/2018.

> defending himself by saying that 'My Father is always at his work to this very day, and I, too, am working.' In other words Jesus is interpreting the seventh day figuratively as referring to the whole extended work of God in creation.[2]

Gill explains the passage in John's Gospel thus:

> He who is my Father, not by creation, or adoption, but by nature, though he ended all his work on the seventh day, and rested from what he had done; yet he did not cease from working at all, but has continued to work ever since, on sabbath days, as well as on other days; in upholding and governing the world, in continuing the species of beings, and all creatures in their being; in providing for them, and in dispensing the bounties of his providence to them; in causing his sun to shine, and showers of rain to descend on the earth; and in taking care of, and protecting even the meanest of his creatures: and much more men; and still more his own people.[3]

What both Ross and Alexander are doing is confusing God's work of creation *ex nihilo* with God's ongoing work of sustaining and upholding creation. Ross also quotes John 17 as a "problem", along

2 Alexander, D.R. (2008), *Creation or Evolution: Do We Have to Choose?*, (Oxford: Monarch), p. 157.

3 Gill, J. (1748), *An Exposition of the New Testament*, online version < https://www.biblestudytools.com/commentaries/gills-exposition-of-the-bible/john-5-17.html >, accessed 12/15/2018.

with two other passages, which also specifically refer to the ongoing sustaining work of God, and not the completion of creation.

> The picture of an ongoing seventh day receives mention in other portions of Scripture. Psalm 95:7–11, John 5:16–18, and Hebrews 4:1–11 (each by a different author) indicate that the seventh day began, from an earthly perspective, after the creation of Adam and Eve and extends through the present era to a future time.[4]

In Psalm 95:9 the context shows that God is simply referring to all the things He did for the Israelites, while they were in the desert. And in Hebrews 4, the context again shows the comparison between the cessation of the creative work, and the ongoing sustaining work, with the rest from creative work being used as a type of the eternal rest to come. In no wise do any of these passages suggest or require that the world's seventh day did not end. Given that the day has a number, therefore, we revert to the comments we made earlier that when the Hebrew word *yôm* appears with a number, it always refers to an ordinary, 24-hour day.

Cessation of Creation

Genesis 2:1 tells us that the creation of the heavens and the earth had finished. We have already discussed that the phrase "the heavens and

4 *Ob cit.*

the earth" is a *merism*, meaning the whole of everything; the entire universe. The phrase "and all the host of them" is reminiscent of Deuteronomy 4:19, where it refers to the sun, moon, and stars. This seems to be underscoring the fact that the whole of creation is finished at this point, including everything, everywhere in the universe.

It is virtually impossible for us to analyze every event of the Creation Week from a modern scientific perspective. This is because what God was doing in the Creation Week was miraculous. In an article on a possible cosmogony, Dr. Danny Faulkner said:

> As creationists, we ought not to be so resistant to believing in miracles. We might as well enquire as to the physical aspects of the virgin birth or resurrection of Jesus. Both of these events are objective reality, but both were miraculous. Creation by its very nature was a miraculous event/process. As scientists, we are so used to looking at physical mechanisms that we often want to box in the Creation Week in terms of physical/natural processes. While certain aspects of the Creation Week probably were physical and there likely are physical ramifications of creation even today, we ought to realize that there are certain things about the Creation Week that we as scientists cannot fully comprehend.[5]

5 Faulkner, D., *A Proposal for a New Solution to the Light Travel Time Problem*, Answers Research Journal

However, on Day Seven we find that the creative work is finished, so that must be the starting point for all the scientific laws that we have today. Prior to this point, God has made new material out of nothing. After this point, the First and Second Laws of Thermodynamics must have been operative. The First Law states that "energy cannot be created or destroyed – only changed from one type to another". Mass, we have discovered, is really a sort of frozen energy, so this law describes an equivalence between mass and energy. The Second Law states that in every energy change, some energy is converted to low temperature heat, which, therefore, cannot do any useful work. These, and all other laws (such as Gravity) came into being at the beginning of Day Seven, and they have been with us ever since. So it is finishing of the miraculous Creation Week that actually enables the scientific laws, by which God, having previously created His universe, now sustains it by His power.

Rest

If God were not creating anything during Day Seven, and if it were a real 24-hour day, then what was its purpose? The first thing we should note is that God was not tired, after His six days of creation. So this day of rest was not for His benefit, directly. If it were not for His benefit, then it must have been for ours. In fact, as we shall see shortly, the sort of rest, of which this passage speaks, is not a rest,

6 (2013):279–284.

because of tiredness. It is being at rest. It is ceasing normal work activity. God is setting a pattern of six days work, and one day of ceasing to work, as a weekly timescale and rhythm for us. That this is the case is seen in the giving of the Ten Commandments, only one of which has a reason attached to it.

> Remember the Sabbath day, to keep it holy. Six days you shall labor, and do all your work, but the seventh day is a Sabbath to the Lord your God. On it you shall not do any work, you, or your son, or your daughter, your male servant, or your female servant, or your livestock, or the sojourner who is within your gates. For in six days the Lord made heaven and earth, the sea, and all that is in them, and rested on the seventh day. Therefore the Lord blessed the Sabbath day and made it holy. (Exodus 20:8-11)

It is clear that for the Israelites this day of rest was to be the seventh day of the week. This pattern of a seven day cycle was re-instituted at the time of Moses, as shown in the Ten Commandments, and also as previously seen in the cycle of six days' collection of manna in the wilderness, followed by one day when manna was not to be collected.

It has often been said by some that the Fourth Commandment has no binding power on Christians today. As evidence for this, some point to the idea that the other nine commandments are quoted in the New

Testament, but the Sabbath provision is not. It is certainly true that the New Testament shows that we are not saved by our keeping of the Law. However, having been saved, we are to follow Christ by doing what He says – not for salvation, but out of love for Him.

"If you love me, you will keep my commandments," says Jesus in John 14:15. A few verses later He says "Whoever has my commandments and keeps them, he it is who loves me. And he who loves me will be loved by my Father, and I will love him and manifest myself to him". (John 14:21) Of course, it is true that there are strictures against legalism, and one verses in particular makes clear that we are not to be legalistic over opinions on the Sabbath.

> Therefore let no one pass judgment on you in questions of food and drink, or with regard to a festival or a new moon or a Sabbath. (Colossians 2:16)

But that does not mean that there is nothing to say about the facility of a seven day cycle, including one day of ceasing from normal work.

Fifty years ago, my next point would not have been controversial, yet it is today. It is my contention that the most appropriate day for the cessation of normal work is Sunday. This does not mean that Sunday has all the attributes of an Israelite Sabbath, but neither is it to be just another working day, like any other. I like the way that John MacArthur puts it:

> But when you come to the new covenant, you have a new kind of observation, not observing God as Creator, not observing God as law-giver, but in the new covenant God is defining Himself as what? Savior. So the new covenant has its own day, a day in which we focus on God as our Savior.[6]

The phrase "Lord's Day" to describe Sunday is particularly appropriate, therefore. It is a biblical phrase, and it emphasizes that, while Sunday is not like the old Sabbath, nor is it like any other day.

Why Is Sunday Special?

In the 1990s, there was a campaign in the UK entitled "Keep Sunday Special". Alas, it was not terribly successful. Major grocery chains in the UK were trying to get permission to open all day on Sunday. Eventually, a campaign of disobedience by the large grocery chains led to a change in the law in 1994. Prior to that change in the law, trading on Sundays had been illegal, with a few exceptions. After that change in the law, regulations were liberalized – though not to the extent that they are in the US. Living in America, I am now used to the idea of the big grocery chains being open constantly, 24 hours a day, seven days a week. It may be a shock to many of my American friends to know that in England and Wales, 24-hour trading can only

6 MacArthur, J. (2009), *Why Sunday Is the Lord's Day*, < https://www.gty.org/library/sermons-library/90-380/why-sunday-is-the-lords-day >, accessed 12/15/2018.

occur between 12:01am on Monday through 11:59pm on Saturday. On Sundays, large stores may only open for six hours. And it is still illegal for stores to open on Easter Sunday. The rhythm of life has changed a great deal, but, in most parts of the UK, the rhythm still exists.

But even here in the US, there is often something still special about Sundays. It is true that today one can leave the Sunday service and go straight to the restaurant – something that would never have happened for my family, growing up in 1960s England. But church services are still mostly on Sundays. There is still an assumption – largely true – that most people will be able to gather together on a Sunday for worship.

But why Sunday? The New Testament gives us a progression of events.

1. The Resurrection took place on the first day of the week – a Sunday.
2. In Matthew 28:9, we have the first act of Sunday worship – the disciples clasped Jesus' feet and worshiped Him.
3. In Luke 24:13ff, later on the same day, we have Jesus meeting with the disciples on the road to Emmaus. We get the first Sunday Bible Study, as Jesus teaches them about all the places in the Old Testament that refer to Him. And, of course, that

encounter ends with the breaking of bread – probably for the first time, since the Passover meal the previous week.

4. In MacArthur's article, quoted above, he points out that, by the end of that first Sunday, a lot of people know that Jesus has risen. "Peter knows it, John knows it, Mary Magdalene knows it, the other Marys, the other women know it, other disciples know it. And by Sunday evening, all the disciples know it with one exception, who was absent? Thomas."[7] But Thomas meets the risen Jesus the very next Sunday (John 20:26). Sunday is already turning out to be very special.

5. The next important event was Pentecost. This was to be 50 days after the Passover. That means that it was on a Sunday! This was the day when the Holy Spirit was given – and that event was in fulfilment of the prophecies of Jesus "But you will receive power when the Holy Spirit has come upon you, and you will be my witnesses in Jerusalem and in all Judea and Samaria, and to the end of the earth". (Acts 1:8)

6. By Acts 20:7, it appears that, although the disciples liked to meet together every day, they especially liked to break bread together on Sunday.

7 *Ibid.*

7. In 1 Corinthians 16:1-2, the collection for the saints was taken on Sundays – the first day of the week.

8. And in 96 AD, in Revelation 1:9, John gets a vision on "the Lord's Day" - the day of the week, when worship seemed to be most fitting.

So, while it is true that Sunday is not really a Christian Sabbath, in the full meaning of the word, it has taken on many of the attributes of a Sabbath, and this pattern has maintained throughout the history of the Church, even in times of persecution. For much more detail on this matter, please read Iain Campbell's excellent book *On the First Day of the Week.*[8]

So, as we return to the very first of God's special days – Day Seven – which was given long before the law of Moses came into force, we find that the four attributes God gave that day are of particular value for our celebration of the Lord's Day today.

> And on the seventh day God finished his work that he had done, and he rested on the seventh day from all his work that he had done. So God blessed the seventh day and made it holy, because on it God rested from all his work that he had done in creation. (Genesis 2:2-3)

8 Campbell, I.D. (2005), *On the First Day of the Week*, (Leominster, UK: Day One Publications).

1. God did no more work. His creative work was finished. God would be active during Day Seven in sustaining the world, but this was different from His creative work. In the same way, we can cease from our normal weekly work. That does not mean we do nothing, but Sunday's work is special, because it is worshiping the King.

2. God rested. The Hebrew word translated rest is shabath (שָׁבַת), a verb, sharing a root with the noun Sabbath. As we have said, this does not imply that God was tired. Rather, it means that there was an active cessation. In the same way, we must make an active decision that Sunday is not to be a day like any other day. Although I do not want to be legalistic, dare I suggest that we try to do our grocery shopping on Saturday, for example, so that we can devote Sunday to God? Again, that is not a law – this is not legalism. But it is a plea for Sunday to be different – for it to have a different atmosphere.

3. God blessed the day. There must be something special about the day, if it is blessed by God.

4. God made the day holy. He set it apart. If we are going to enjoy the presence of God on Sunday, then we need to set it apart for Him, and treat it as holy, because He is holy.

Many of the thoughts that I have shared here are not popular today. And there were always legalists in my youth, who would consider it a dreadful sin, if you had to go to the convenience store on Sunday to get an extra pint of milk. We should not be about putting so many strictures on people. But, if we set aside this day for God, and for worshiping Him, not just in a morning's service, then we will be all the richer because of it.

Genesis 2 Part 2 – In the Garden

(Genesis 2:4-25)

Toledoth (תּוֹלְדָה)

> These are the generations of the heavens and the earth when they were created, in the day that the Lord God made the earth and the heavens. (Genesis 2:4)

The book of Genesis has a structure to it. Every so often, we read a phrase, such as "these are the generations of...". The ESV, quoted above, uses the word *generations*, as does the KJV. The NIV uses the word *account,* while the NKJV has *history*. All of these are legitimate translations of the Hebrew word *toledoth.*

Many commentators have suggested that these mark out sections of the book of Genesis, probably compiled in written form or oral form, by the patriarchs around at the time of their authorship. None of this is to undermine the Mosaic authorship of Genesis. We can see Moses as writing the accounts down as a sort of inspired editor, under the inspiration of the Holy Spirit. It was Moses's work from Moses's pen, but perhaps information had been carried down through the years by these patriarchs.

If we accept this toledoth structure, our next question has to be whether the phrases mark the heading at the start of a section, or a back-heading at the end of the section preceding. In *The Genesis Record* Henry Morris argued that the toledoth phrases were at the end of sections.[1] I accepted this argument, in my book *The Six Days of Genesis* (originally titled *Just Six Days*).[2] I now believe I got this the wrong way round. In his *The Genesis Account*, Jonathan Sarfati concludes that the phrase indicates something generated by what went before. That puts the phrases as headings for the section that follows. He quotes a number of experts in Hebrew grammar that back up his position – which is the majority opinion among those with a high view of Scripture. Sarfati shows, for example, that the toledoth in Ruth 4:12 is clearly a heading for the short genealogy at the end of Ruth 4 – following the toledoth.

For these reasons, I will be using Sarfati's toledoth divisions, which, to be fair, are the divisions quoted by a large number of other commentators. I would recommend reading the relevant section of Sarfati's commentary for more information, including references to the works of other experts.[3]

Here, then, are the toledoth divisions that I am using, as compiled by Sarfati.

1 Morris, H.M. (1976), *The Genesis Record*, (Grand Rapids, MI: Baker Book House), p. 26ff.
2 Taylor, P.F. (2007), *The Six Days of Genesis*, (Green Forest, AR: Master Books), pp. 83-84.
3 Sarfati, J. (2015), *The Genesis Account*, (Powder Springs, GA: Creation Book Publishers), pp. 17-22.

0. Precursor (not a toledoth) Genesis 1:1-2:3. The Creation Week.
1. Toledoth of the heavens and earth. Genesis 2:4-4:26. This is what followed creation.
2. Toledoth of Adam. Genesis 5:1-6:8. Leading up to the Flood, including the first chrono-genealogy.
3. Toledoth of Noah. Genesis 6:9-9:29. The Flood and its aftermath.
4. Toledoth of the sons of Noah. Genesis 10:1-11:9. The table of nations, and the account of Babel.
5. Toledoth of Shem. Genesis 11:10-26. The second chrono-genealogy.
6. Toledoth of Terah. Genesis 11:17-25:11. The calling of Abraham, and the Abrahamic Covenant.
7. Toledoth of Ishmael. Genesis 25:12-18. Almost an aside, of the descendants of Ishmael.
8. Toledoth of Isaac. Genesis 25:19-35:29. Jacob's line, and his struggle for blessing.
9. Toledoth of Esau. Genesis 36:1-8. The side-line of Esau.
10. Toledoth of Esau part 2. Genesis 36:9-37:1. The ancestry of the nations of the Edomites, Horites, and Amalekites.

11. Toledoth of Jacob. Genesis 37:2-50:26. The 12 tribes, and the account of Joseph. This sets the scene for the account of the Israelites in Egypt and the exodus to follow.[4]

There are some commentators who proceed to make a lot of the fact that this verse refers to "in the day that the Lord God made the earth and the heavens". The making of the earth and the heavens took six days in Genesis 1, so it is proposed by some that the phrase "in the day" indicates that the days of creation were figurative, rather than literal. This is not so. The word *yôm* can indeed be figurative, when it is applied by itself, but as we discussed earlier, *yôm* always refers to an ordinary 24-hour day, if it is accompanied by a number. Therefore, the occurrences of the numbered days in Genesis 1 were literal 24-hour days, but this mention of "day" in Genesis 2:4 does not refer to a literal 24-hour day. There is no contradiction caused, by making these assumptions.

Plants of the Field

In verse 5, some versions refer to "plants of the field" and "herbs of the field" (e.g. KJV and NKJV), while others refer to "bush or shrub of the field" and "plants of the field" (e.g. ESV, NASB). The first used phrase is *siach hassadeh* (שִׂ֣יחַ הַשָּׂדֶ֗ה) and the second is *eseb hassadeh* (עֵ֥שֶׂב הַשָּׂדֶ֖ה). The word *hassadeh* ("of the field") implies that these were

4 *Ibid.* pp. 18-19.

cultivated plants. So the *siach hassadeh* probably refers to fruit-bearing shrubs, while *eseb hassadeh* probably refers to small edible plants. Their mention here, in Genesis 2:5, is not a contradiction of the creation of plants on Day Three (Genesis 1:11). The events about to be described in Genesis 2 are a detailed description of the creation of the first humans, and so must have been on Day Six, but God would only make these cultivatable plants at this point, as He was about to make the people to cultivate them.

LORD God

Throughout Genesis 1, God was referred to as *ĕlōhîm* (אֱלֹהִים). In Genesis 2 – 3, we read of *yahweh ĕlōhîm* (יְהוָה אֱלֹהִים). There are commentators who wish to use this change to suggest that Genesis 2 is a different creation account to that in Genesis 1. Moreover, they suggest that they came from different writers, in a theory known as the Documentary Hypothesis, which suggests that the Pentateuch was compiled during Babylonian Captivity by four scribes, known as J, E, P, and D. Under this hypothesis, sections that refer to *ĕlōhîm* were written by E – the "elohist" scribe. Sections that refer to *yahweh* were written by J – the "jehovist" or "yahwist" scribe. However, we have already indicated that the authorship of the Penteteuch was one person – Moses – even if he used originators of the *toledoths*, under inspiration. Also, we maintain that Genesis 2 cannot be a different creation account to that in Genesis 1, because God created the world just once. We find that, when we start with this presupposition of the unity of Genesis 1 and 2, it is just as easy to read Genesis 2 in that way. Jesus treated both accounts as one, for example, when He quoted from both chapters in His argument about marriage, in Matthew 19:4-5.

A better explanation of the difference in divine name is that Genesis 1 is written from God's point of view, on the whole Creation Week, whereas Genesis 2 fills in details of what God did, written more from the human perspective.

Most English translations use the form LORD with small caps to represent the Hebrew word *yahweh*, whereas *Lord*, with small letters, represents the Hebrew word *adonai*.

The use of the word LORD often indicates that it is the Second Person of the Trinity to whom we are referring. This is not always the case, but it probably is here, remembering that Colossians 1:16 tells us "For by [Jesus] all things were created, in heaven and on earth, visible and invisible, whether thrones or dominions or rulers or authorities—all things were created through him and for him." The Divine Name *yahweh* is probably better represented as *YHWH*, as this includes four letters, and the Hebrew word also includes four letters. The word is explained more fully, when the LORD God appears to Moses in a burning bush.

> God said to Moses, I AM WHO I AM. And he said, Say this to the people of Israel, I AM has sent me to you. (Exodus 3:14).

"I AM", you will recall, sounds very like the word YHWH. Hence, when Jesus says things like "I am the good shepherd" (John 10:11), it caused such a lot of outrage. By the use of the phrase "I am", Jesus is claiming to be God, especially as that whole phrase sounds so much like the beginning of Psalm 23: "The Lord is my shepherd".

Was there Rain before the Flood?

Genesis 2:5 clearly tells us that there was no rain, during this Creation Week. In the past, many creationists have suggested that this means there was no rain before the Flood. This latter assertion was tied in with the belief in the vapor canopy model, whereby a canopy of water vapor was postulated, which would have surrounded the Earth.

I have already made clear that I, in common with most creationists, do not accept the Canopy Theory anymore. Therefore, there is no necessity to suggest that there was no rain after the Creation Week.

I have previously written that I suspected there may not have been rain before the Flood, even without accepting the Canopy Theory[5]. This is because the rainbow was used as a sign of the Noahic Covenant after the Flood. However, there have been other occasions where God

5 Taylor, P.F. (2007), *The Six Days of Genesis*, (Green Forest, AR: Master Books), p. 85.

has placed meaning on something that already existed. So, I now think that it is simply impossible to say, from the text, whether or not there was rain after Creation and before the Flood.

This leaves us with a brief discussion on what was happening in Genesis 2:6. The verse says "a mist was going up from the land and was watering the whole face of the ground". The word translated *mist* is *ed*, and this could refer to a mist or a spring. In some way, there was already a cycling of water in this perfect Creation Week world. God has provided a water cycle, to keep water fresh and pure, by evaporation and condensation – it is a planet-wide distillation process. This shows the wisdom and economy of God. He did not just create things; He also created systems.

It is worth pausing to emphasize the importance of water to God's economy, and the sustaining of life on Earth. Water has a very narrow temperature range for its liquid phase; just 100°C or 180°F (between 32 and 212). This means that the Earth had to be created in exactly the right place, distance-wise, from the Sun, in order to maintain all three phases of water in equilibrium. It is clear that, if the Earth were too close to the Sun, or too far from it, there would be no liquid water. The existence of all three phases on Earth is part of a dynamic system, because the continual evaporation and condensation of water, beginning right there in Genesis 2, is the means by which God keeps water clean and pure – just right for human life, and indeed all kinds of life.

The Creation of Adam

"The LORD God formed the man of dust of the ground..."

The first thing we should notice from this declaration is that this was a positive action of God. It does not say that God sat back and watched Adam evolve from ape-like ancestors. But some commentators read evolution into this statement, by assuming that the "dust of the ground" is a euphemism for naturalistic processes, leading to the evolution of human beings. John Walton says:

> The other element that often leads us to think that Genesis 2:7 is speaking in material terms is the reference to dust, presumed by many to be a material ingredient. By now, however, we have learned that we must think this through before jumping to conclusions.[6]

Walton's view is that the dust refers to mortality.

> We find the decisive clue in Genesis 3:19: "For dust you are and to dust you will return."[7]

6 Walton, J. (2015), *The Lost World of Adam and Eve*, (Downers Grove, IL: InterVarsity Press), p. 72.
7 *Ibid. p. 73.*

Walton's assumption is that dust is synonymous with death. But there is no reason to read this into the verse. In Genesis 3:19, we will see that God is simply reminding Adam of where he came from, and where he will now return to. Walton goes further, and argues that Adam and Eve, or whatever he conceives of as being the first humans, must have had the capability to die.

> Besides the likelihood that Genesis 3:19 suggests people were created mortal, another piece of evidence in Genesis offers even stronger evidence. In the garden, God provided a tree of life. *Immortal people have no need for a tree of life.* The provision of one suggests that they were mortal. (emphasis mine)[8]

Walton's error here is to assume that the fruit of the tree of life would have some magical powers to keep those who eat it alive. This is not so. Look at the very last chapter of the Bible.

> Then the angel showed me the river of the water of life, bright as crystal, flowing from the throne of God and of the Lamb through the middle of the street of the city; also, on either side of the river, the tree of life with its twelve kinds of fruit, yielding its fruit each month. The leaves of the tree were for the healing of the nations. (Revelation of John 22:1-2)

8 *Ibid.*

When God has remade the heavens and the earth perfectly, and we dwell in them forever, we will not need to eat fruit from the tree of life to stay alive. So what is the purpose of this fruit? We note that this fruit had led (past tense) to the healing of the nations, which implies a reconciliation of peoples from all parts of the globe to God. Our perfection of state is accomplished only by the sacrifice of Jesus Christ, and the fruit of the tree of life does not give us immortality, which has already been won for us, but it is symbolic of the work of Jesus. And for us to partake of it every month is an act of fellowship. In this regard, therefore, it is very analogous to the communion. The elements of bread and wine do not achieve our salvation, or any merit for us. That is achieved by Jesus, whose death and resurrection we celebrate by communion. Nevertheless, we are commanded to partake of the communion as an act of fellowship, and, indeed, incorrect or inappropriate partaking of the communion brings judgment. In the same way, the tree of life in the Garden was not to give eternal life, but to be symbolic of it, and our fellowship with God. So the hypothetical inappropriate consumption of fruit of the tree of life, after the Fall (Genesis 3:22) would have led to a terrible curse - an imperfect sinful body, without the ability to die. This digression should be sufficient, it is hoped, to show that Walton is wrong to equate dust with mortality. Simon Turpin emphasizes this point, when he says:

> Dust in Genesis 3:19 cannot be referring to Adam's mortality, as Walton argues, because this 'mortality' comes in the context of a curse upon Adam and his wife because of their disobedience.... According to the Bible, death is not a biological necessity but the wages of sin (Rom. 6:23)[9]

Another clear reason to suppose that the dust is a material is in the text. The text itself contains a play on words, such as we have seen before. We have already said that the word for *man* is *adam*. But the word for *ground* is *adamah*. The words have the same root, and the reason for that is that Genesis is emphasizing that Adam was created out of a physical material from the ground. The problem with Walton and others is that they have started by wanting to believe evolution – a false presupposition – and they have allowed that to influence their exegesis. Their interpretation of the text has been led by their scientific opinion. By this, they have shown that their view of Scripture is not a high one, as they have maintained. Walton is part of what Turpin describes as "evangelicalism that has compromised".[10]

Evolutionism and Docetism

Does it really matter whether we believe that God made Adam from literal material from the ground, or by a material-based process of

9 Turpin, S. (2018), *Adam: The First and the Last*, (Leominster, UK: Day One Publications), p. 30.

10 *Ibid*. p. 28.

evolution? Indeed it does matter. It is of great theological significance, to the Gospel itself, that we understand that Adam was created perfect, both spiritually and biologically.

Most evangelicals are aware of the problems of unitarianism. Unitarianism teaches that Jesus was not God, but merely a very good man. The Bible teaches that Jesus was and is both human and divine. However, Jesus is not 50% human and 50% divine. He is 100% human and 100% God. He is said to have two natures, united in one person. This is a doctrine known as the Hypostatic Union. A unitarian believes that Jesus is 0% God and 100% human. What many people do not realize is that there is an equal and opposite heresy to unitarianism, which is known as docetism. I have written at length on the subject of docetism, in my book *Itching Ears*.[11] The argument in brief is this: docetism teaches that Jesus was 100% God and 0% human – or at least not fully human.

Now, if we believe that human beings have always had biological flaws, from the moment we allegedly evolved, then Jesus, as the perfect Last Adam, cannot fully represent us, as He has a human nature unlike that of Adam. Therefore, Jesus is not human. He is superhuman.

11 Taylor, P.F. (2014, 3rd edn), *Itching Ears*, (Castle Rock, WA: J6D Publications), chapter 2, *The Deity of Christ*.

However, if Adam was created without physical death, biologically perfect, then we have a previous model of biological perfection, and Jesus' nature is fully human, as Adam's was. Therefore, the doctrine of the Hypostatic Union can only work if God made Adam exactly as He said He did. I repeat, if Adam was simply at the head of a long process of evolution, death, and disease, then Jesus was not fully human. Theistic evolutionists therefore unwittingly adhere to a mild form of the docetic heresy.

The Garden of Eden

In contemporary culture, Eden has become synonymous with the concept of a primitive paradise. Evolutionists thus co-opt the word for their own use. A beautiful, unspoilt area of the world might be described as an Eden. But the Garden of Eden was not meant to be "unspoilt", in the way that evolutionists use the term. They refer to edenic areas as "unspoilt", if they show no signs of being worked by human beings. Of course, Eden was definitely unspoilt in the sense that, at its creation, there was nothing wrong with it. It was made perfect. But it was not made to be without a human touch. As we will see, God intended it to be a place where humans were to be set to work. As for it being a paradise, that is a better use of language. Paradise, etymologically, refers to an enclosure, implying a garden. The word is, of course, used to imply a heavenly afterlife, and we can assume that when God makes the new heaven and new earth mentioned in Revelation (and in Isaiah), that this is akin to a return to Eden. *Paradeisos* (παραδεισος) is the Greek word used to translate the word garden in the LXX.

We have already referred to the mention of Eden in Ezekiel 28. In support of the Gap Theory, many have assumed that the Ezekiel Eden was different from that in Genesis 2, because the Ezekiel Eden does not mention plants, but, instead, refers to precious stones.

> You were in Eden, the garden of God; every precious stone was your covering, sardius, topaz, and diamond, beryl, onyx, and jasper, sapphire, emerald, and carbuncle; and crafted in gold were your settings and your engravings. On the day that you were created they were prepared. You were an anointed guardian cherub. I placed you; you were on the holy mountain of God; in the midst of the stones of fire you walked. (Ezekiel 28:13-14)

However, Genesis 2 also mentions minerals in verses 11 and 12. It seems likely that Ezekiel 28 is simply giving more details about some of the minerals found in Eden, remembering that Genesis 1 and 2 do not give us a full list of every single item that God has made, while insisting that God did indeed make every single item, and did so in the six days of the Creation Week.

Many people want to know where Eden is located. The answer is that it is not located anywhere anymore. It must have been destroyed in the Flood, as was the rest of the surface of the Earth. In Genesis 2, however, we are told that Eden was "in the East". We can, perhaps, read too much into the exact geography of this created place, but, at a minimum, we can suggest that God did not create Adam in Eden, but somewhere else. Then God took Adam and placed him in the garden.

As we have already discussed, the trees that God placed in the Garden were there for food. The fruit of those trees was to be "pleasant to the sight and good for food". And two special trees were placed in the center – the tree of life, and the tree of the knowledge of good and evil. We will discuss the purpose of these trees, when we meet them in chapter three.

One matter about the geography of Eden can be discussed, however. The Garden was almost certainly on top of a hill. How do I know this? It is because "a river flowed out of Eden". This river divided into four rivers. Water flows downhill, which means that the garden itself must have been uphill!

The idea of gardens on top of hills is a theme in ancient mythology. For example, the Hanging Gardens of Babylon were thought to have been constructed by Nebuchadnezzar to remind his wife of the beautiful hilltop gardens of her homeland. I like C.S. Lewis's garden imagery. In *The Magician's Nephew*, Digory, having found himself at the creation of the Narnian world, is sent by Aslan to a garden, to collect the fruit of eternal youth, to provide healing for his mother[12]. This garden is a walled garden on top of a hill. It goes without saying that Lewis was very familiar with the account of the first garden here in Genesis 2.

The Rivers from Eden

There are those today who suggest that Eden must have been somewhere in Mesopotamia - much of which is in modern Iraq. Their reasoning is that two of the four rivers, which divide from the Edenic river, are the great Mesopotamian rivers: the Tigris and the Euphrates. Some place Eden near the confluence of the rivers, while others place it near the river sources. The study notes in the ESV Study Bible suggest these locations. Although I have a great respect for the ESV Study Bible, this note alone reminds us that it is the Bible text which is inspired, and the study notes are not! As we have already mentioned, the Garden of Eden was destroyed, along with the rest of the Earth's surface, at the time of the Flood. So why are the Tigris and Euphrates mentioned? If you think about it, the answer is obvious.

Searching one day on a travel booking site, I was trying to find flights to my home city of Manchester, which has the only airport in England outside London where transatlantic planes land. At first, I thought the

12 Lewis, C.S. (1955), *The Magician's Nephew*, (Puffin).

price of the flights was ridiculously cheap until I realized I had searched not for Manchester, England, but Manchester, New Hampshire! It should be obvious that Manchester, NH, is named after the English city. There are many other examples of cities and regions named after cities and regions elsewhere. In the same way, the post-Flood Tigris and Euphrates were so named after the pre-Flood Tigris and Euphrates. So, there is no reason to suppose that the modern rivers are anywhere near where the pre-Flood rivers were. In any case, the Edenic Tigris and Euphrates had a common source – the Edenic River – whereas the modern rivers do not. Moreover, the writers of the ESV Study Bible notes have forgotten to take account of the other two rivers – the Pishon and the Gihon.

Working the Garden

There is an old comic song, by Michael Flanders and Donald Swan, called "The Second Law of Thermodynamics". It contains these wonderful lines:

> Heat is work, and work's a curse
> And all the heat in the Universe
> Is gonna cool down... 'cos it can't increase
> Then there'll be no more work, and there'll be perfect peace!

It's an amusing point, but, of course, it is not correct. Work is not a curse. Toil is a curse, and work became toil after the Fall. But, in Genesis 2:15, we read "The LORD God took the man and put him in the garden of Eden to work it and keep it." We need to remember that, at this point in history, it is still inside the Creation Week. There is, as yet, no sin. Therefore, work is not a punishment. Work is the natural order of things.

This clearly has implications for the way we operate our lives. There is a tendency to think of work as something difficult, but necessary, always with a view t getting it finished and out of the way. The last couple of generations have worked towards the goal of retirement, with the idea of doing no further work. This would appear to be an unbiblical aim. There is nothing wrong, of course, with leaving one's paid employment in one's 60s or 70s, and moving to more vocational work, that might even be unpaid. And there would be nothing wrong in taking more leisure time. But the idea of giving up work altogether would seem not to be an option.

So Adam was given the task of working the Garden and keeping it. We are going to read about weeds in Genesis 3, but even though there were no weeds, it would be possible for this Garden to get out of hand, considering how fertile the ground would have been. Even in a perfect world, there was work to do, to stop the Garden getting overgrown. Bunyan points out that, by being set this work, Adam was being a type of the Last Adam, Jesus Christ. In his commentary on Genesis, Bunyan quotes Isaiah 27:3, rightly prophetically applying it to Christ.

> I, the LORD, am its keeper; every moment I water it. Lest anyone punish it, I keep it night and day; (Isaiah 27:3)

> "In this also Adam was a figure of our Lord Jesus Christ, as pastor and chief bishop of his church."[13]

God's Law for Adam

Immediately after giving Adam his first instructions, God also gave him his first restrictions. It has been rightly pointed out that Genesis 2:16-17 contains the One Commandment that humanity in their perfection were supposed to obey. The fact that there was a commandment given before sin came about is also significant. Adam was designed to obey, and, hence, so was every other human being, including Eve. But Adam was the Federal Head, through whom all of this obedience was to flow. This conferred on Adam – and therefore on all the rest of humanity – a responsibility. This responsibility existed before sin came into the world. It follows that the failure to uphold his part in that responsibility was to have eternal consequences, and race-wide consequences. Adam's sin was not

13 Bunyan, J. (ed. Paul Taylor, 2010), *Genesis: An Exposition of Chapters 1 to 11*, (Castle Rock, WA: J6D Publications), p. 53.

merely his own. He represented us, because he was given the One Commandment.

We should further note that the One Commandment began with permission. God said "You may surely eat of every tree of the garden". It was not to be taken for granted that Adam could eat what he liked, until God gave him this permission – even in a perfect world. Too many Christians today major on the freedoms that God has given us, therefore treating God with something approaching familiarity. God is addressed as if He were our mate, or our buddy. "God is crazy about you", we hear preachers say. Of course, it is true that God loves His people, and we must never lose sight of that, but there is altogether too much familiarity and not enough respect in the way we think we can relate to God. Even a perfect human being could only have his freedoms because God had given them to him. God is Sovereign. He is not our buddy, or our mate. He is our loving Heavenly Father, and we can have confidence in His presence, but there still must be an awe and respect.

Also note that in this permission, God says "you may *surely eat*". The nature of this permission is summed up in this phrase. In fact, in the Hebrew, the word for "eat" is repeated. What the verse actually says is "You may eat eat of every tree in the garden". As we will see in the next verse, this repetition of a word is significant, and implies that a process has begun, which is going to continue. So we eat by God's good grace, and, while I cannot find a specific verse telling us to pray before we eat, this verse at least shows that the process of having meals, and having regular food, was inaugurated by God, so it makes sense to thank Him before we eat.

Following the verse giving Adam permission to eat came a verse that qualifies that permission, by introducing a restriction. Again, we should notice that this restriction was to be in place in a perfect world. Mankind's freedoms are not inherent to himself, and nor do they emanate from other human beings. Our freedoms, and our restrictions, are sanctioned by God. Therefore, God told Adam "but of the tree of the knowledge of good and evil you shall not eat".

Some have got confused at this point. Why did God give Adam a rule that he was bound to break? It is only human nature that, when we are told not to do something, we will want to do it, isn't that so?

No, it is not so. Yet again, we must remember that this was a perfect world. Adam was not born into sin. He had every ability to keep this rule, simply by doing nothing. I repeat – Adam could have remained in a state of grace, simply by doing nothing. It was the *something* that he did which caused the problem.

So what was the purpose of the rule? Why should it matter that Adam did not eat the fruit of this one tree? Was there something magical or dangerous in it? I would suggest there was nothing magical or dangerous about the tree. Its fruit was not poisonous. In C.S. Lewis's novel, *Perelandra*, the Queen of Perelandra tells Ransom that she and the King were not allowed to stay on the fixed island overnight. Ransom puzzled over the rule, but eventually came to the conclusion that the purpose for the rule was that there had to be a rule to be obeyed. He suggested that this was the same with our own Adam and Eve, given a rule about this one tree, in order that obedience should be active.

This brings us to the point that God told Adam in advance what the sanction would be for disobedience. "In the day that you eat of it you shall surely die." The question that this raises is this: how could Adam (and later Eve) know what this sanction meant, if they had not experienced death?

With respect, I think the question is a non-starter. God had given Adam language. Adam had understanding. And Adam knew words. So, God gave Adam an instruction that he understood, with a sanction that he also understood. Sarfati maintains, rightly, that "It's preposterous to argue that Adam would need to see something to comprehend it." If God used the concept of death in His command to Adam, then we should assume that God knew that Adam would understand what was being said, and would be able to choose his actions accordingly.[14]

The Wages of Sin

Verse 17 contains another repetition. This time it is the word *die* that is repeated. God tells Adam that, on the day he eats that forbidden fruit, he will "surely die" - or he will die die. This means that the process of death was going to begin – and would begin immediately. So, although Adam would be alive another 930 years, Adam's death was inevitable, from the moment he disobeyed God. Again, Adam's death did not come about because he ate some bad fruit. Adam died because He disobeyed God.

The Reformers were not so much concerned with issues to do with the length of the Creation days, because it did not occur to them that someone would fail to believe the days were 24-hours long. But they were concerned with issues to do with the correctness of the Gospel message. Hence, Calvin tackles the issue of why physical death did not occur immediately for Adam, upon his sin.

> Wherefore the question is superfluous, how it was that God threatened death to Adam on the day in which he should touch the fruit, when he long deferred the punishment? For then was Adam consigned to death, and

14 Sarfati, J. (2015), *The Genesis Account*, (Powder Springs, GA: Creation Book Publishing), pp. 320-321.

> death began its reign in him, until supervening grace should bring a remedy.[15]

We have noted above that God had given Adam – and, therefore, Eve, once she had been created – a commandment. He had also told them the penalty for disobeying that commandment.

The apostle Paul said "So then, the law was our *guardian* until Christ came, in order that we might be justified by faith." (Galatians 3:24 – emphasis added). The Greek word translated as *guardian* in the ESV is translated *tutor* in the NKJV, and *schoolmaster* in the KJV. It is the word *paidagogos* (παιδαγωγός), from which we get the English term paedagogy, or "teaching method". This paedagogue was a very unusual type of teacher. He was actually a bondservant to the family. It was his job to observe the student in his studies. If the student got lost in a day dream, the paedagogue would hit him to get him back on target!

Paul is saying that the Law is our paeadgogue, to wake us up sharply, if we think we are getting by in our own merit. The Law's paedagogy reminds us that we cannot save ourselves. We will never be good enough to keep God's Law.

15 Calvin, J. (1847 translated edition), *A Commentary on Genesis*, (Edinburgh: Banner of Truth), pp. 127-128.

But, of course, Adam was indeed good enough. He was created perfect. So some theologians have pondered about whether God should have made Adam incapable of sinning. Why did God allow sin into the world? I do not know the answer to this. Adam seems to have had a choice, and yet the big lesson of the Creation is that God is Sovereign. Clearly, it goes without saying that God knew what He was doing, and why. God was not caught out by this. Adam's sin was not something that took God by surprise. Yet it is also true that Adam therefore bore the responsibility for his sin, and we will need to investigate this further when we discuss Genesis 3.

Man Gave Names to all the Animals

In his Gospel music period of the late 70s and early 80s, Bob Dylan wrote a song entitled "Man Gave Names to all the Animals", on his album *Slow Train Coming*. Despite the fact that Dylan seems to have turned away from the faith, I still love that album. This song about the animals, however, comes across as a nursery rhyme, and this might diminish its impact – though I like the last stanza:

> He saw an animal as smooth as glass
> Slithering his way through the grass.
> Saw him disappear by a tree near a lake . . .[16]

16Dylan, R. (1978), *Man Gave Names to all the Animals*, from the album *Slow Train Coming*, CBS Records.

In my opinion, it is particularly clever that he deliberately does not complete the rhyme.

Because of the confusion over this naming process, I think we should quote the next three verses of Genesis 2 in full here.

> Genesis 2:18-20
> (18) Then the LORD God said, "It is not good that the man should be alone; I will make him a helper fit for him."
> (19) Now out of the ground the LORD God had formed every beast of the field and every bird of the heavens and brought them to the man to see what he would call them. And whatever the man called every living creature, that was its name.
> (20) The man gave names to all livestock and to the birds of the heavens and to every beast of the field. But for Adam there was not found a helper fit for him.

The concern that some people have is with the realism of the event. In fact, some are so convinced that these events are impossible, that they use these verses as their "evidence" that the Bible is not true. The argument is that there was not enough time in Day Six for all these events to occur, especially if Adam had to name ALL the animals.

The naming of the animals happened before God made Eve. Yet God must have made Eve on Day Six, as we were told that God made *man* male and female – so the events of Genesis 2 are all part of Day Six of the Creation Week.

We saw at the end of Genesis 1 how the phrase "very good" referred to perfection, in the sense of completeness. The term "good" had been used in Genesis 1 several times, to denote that what God was making was good, but not yet complete. Now God says that it is not good that the man should be alone. This does not imply that Adam's current singleness was a bad thing – merely that God had not yet completed His creation of mankind. So why did God not make Eve immediately? And why did God bring the animals to Adam? Adam did not find a helper among the animals. Did God think that there may have been a helper among the animals for Adam? Absolutely not! God always intended to make Eve. That was His Sovereign Will, expressed in His declaration "I will **make** him a helper fit for him". Yet, on the surface, it does seem as if God was offering Adam a choice of companion from the animals. In a sense, He was – even though God always intended to make woman. But God was very openly, and very deliberately, showing Adam that he was not an animal. God was actually refuting the theory of evolution right at this very point! Of course, God's purposes were much bigger than just refuting evolution. But God knew that there could easily be confusion for Adam, as he saw the similarities that God had placed in His creation between all these animals, and, for example, the way they all ate the same kind of food. Adam was to share the world with these animals, but God was making clear that Adam was not one of them.

Now note the tense used in verse 19. In the ESV, the pluperfect is used. These are animals that God *had* made. The NIV and TLV also use the pluperfect. Other versions merely use the past tense. So which is it?

Sarfati clearly shows that the correct rendering of the Hebrew word concerned – *wayyitser* (ויצר) - is *had formed* – that is to say, the pluperfect, and he marshals a number of experts in his support[17]. This matter is important, because, without the use of the pluperfect, there are some who would see an apparent contradiction between Genesis chapters 1 and 2. In chapter 1, God made animals before people. There are those who suggest that chapter 2 is telling us that God made Adam before He made animals. However, this is not so. Genesis 2 is simply telling us that God brought to Adam animals that He had already made. There is no contradiction. And as an aside, we should note that a correct rendering of Scripture will always be that which does not allow for contradictions.

Now to the argument that Adam would not have had enough time to name these animals. It is usually suggested that Adam could never have coped, finding and naming millions of species. But that is not

17 Sarfati, J. (2015), *The Genesis Account*, (Powder Springs, GA: Creation Book Publishers), pp. 323-324.

what he would have had to do. God brought the animals to Adam, so there was no need to catch them. And we have already discussed how the term *kind* or baramin is much broader than the modern word *species*. And, finally, God did not bring all animals to Adam. He brought only "every beast of the field and every bird of the heavens". These were all land vertebrates, so no need to name marine vertebrates, and no need to name any invertebrates. The list does not even include the "creeping things". Finally, it is probable that "beasts of the field" comprise a smaller group than "beasts of the earth" mentioned in Genesis 1:24. Sarfati estimates that this naming process – for a perfect man with a perfect brian – could easily have been accomplished in four hours, which would be just enough time to convince Adam that he was not one of the animals.

The Creation of Eve

The climax of Genesis 2 is the completion of the creation of human beings. As we have already seen, the creation of Adam alone was that of an incomplete humanity. But God was always going to create Eve, but He chose to delay, in order to emphasize to Adam his separation from the animals. Not only that, but His commandment, about the tree of knowledge, was relayed to Adam alone, which underlines Adam's authority within the marriage that was about to begin. It was the man who held the direct words of God, and it was his responsibility to relay these to his wife.

God now put Adam into a deep sleep. I am quite sure that normal sleep was part of the normal, intended life-cycle of humanity, as it is for many animals, and as work was part of humanity's normal practice. So, the reason that a deep sleep, given directly by God, is mentioned is to show how important this sleep was to be. It sounds like the same kind of sleep that God put on Abram in Genesis 15:12, and this deep sleep led to a one-sided covenant, made by God, to be between God and Abram, but "signed", as it were, by God alone. In the same way, Eve was to be at the heart of a covenental relationship with Adam and with God, both in the institution of marriage, and in her relationship to God as co-heir, equal with Adam.

When God made animals, it does not tell us how many of each kind God made. And it does not suggest in any way that female animals were made from male animals. It is logical that God could have made as many animals as He chose of each kind, and that He determined the sex of each one, when He made them. However, in the case of human beings, there was to be a very special approach to their creation.

If God had made Eve in exactly the same way that He made Adam, then Eve would have been separate from Adam, and not "descended" from him. Eve would, therefore, have needed a separate savior. But Eve was, instead, fashioned from one of Adam's ribs.

There is a sense, then, in which we can say that Eve was a sort-of descendant of Adam. This is of huge theological importance. It means that Adam and Eve – and, hence, men and women – can have a common savior. Jesus has the right to be our Savior, because He is related to every one of us. There never was a human being – not even Eve – who was not descended from our original Federal Head, Adam. Adam originally contained all the genetic material of the human race. That is why he could say "This at last is bone of my bones and flesh of my flesh; she shall be called Woman, because she was taken out of Man." He represented the *whole* human race. Therefore, we now need a Last Adam; a new representative, Jesus Christ. That is why Jesus is the new Adam. "For as in Adam all die, so also in Christ shall all be made alive." (1 Corinthians 15:22).

It had to be Adam who was first. If Eve had been created first, it would have been as if Adam had been *born* of Eve. But with Adam created first, and Eve supernaturally fashioned from him, the creation of humanity fits with everything we know from the rest of the Bible about God's wonderful plan of salvation for our lives. This order of the creation of the first couple is mentioned by Paul, in 1 Timothy 2:13, where he emphasizes "Adam was formed first; then Eve".

Adam, Eve, Marriage, and Jesus

Finally in this chapter, we come to the inauguration of marriage. "Therefore a man shall leave his father and his mother and hold fast to his wife, and they shall become one flesh". (Genesis 2:24) Another reason that Eve had to be created from Adam was so that they were one flesh. This pattern is now the case for all marriages. That this institution is placed at the end of the section on the creation of Adam and Eve is very important. This is the purpose for which they were created, to be a married couple.

It follows, then, that all the novel and artificial forms of relationships invented by people over the centuries – and especially in the last ten years – are null and void to God. It is not up to a Parliament, a Prime Minister, a President, a Congress, or a Supreme Court to define marriage. The only definition of marriage that counts is the one that God gave us. And as the Bible goes on to show, this is because biblical marriage – and ONLY biblical marriage – is the pattern or type for the marriage of Jesus and His Bride, the Church, the people of God.

Note also that the new relationship is to happen when the man leaves his father and mother. It does not say that he is to go and join his new wife's father and mother. The implication is that this pattern is good enough for all mankind, men and women. An important step for all young couples is to set up their own household. I see a lot of conservative couples today, still very much under the control of either the wife's or the husband's parents. That is not to be the pattern.

It should also be noted that Jesus quoted this passage, and Genesis 1:27, when He discussed marriage. As a side note, we should observe that Jesus, therefore, did not think that Genesis chapters 1 and 2 were two different creation accounts. He considered them the same – and so should we.

So Adam and Eve end Genesis 2 as a perfect couple. They had no need for clothes, because there was no sin, and therefore there was no shame.

Summary

In this section, we have looked at the meaning of the word *toledoth*, which marks the divisions within Genesis. We also looked at what is meant by *plants of the field*, and by the introduction of the phrase LORD God. After the a brief comment on whether or not there was rain before the Flood, we looked at the creation of Adam, and issues to do with the Garden of Eden. We saw how Adam was given a commandment, and what it meant for him to name the animals, proving that he did not evolve from animals. Then we considered the creation of Eve, and the establishment of the institution of marriage.

Genesis 3 Part 1 – Sin Enters the World

(Genesis 3:1-8)

An ancient medieval Christmas carol goes as follows:

> Adam lay ybounden,
> Bounden in a bond;
> Four thousand winter
> Thought he not too long.
>
> And all was for an apple,
> An apple that he took.
> As clerkës finden written
> In their book.
>
> Ne had the apple taken been,
> The apple taken been,
> Ne had never Our Lady,
> A-been heaven's queen.
>
> Blessed be the time
> That apple taken was!
> Therefore we may singen
> *Deo gratias!*[1]

1 The traditional words have been modernized somewhat by Rickert. Reference: Edith Rickert, *Ancient English Christmas Carols: 1400–1700* (London: Chatto & Windus, 1914), p.163.

The carol is a lesson in the difficulties Christians have had, down the centuries, trying to make sense of the events of Genesis 3. The chapter refers to great evil, and there are many other evil episodes in history, but this is unique, because it is the first evil action. So how can we explain it? Evil done by evil people – and all people are evil, born in original sin – is somewhat understandable. But, prior to this evil, the protagonists were good. They had been created perfect. How, then, did they become evil?

Perhaps the problem is even more difficult for those of us, who strongly adhere to the doctrine of the Sovereignty of God. If God is in charge, then how could He have allowed the world to go evil? And, since the world obviously is indeed evil, does this not suggest that God is not in charge, or has no control over these events? Yet, if god is indeed in control, then is it fair of God to hold Adam, and through him the whole human race, responsible for the evil which occurred? These are the questions, which we will have to answer, as we exegete the text.

The medieval caroler thinks that good things have come from that first evil. For example, the medieval English church venerated Mary (a practice which we reject and refute), and the third stanza suggests that Mary would not have achieved her "position", had Adam not sinned by taking the fruit (which the caroler assumes was an apple).

The caroler even calls the taking of the apple "blessed", and sings "Thanks be to God"!

While we have to reject these traditional nuances – the first sin was not a blessed time – we will, nevertheless, see God's purposes being worked out, through the events of Genesis 3.

Theodicy

One of the most difficult issues to address is why evil began in the first place. All sorts of unworthy thoughts can cloud our judgment on this matter. Did God make a mistake? Did God create Satan with a serious flaw? Did God give us all free will, so that we could choose to do things He did not expect? Basically, we are asking – was God out of control?

The very idea does not compute in my brain. The concept of the Sovereignty of God would appear to be of vital importance, because without God being Sovereign, how can He really be God at all?

Given that God being Sovereign is one of the most important presuppositions, how, then, do we explain the origin of evil? The attempt to answer this important question, of how a good God allows the manifestation of evil to exist, is known by the technical term *theodicy*. Whole books have been written on the subject of theodicy, so, clearly, I am only going to be able to scratch the surface here.

In conversations, one of the most popular arguments used against the Christian, to try to shut the conversation down, is this: if God is a good God, why does He allow so much suffering and evil in the world?

Most Christians are frankly at sea with such a comment, and will usually try to answer it at face value. But it is always important to look for false presuppositions, in such situations. The presupposition behind this question is that evil exists. That is a correct presupposition. The problem is that the atheist has no definition for evil. There is always going to someone else who will call evil good, and good evil. We cannot let the atheist off the hook by simply agreeing with them that, for example, the abuse of children is morally wrong. Of course it is morally wrong, but we have an absolute definition, against which to measure such an evil, and the atheist does not. If, on other grounds, they would argue tolerance, then there is no logical ground for drawing a line anywhere. It is not even sufficient to say that "murder is wrong, because the majority say so." The majority can be, and have previously been, wrong on moral issues. It is important that we deny atheists access to our weapons of warfare. We should not allow them to use arguments of morality, because morality cannot exist, without presupposing the existence of God.

With biblical presuppositions, we show that evil exists, because it is the opposite of good, and good is what is according to the nature of God.

So far, so good. But there is a further problem, when we look at Genesis 3, and it is this: "why did God allow evil to start?" It is one thing to say that today, evil is what is opposite to the nature of God, but if God is Sovereign, why did He allow evil to begin? Why did He create Satan, and then Adam and Eve, with the ability to sin?

When I wrote my previous commentary on Genesis, I put a great deal of store, as do many other apologists, in the free will of human beings. God gave us free will, I argued, so that we could choose to obey, because if we were not able to choose, then our "obedience" would not really be obedience. However, this argument proves inadequate for purpose. There is a danger inherent in the argument, as it can undermine the Sovereignty of God. Are we suggesting that God gave Adam free will, and was not in control of what choice Adam would make? We might say that God knew what choice Adam would make, but that still leaves God weak. He is not in control of events. Adam has the right to choose, and He can choose what God does not want.

I have argued for decades, even before writing my previous commentary, that the Sovereignty of God is one of the founding principles of all doctrines. God, whose creation of the world in six literal 24-hour days we have just been following, is not then taken by surprise by an autonomous human being, whom God had created. The problem was summarized by the 18th Century atheist, David Hume, who said:

> Is God willing to prevent evil, but not able? Then he is impotent. Is he able, but not willing? Then he is malevolent. Is he both able and willing? Whence then is evil?[2]

Greg Bahnsen, one of the brightest and best commentators on Presuppositional Apologetics, quoted Hume's comment. It therefore makes sense to summarize Bahnsen's arguments here, to show how he derives them. He started where I started, by showing that the existence of evil cannot be explained without the existence of the God of the Bible. The distinction on which God we are talking about is important. For example, Muslims would suggest that Allah is the source of both good and evil, while other religions postulate a god who is not fully in control. As I have discussed elsewhere, there are really only two worldviews possible – that of acknowledging the existence of the God of the Bible (Christianity) or not (atheism, and all other religions).[3]

Having thus neutralized the atheist, or non-Christian foundation, Bahnsen shows that we have two propositions.[4]

2 Hume, D., (ed. Pike, N. 1981), *Dialogues Concerning Natural Religion*, (Indianapolis: Bobbs-Merril Publications), p.88.

3 See Taylor, P.F. (2016), *Only Believe*, (Castle Rock, WA: J6D Publications), pp. 45-61.

4 The argument, which follows the position of this footnote, is from Bahnsen, G. (1996, ed. Bahnsen, R. and V.), *Always Ready*, (Nacogdoches, TX: Covenant Media Foundation), location 2840 – 3101, Kindle edition.

1. God is all-good.
2. God is all-powerful.

But we still need to understand where evil came from. So, we add a third proposition.

3. Evil exists.

Although, at face value, the addition of this third proposition seems to be problematic, it can be resolved. We simply need to know why God allowed evil to exist. This becomes more logical, now that we have shown the incoherence of the atheistic or non-Christian positions. We can therefore add proposition 4.

4. God has a morally sufficient reason for the evil which exists.

This fourth proposition is inferred from the other three, but only after we have neutralized the incoherence of the non-Christian position. We now realize that we are unlikely ever, in this life, to know what that morally sufficient reason is, but we are now entitled, biblically, to take it on trust that it exists. This was, after all, the substance of the reason for the Book of Job. Job's suffering was immense. There is no evidence, within the book, that Job ever, in his lifetime, found out about the conversations between God and Satan in Heaven. Those conversations are included for our benefit, so that we can see that Job is to be led to a point where he worships God for who

God is, not for what he, Job, can get out of the relationship. Thus, the book ends with Job confessing "I have uttered what I did not understand, things too wonderful for me, which I did not know." (Job 42:3). It was not necessary for Job to have all the reasons. It was necessary for Job to acknowledge that those reasons exist.

A final comment on a presuppositional approach to theodicy would concern Adam's ability to choose – and, for that matter, Satan's ability to choose. The problem of the situation is expressed thus:

1. God predestined that Adam would take the forbidden fruit.
2. Therefore, Adam could not do otherwise than take the forbidden fruit.
3. Therefore, Adam was not responsible for his sin; God was.

I have heard this argument used, not only by atheists against Christianity, but also by some Christians, who wish to oppose Presuppositional Apologetics. But as with previous statements, we need to unpick the false presuppositions behind the argument. Proposition 2 is that God has foreordained an action. Proposition 3 is that Adam was coerced into the action by that foreordination. Once again, we can refer to Bahnsen, who shows that foreordination does not imply coercion. It is clear, logically, that if foreordination does not imply coercion, then proposition 3 does not follow from proposition 2, and Adam was fully responsible for the action that he took.

The problem with stating the propositions as above is that we fail to acknowledge that God does not merely predestine the end – He also predestines the means. For example, if God only predestined the end, then we might argue, with the hyper-Calvinists, that there is no need to evangelize, because those whom God will save, God will save, without our interference. This is unbiblical. God has also ordained that the means, by which someone will be saved, is by the "foolishness of preaching". God has ordained that we should preach the Gospel, and, therefore, we are responsible for doing so. In the same way, God was and is Sovereign, so that what happened in the Garden in Genesis 3 was His plan, for a morally sufficient reason, that we do not understand – and yet Adam was responsible for his sin, Eve was responsible for her sin, and, before them, Satan was responsible for his sin.

With that important argument now settled, we can examine what actually happened.

Satan's History

In my previous book, I gave a traditional description of the supposed history of Satan. To do so, I examined passages in Isaiah 14 and Ezekiel 28 that seem to refer to Satan. These passages have traditionally been used by creationists, to refer to how Satan became sinful and wicked. However, it must be acknowledged that not every scholar accepts that these passages refer to Satan. A very senior apologist and theologian from the UK once reminded me, personally, that not all scholars accept that Isaiah 14 or Ezekiel 28 refers to Satan. It should also be mentioned that Calvin, in his commentary on Isaiah, suggests that Isaiah 14 refers only to the King of Babylon, and not to a heavenly being. Yet, in his commentary on Genesis, Calvin writes "The revolt of Satan is proved by other passages of Scripture", so we are left wondering, to which passages of Scripture is he referring? Calvin continues "We must conclude that the principle of evil with which Satan was endued was not from nature, but from defection, because he had departed from God."[5] We can therefore certainly conclude the following:

- Satan, whatever his name might have been originally, is a created being, as are all other spiritual beings, angels, etc.
- Everything was created during the Creation Week of Genesis 1, whether or not Genesis 1 specifically gives details or not about any particular class of object or being, so Satan did not exist before the Creation Week, let alone sin before the Creation Week.

5 Calvin, J. (Geneva Commentary edition, 1965), *A Commentary on Genesis*, (Edinburgh: Banner of Truth), p.142.

- At the end of the Creation Week, everything was declared by God to be "very good", so it follows that Satan had not become evil before the end of the Creation Week.
- At the start of Genesis 3, we find that the serpent, who we later learn is Satan (Revelation 12:9), is already evil.
- Therefore, Satan's Fall occurred some time between the end of the Creation Week, and the beginning of Genesis 3, but we are not given the exact details on what happened.

For these reasons, I do, in fact, think we are entitled to look at passages such as Isaiah 14 and Ezekiel 28 and draw some conclusions, while continuing to acknowledge that godly men of the past and present disagree with us.

So, when Isaiah 14:14 refers to the King of Babylon wanting to ascend above the heights of the clouds, and make himself like the Most High, it does seem to me that something greater than a human being is being described. That something is called, in Isaiah 14:12, the "Day Star". The concept of the Day Star refers specifically to the planet Venus, as the brightest "star" in the sky. We also find that the phrase is used elsewhere in Scripture of the Messiah, yet here is referring to someone evil. It makes sense, therefore, to suppose that this is referring to an antichrist.

The Latin Vulgate Bible used the word *Lucifer* in verse 12, because that is the Latin word for Day Star. It should not be presumed that this is the name for the being, who would become Satan. This idea has developed because of the KJV's inappropriate use of the word in its rendering of Isaiah 14:12.

Likewise, the oracle against the King of Tyre, in Ezekiel 28:11-19, also seems to be referring to someone who is more than a man. This is the "anointed cherub", and the use of the word "anointed" again suggests an anti-type of the Messiah – the antichrist – because the Hebrew for Messiah is derived from the Hebrew word for anointed. And this anointed cherub, we are told, was in Eden at the start of things.

So something happened between the Creation Week and Genesis 3 to Satan, who had been created good, just as everything else had. It seems likely to me that we are given an insight into what happened to Satan in Isaiah 14 and Ezekiel 28, but it is not necessary, for the purposes of this study, to continue to insist on this interpretation.

Satan, the Devil, and the Serpent Are the Same

In Revelation 12:9, we read about Satan being thrown out of heaven.

> And the great dragon was thrown down, that ancient serpent, who is called the devil and Satan, the deceiver of the whole world—he was thrown down to the earth, and his angels were thrown down with him.

This verse equates the dragon, Satan, the devil, and the serpent. So these are all names for the same being. This being is a person. It is popular, today, to think of evil as a force, as we find in the Star Wars franchise. This is not the case. The devil is a person, and therefore speaks as a person, and reacts as a person, albeit one of complete and utter evil.

Jesus told us that the devil has always been a liar, and that he was evil from the beginning.

> You are of your father the devil, and your will is to do your father's desires. He was a murderer from the beginning, and does not stand in the truth, because there is no truth in him. When he lies, he speaks out of his own character, for he is a liar and the father of lies. (John 8:44)

We have already discussed that Satan was still good, at the end of the Creation Week. In order for Satan to have been evil "from the beginning" (*apo arche* - ἀπ ἀρχῆς), it follows that the events of Genesis 3 cannot have been very long after the close of the Creation Week. I have heard some suggest that Genesis 3 could have been hundreds of years after creation. I do not think that this can be true, because of what we reported above, that Jesus said.

Satan Is Dangerous and Powerful

Too many people take Satan for granted. Yet Peter said "Be sober-minded; be watchful. Your adversary the devil prowls around like a roaring lion, seeking someone to devour." (1 Peter 5:8). We must be aware that our enemy is both powerful and dangerous. Too many people make fun of Satan. I have even heard Christians do this. This is very dangerous, because he is real, and powerful.

However, Satan's power is not infinite. It is only God who possesses infinite power. The point of the Gospel is that Jesus has the victory. Though Satan is powerful, Jesus, being God, is infinitely more powerful.

> But thanks be to God, who gives us the victory through our Lord Jesus Christ. (1 Corinthians 15:57)

> Little children, you are from God and have overcome them, for he who is in you is greater than he who is in the world. (1 John 4:4)

The Serpent

Genesis 3 does not open, by directly introducing Satan. Instead, we are told that "the serpent was more crafty than any other beast of the field that the LORD God had made." The sudden appearance of a talking serpent has been a mystery for many people, and that has caused many people to stumble over the text at this point. As a child, I was taught, both at school, and in church Sunday school, that this account was a mythology, because, obviously, a talking snake could not be real, so it was just an allegory of evil. The event, I was assured, did not really happen, but was a symbolic explanation of how evil came into the world. But, when I was saved, I had a new respect for God's word. There was, after all, a real devil. Someone told me that very early in my Christian life - "if you didn't know before that the devil was a real person, you will certainly find out for sure soon, because he is not happy at losing another soul." I soon found that to be true, but I also found out that "he who is in you is greater than he who is in the world" (1 John 4:4).

As is my pattern today, we should start by accepting that what the Bible says is true, and then we will look at the implications afterwards. So Genesis 3 opens with a serpent talking to Eve. Could this have been a real snake?

Well, we have to be careful with our terms. The Bible says that this animal was a serpent, not a snake. Of course, it could have been a snake, because a snake is a serpent. But the word serpent could, in fact, have been applied to a wide variety of reptiles – not just a snake.

We must notice that the Bible describes the serpent as a "beast of the field", and also states that it was made by the LORD God. So this must have been a real animal. Does this mean that animals could talk in the beginning? I don't think so. Because this animal is associated with Satan, it seems likely that Satan, as an evil spirit, had possessed this animal. There is nothing inherently evil about a serpent or snake, even though I cannot say that I like them! Yet it is certainly a crafty animal, in its fallen state, as it can strike quickly, and almost mysteriously, and, if it was actually a snake, many of them might be venomous, though, presumably, that venom was not originally something dangerous, when God created it. But craftiness is not necessarily a fault. Obviously, craftiness can indeed be a fault in the wrong hands, such as those of Satan, yet Jesus exhorted His followers to be "wise as serpents and innocent as doves" (Matthew 10:16).

Some atheists have suggested that the account is absurd, because Eve expresses no surprise that she is hearing a talking snake. But there is no evidence from the passage that Eve was not surprised. Indeed, her inability to answer correctly could have been due to her surprise. And if you think my point is conjecture – which it is – don't forget that the atheist point about Eve not being surprised is also conjecture. Neither of us can prove for sure one way or the other from the text itself. The reality of the account, however, is confirmed in many places in the New Testament – for example, John 8:44, Romans 5:12, Romans 16:20, 2 Corinthians 11:3-4, and 1 Timothy 2:14.

So this serpent was possibly a possessed animal, able to speak only by Satan's promptings. Satan did not make the serpent – only the LORD God can create. But the words spoken by the serpent were the words of Satan, permitted by God to be spoken, for His morally sufficient reason that we have discussed before.

Did God Actually Say?

Writing to the Christians at Corinth, Paul described the serpent as "cunning" (2 Corinthians 11:3). In this first ever temptation, Satan was too clever to start by directly opposing what God had told Adam and Eve. So he started by saying to the woman "Did God actually say, 'You shall not eat of any tree in the garden'?" There are so many issues to note here. We should note that all of Satan's tactics in this first temptation are still used by him today.

First, Satan addressed the woman. This was an immediate plan to divide and conquer. A non-sinful being would have addressed Adam, as the federal head of the human race. But Satan, being subtle, had the plan to divide Eve from Adam.

Second, Satan's question is obviously less than honest. By asking "Did God actually say…", he was deliberately sowing seeds of confusion and doubt in the woman's mind. The wise man of God today will not entertain questions about Scripture, beginning with "Did God really say…?" While it is our duty to search the Scriptures, and to make sure we understand exactly what they say, we should not be entertaining doubts about the substance of God's word. In other words, it is okay to say "This is what God said, now let's study what He meant by that, so that we can act upon it." That is very different from allowing that what is written might not be what God said.

The next issue is the question that Satan asked. "Did God actually say, 'You shall not eat of any tree in the garden'?" We should pay attention to how Satan phrased his question. He quotes the law that God gave, so we should look again at how God phrased it.

> And the Lord God commanded the man, saying, "You may surely eat of every tree of the garden, but of the tree of the knowledge of good and evil you shall not eat, for in the day that you eat of it you shall surely die". (Genesis 2:16-17)

God's command was a positive command with an exception, and a clearly understood sanction. Satan's report turned God's command into something negative. The implication behind the command is that Adam and Eve are missing out on something important, that might be of interest to them. God's command was given for Adam and Eve's protection. Satan made it sound like God was hiding secret knowledge, that the humans would enjoy finding out.

So Eve replied to Satan, and here we should notice the first mistake. Eve should not have replied. In the order of things, from before the sin that is about to happen, Eve was still designed to be a helper to Adam, and was taken out of Adam's side – he was to be the federal head. So it was inappropriate for Satan to address the woman, instead of the man, but we expect no better of him. Likewise, it was inappropriate for Eve to answer the serpent. She should have deferred to Adam. Adam, for his part, should have protected his wife, and refused to engage in this conversation.

Even so, there was one good point to Eve's reply. She denied the negativity of the serpent's first statement, explaining the positive angle, from which God's pronouncement should be viewed. So, she understood that Satan's quotation of God's law was wrong, but she should not have been attempting to argue the point. That argument, and her decision to work autonomously, would lead to her greater mistake. In her reply to the serpent, which was so ill advised, she both added to and subtracted from Scripture. This is what God had said:

> And the LORD God commanded the man, saying, "You may *surely* eat of every tree of the garden, but of the tree of the knowledge of good and evil you shall not eat, for in the day that you eat of it you shall surely die." (Genesis 2:16-17, emphasis added)

This is what Eve replied:

> And the woman said to the serpent, "We may eat of the fruit of the trees in the garden, but God said, 'You shall not eat of the fruit of the tree that is in the midst of the garden, *neither shall you touch it*, lest you die.'" (Genesis 3:2-3, emphasis added)

We have already discussed that God repeated the word *eat*, and the ESV has translated this repetition by using the word *surely*. This emphasizes the freedom the humans were to have in eating the fruit. Then, in her report of God's sanction, she adds the words *neither shall you touch it*. At no point did God forbid the humans from touching the fruit. This episode emphasizes the reason why God has, elsewhere, stated that we should neither add to nor take away from His word (Deuteronomy 4:2; Proverbs 30:5; Revelation 22:18-19)[6].

We have already remarked that Satan's strategy has not changed. So far, in Genesis 3, he had tempted Eve to exercise autonomy, by addressing her instead of Adam, and she had succumbed. He then deliberately sowed the seeds of doubt in God's word, while slightly misquoting it, shifting it from positive to negative. His strategy had succeeded, in that, although Eve had contradicted his negativity, she did so by exercising autonomy, and then wobbled on her reporting of God's words, with a minor addition and subtraction. Satan was now ready to pounce, by directly contradicting God's words.

6 See Morris, H.M. (1976), *The Genesis Record*, (Grand Rapids, MI: Baker), p.111.

> But the serpent said to the woman, "You will not surely die."

God had said that Adam and Eve would *surely die* if they ate of the fruit concerned. Satan contradicted God. But he had already got Eve into a place, where she might want to hear what came next. Satan even repeated God's phrase "surely die", which we have said was actually the word *mûth* repeated. This indicates that Satan knew that the sanction did not refer to immediate physical death, but the beginning of the process of death. Then, Satan followed up this contradiction with what we would term to be Gnosticism.

> "For God knows that when you eat of it your eyes will be opened, and you will be like God, knowing good and evil."

Eve, do you want to be like God? God has some hidden knowledge. Do you want to share it? We read through these words too quickly, sometimes. Read them again, and again, and catch the sense of how evil these words are, and yet how enticing. The irony is that Eve already knew what good and evil was. She had to know what they were, in order to understand the language. Good is what is in accord with the character of God, and evil – even though she had not seen or experienced it – is what is in opposition to it. Therefore, she already had the tools to be able to define Satan's words as evil. She did not need a fruit to exercise this knowledge!

The Original Sin

Even at this stage, the matter could, theoretically, or from a human point of view, have been brought to a close. But the next verse is the most terrible verse in the whole of the Bible. It is the verse, which records the Fall of humanity. Every clause of the verse is replete with meaning.

> So when the woman saw that the tree was good for food, and that it was a delight to the eyes, and that the tree was to be desired to make one wise, she took of its fruit and ate, and she also gave some to her husband who was with her, and he ate. (Genesis 3:6)

The woman saw that the tree was good for food. Remember that there was nothing evil or poisonous about the fruit. The fruit was good. The sin would be to eat the fruit that God had forbidden. Adam and Eve would die, because of breaking God's law, not because of a fruit. So, Eve saw that the fruit was "good for food". There is no contradiction here. The difference is that Eve was looking at the fruit, having been deceived by the serpent.

It was a delight to the eyes. This fruit was something that God had made, so of course, in this perfect world, it was a delight to the eyes. It looked good. Fruit can be very attractive. Back in the 1980s, when I was a schoolteacher, I was involved in the high school production of a musical play, called Secrets, written by seven teachers, including myself. On the last night, the authors and composers were called on stage. The ladies were given bouquets of flowers, while we male teachers were given fruit baskets. I think the men had the better deal! The fruit baskets looked just as attractive as the flowers, but the ladies couldn't eat the flowers. God has made many, many fruits to be very attractive, and I would hazard a guess that all the fruits in the Garden of Eden were pleasant to the eye. But this fruit transfixed Eve, because the serpent had deceived her.

The tree was to be desired to make one wise. This is a peculiar phrase. How could a tree look as if it would make one wise? I suggest that it looked so, because Eve was looking through deceived eyes, ready to want to believe that there was hidden wisdom or knowledge in the eating of that fruit. So this phrase speaks more of Eve's state of mind. Calvin says:

> It is, therefore, a sign of impious defection, that the woman now judges the tree to be good for food, eagerly delights herself in beholding it, and persuades herself that it is desirable for the sake of acquiring wisdom; whereas before she had passed by it a hundred times with an unmoved and tranquil look. For now, having shaken off the bridle, her mind wanders dissolutely and intemperately, drawing the body with it to the same licentiousness. The word להשכיל (lehaskil) admits of two explanations: That the tree was desirable either to be

> looked upon or to impart prudence. I prefer the latter sense, as better corresponding with the temptation.[7]

She took of its fruit and ate. This was her sin. This was Eve's sin, and her sin alone. We are never told what would have happened, and we have to know that God had a purpose, even in this dreadful event, but we read elsewhere that Eve sinned, because she was deceived[8]. So her sin was her own, and not anyone else's. So her next step was to give some fruit to her husband, *who was with her.*

We must pause for a moment, and reflect on Adam's awful dereliction of duty at this point. He, not Eve, was the representative of the human race. He was the one, if anyone, who should have answered the serpent, and sent him packing. Yet he did not do so, even though he was with her.

Now, not everyone accepts that Adam was actually alongside Eve the whole time the temptation was taking place, but I think that 1 Timothy 2:14 strongly implies that this must be the case.

> Adam was not deceived, but the woman was deceived and became a transgressor. (1 Timothy 2:14)

Adam knew exactly what was going on. He was not deceived. In order to know what was going on, I suggest that he was a close witness. So

7 Calvin, J., *The Book of Genesis*, (Edinburgh: Banner of Truth), p. 151.
8 1 Timothy 2:14.

the awful wonder of this event is that, despite knowing what was going on, despite walking into this event with eyes open, Adam still took the fruit and ate. The ESV contains just three words that catalog the event that would change the universe.

And he ate.

In the past, there have been those who have tried to minimize Adam's involvement. Milton, for example, suggested that Adam had only eaten the fruit as an act of love to Eve, because he could not bear the thought of Eve undergoing aging and death, while he remained forever immortal.

So saying, she embrac'd him, and for joy
Tenderly wept, much won that he his Love
Had so enobl'd, as of choice to incurr
Divine displeasure for her sake, or Death.
In recompence (for such compliance bad
Such recompence best merits) from the bough
She gave him of that fair enticing Fruit[9]

This view, however, misses the point, that it was Adam's sin that was, in fact, the greater. Eve sinned, Paul says, because she was deceived. Adam sinned, even though he was not deceived. Adam was our

9 Milton, John (1674 version), *Parafise Lost, Book 9*, < https://www.poetryfoundation.org/poems/45745/paradise-lost-book-9-1674-version >, accessed 4/9/2019.

Federal Head – Eve was not. Eve's sin was just her own, but Adam sinned on behalf of all of us, and his sin was and is imputed to every one of his descendants – save one.

Therefore, our deaths are due to the responsibility of Adam, not Eve. We do not need a female savior. We need a Last Adam, that is Jesus Christ (Romans 5:12-21, 1 Corinthians 15:20-23).

Is This History?

At this point, we need to note that there are a number of theologians, who self-identify as conservative evangelicals, who have a problem with considering Genesis 3 to be actual history. Many of those who thus struggle would come under the theological covering, as it were, of BioLogos. There are three methods of navigating their objections, and these are best exemplified by the principle proponents of each idea, John Stott, Peter Enns, and John Walton.

Stott: In 1986, I attended a lecture in Yorkshire, England (I think it was York, though I know I have written elsewhere that it was Leeds), to hear the legendary evangelical Anglican preacher Dr. John Stott. He had just published his seminal book, *The Cross of Christ*. During his talk, he emphasized that it was very important to believe in a real historical Adam, because of the passages in Romans 5 and 1 Corinthians 15. This puzzled me, because I had heard that he believed in the theory of evolution. I had the privilege of asking the first question, so I quizzed him on this matter. In his reply, he suggested that God had taken one of the semi-evolved ape-men and breathed His spirit into him, so that he became what Stott referred to as *homo divinus*. It was his opinion that the phrase "the dust of the earth" referred to the naturalistic evolution of human beings from ape-like creatures. Nevertheless, Stott believed that all human beings had to be descended from Adam and Eve, because of the Romans and Corinthians passages.

Walton: As we have seen, Walton does not believe that the actual historicity of the early chapters of Genesis matters. It is not what is important to him, as he believes that the account comes from an Ancient Near Eastern mythology. Nevertheless, in his book about Adam and Eve, he maintains, strangely, that Adam and Eve were real people. His reason for stating this is not theological, but historical. Adam is found in the genealogies, so Walton reasons that this is enough to identify Adam has historical.[10] However, Walton differs from Stott, in that he does not insist that Adam and Eve were the literal ancestors of everyone. Walton refers to the so-called Mitochondrial Eve and Y-chromosomal Adam. Genetic research has suggested that all current humans are descended from a single female, due to researching the mitochondrial DNA. Other research on Y-chromosomes suggests that all humans are descended from a single

10 Walton, J.H. (2015), *The Lost World of Adam and Eve*, (Downers Grove, IL: InterVarsity Press), p. 102.

man. But the Mitochondrial Eve has an evolutionary date of 180,000 years ago, while the Y-chromosomal Adam has an evolutionary date of 210,000 years ago, which puts them 30,000 years apart. So, believing as he does in evolution, Walton simply suggests that the historical Adam and Eve were part of an initial population.

We will come back to our objection to this analysis later.

Enns: I find that one has to listen to Peter Enns several times, or read over his articles multiple times, until one can be absolutely sure what he is saying. He comes across as an intellectual figure, who is loath to make a definitive statement on anything. On the subject of what Paul believed, Enns is, however, quite clear.

> There is really little doubt that Paul understood Adam to be a real person, the first created human from whom all humans descended.[11]

This makes it all the more remarkable when Enns, as a self-identifying evangelical, claims that this does not matter. This is because Enns's starting point is that the theory of evolution is true, and, therefore, we must adjust our theology to cater to that fact. He writes:

> I accept evolution as the explanation for how life on earth came to be. The scientific community, which includes

11 Enns, P. (2010), *Paul's Adam*, < https://biologos.org/articles/pauls-adam >, accessed 4/9/2019.

> Christians in general and as well as evangelicals, is in harmony on this point: there is no "first human."
>
> This scientific conclusion is not a trend, nor is it a "theory" teetering on the crumbling foundation of godless thinking. It is well established and utterly uncontroversial, and for that reason requires serious engagement by any who seek to take seriously both Scripture and the advance of human knowledge.[12]

This is consistent with Enns's view that the Bible does not speak to us today, but rather spoke only to the ancient world, and we have to understand everything in that context. This is how he copes with the fact that Paul refers to Adam in Romans 5. He can dismiss the truthfulness of Paul's comments by telling us that Paul was an ancient man in an ancient world. Enns clearly wishes Paul had had nothing to say about Adam.

> If Adam had just stayed in the Old Testament, we would not be here talking about him.[13]

But this is not how we are to treat Scripture. Enns would obviously prefer to treat evolution as non-negotiable, and twist his Scripture

12 Enns, P. (2015), *The Historical Adam: It's Time to Stop Hiding Under a Theological Security Blanket*, < https://peteenns.com/the-historical-adam-its-time-to-stop-hiding-under-a-theological-security-blanket/ >, accessed 4/11/2019.

13 Enns, P. *The Challenge of a Historical Adam*, < https://www.youtube.com/watch?v=VV4Sf2_l3nI >, 21:20, accessed 4/11/2019.

reading to it. In fact, we are to start from Scripture, and if a theory is completely opposed to what Scripture says – as is the case with evolution – then it is the science that we should reject, not the Scripture. Simon Turpin points out the dangers of such an approach, in his excellent book, *Adam: The First and the Last.*

> A growing number of evangelical scholars today are undermining Scripture by uncritically accepting the conclusions of critical scholarship. As Christians we need to stand on the God-breathed truth of Scripture.[14]

In the light of that, Turpin opines:

> The history of Adam runs through Scripture, holding the doctrines of sin, salvation and christology together. We cannot lose the historicity of the Bible without losing the theology—in other words, the salvation that comes from it. The Bible has linked them intimately together.[15]

In reverse order, Enns has turned Adam into a mythology, but it is not possible to divorce the reality of Adam from the theology. Walton has populated the world with other people, yet Eve is described as the "mother of all living" (Genesis 3:20), and even Enns and Walton themselves admit that Paul believed there was a real Adam, the

14 Turpin, S. (2018), *Adam: The First and the Last,* (Leominster, UK: Day One Publications), p.55.
15 *Ibid*, p.78

progenitor of the entire human race. So Walton's Adam is a non-Adam, unnecessary by his theology, and not in accord with what the Bible says about him.

One major problem with the positions of both Enns and Walton is that they prefer to try to interpret each passage of Scripture as if it were separate. Scripturally, it actually matters that there was a real Adam, and only one. If this were not so, then there could be pockets of humanity unrelated to others. The message of the book of Ruth is that there can be redemption, but the Redeemer has to be a Kinsman. Jesus is kin to all of us, if Adam were the ancestor of all, and hence there is a legal salvation for anyone who repents and believes. If Jesus were not kin to all humanity, then there could be pockets of humanity who could not be redeemed.

Immediate Consequences

Adam's sin had consequences, and these consequences fall into two groups. There are, first, some immediate, almost natural consequences, which they noticed immediately. Then, there were consequences directly decreed by God. To label this latter group that way does not imply that the "natural" consequences were not decreed by God. All these consequences were as a result of God's decree. But the account in Genesis seems to divide them up into these two groups, so we will analyze them in that way.

Satan had told Eve that, if they ate the forbidden fruit, their "eyes would be opened". This is indeed what came to pass, but the experience of it was not what Satan had led them to believe. Before they sinned, Adam and Eve actually already had the knowledge of good and evil that they needed. Good was according to God's character, and evil meant disobeying God. Of course, they had not yet disobeyed God, so they had no experience. But it is not necessary to experience something to have sufficient knowledge of it. Sarfati helpfully explains it thus:

> The results were diametrically opposed to what Satan led them to believe. In the original creation, God knew evil in the same way as an oncologist knows about cancer – not by personal experience but by knowledge about it (in God's case by foreknowledge). But after Adam and Eve sinned, they knew evil in the same way as a cancer sufferer knows cancer – by sad personal experience.[16]

With their newly "opened eyes", Adam and eve now knew that they were naked. This does not imply that they did not previously know that there was nothing covering their skin, but they now felt a self-consciousness and sense of shame about their nakedness.

16 Sarfat, J. (2015), *The Genesis Account*, (Powder Springs, GA: Creation Book Publishers), p.354.

Their reaction to this shame at their own nakedness was to cover themselves. They made loincloths, or aprons, out of fig leaves. These would have provided minimal cover, but they would have covered what we now refer to as our private parts. These were the source of greatest shame. Shame is, today, not a bad emotion to feel, because, if responded to correctly, it drives us to repentance. However, it can also drive us to try to cover our guilt. That is what Adam and Eve now experienced. They had, in their nakedness, the outworkings of their guilt and shame. So they attempted to cover their own guilt by their own actions. Therefore, their attempt to make loincloths out of fig leaves was a vain activity, and could not, in fact, ever really work – as we now see.

A third "natural" consequence of their sin was broken fellowship with God. Verse 8 tells us that they "heard the sound of the LORD God walking in the garden in the cool of the day". There is something very pleasant sounding, about the cool of the day. This phrase sounds refreshing, and possibly refers to evening. If the LORD God was walking in the garden at that time, we learn, or at least surmise, several things. First, God was not being secretive. His arrival was announced, by the sound of Him walking. Second, if He was walking, this implies that He was making an appearance as a man. The technical theological word for this is a *theophany*. This is a pre-incarnate appearance of the Second Person of the Trinity in human form. Something that God says a little later will confirm to us that this was, in fact, Jesus speaking; I am not sure whether or not we should refer to Him as Jesus here, as this was before He was born as a baby and named, but He is the same person of the Trinity – the eternal Son of God. If we put these factors together, it sounds like there was something very refreshing and inviting about the LORD God walking in the garden. His walk was announced, and we can therefore assume that these walks were regular, and Adam and Eve were invited to be part of them. This was, we assume, a sweet time of fellowship between God and His people.

How long had this been going on, before this dreadful day of the Fall? We do not know for sure. In my previous book, I had suggested that the Fall could have happened as early as Day Eight.[17] But if we assume that this fellowship between Creator and creatures had occurred before, I suggest we must postpone the day of the Fall. We cannot, however, postpone the Fall too far. The Commission given to Adam and Eve by God, in Genesis 1:28 instructed them to "be fruitful and multiply", yet we know that Cain was not conceived until after the Fall. If the delay between the Creation Week and the conception of Cain had been too long, then this would have been another act of rebellion by the humans – but this does not appear to have been part of their sin. So, if the Fall could not be Day Eight, but could not be too

17 Taylor, P.F. (2007), *The Six Days of Genesis*, (Green Forest, AR: Master Books), pp. 101 – 108.

far after the Creation Week either, when would it be? I offer this conjecture: James Ussher, the famous 17th Century Archbishop of Armagh, suggested, in his *magnum opus, the Annals of the World*, that the Fall took place on Day 10.[18] This would allow for God to have been fellowshiping with His creatures on Days seven, eight, and nine, but does not extend the time of the fall too far. We will return to Ussher's reasons for this date in the next section, when we consider the Curse and Salvation.

However pleasant this communion with God had been on days seven through nine, it was no longer pleasant. Adam and Eve had sinned, and, even though they had tried to cover their own guilt, it had not worked. They now knew they were guilty before God, and fellowship was broken, so they tried to hide themselves from the presence of the LORD – as if they could! The psalmist says of this impossibility

> Where shall I go from your Spirit?
> Or where shall I flee from your presence?
> If I ascend to heaven, you are there!
> If I make my bed in Sheol, you are there! (Psalms 139:7-8)

There is a longing in Psalm 139 that must also have been in Adam and Eve's heart, and it is this: How can this sweet fellowship between God and man be restored?

18 Ussher, J., revised and updated Pierce, L. and Pierce, M. (2003), *The Annals of the World*, (Green Forest, AR: Master Books), p.18, §11.

And that, of course, is the subject matter for the entire rest of the Bible! That true story of restoration culminates in the New Heavens and New Earth, when we read:

> Behold, the dwelling place of God is with man. He will dwell with them, and they will be his people, and God himself will be with them as their God. (Revelation 21:3)

Genesis 3 Part 2 – Curse and Salvation

(Genesis 3:9-8)

Why does God ask questions? Isn't He supposed to be almighty, all-present, and all-knowing? Yes, He is all of these things – usually referred to as God's omnipotence, omnipresence, and omniscience. So, His questions are not for the purpose of gaining information. God already has that information; indeed, He has planned everything from the beginning – no, from before the beginning.

If God's questions are not for gaining information, then they are not for His benefit. Therefore, the questions must be for the benefit of the ones questioned. God was about to ask some deep questions of Adam and Eve, so these questions must have been for the benefit of Adam and Eve. As we will see, God would not have asked the questions, if there was no hope for these humans that He had created. Therefore, His questions point, not only to the Curse, but also to the way of Salvation beyond.

God's Questions to Adam

The serpent had deliberately and disobediently ignored the correct order of communication with the First Couple. He had addressed Eve first. The LORD obviously does not do this. He begins with Adam, because Adam is the Federal Head, and therefore has a headship over

Eve, and, indeed, the whole of the human race to follow. His first question is seemingly innocuous. "Where are you?" But remember, God knows where Adam and Eve are, and why they are hiding. So His question both invites the fellowship that they have broken, and commands them to face up to their responsibilities. Adam is obliged to reply, and his answer shows that he knows the fact of and the reason for this breakdown in sweet fellowship.

> "I heard the sound of you in the garden, and I was afraid, because I was naked, and I hid myself."

He was afraid. There had been no fear in the previous times of fellowship, which had been pleasant, in the cool of the day. But now, it was not possible to be in the presence of God, in his own strength. Adam could only stand before God, because God had commanded him to do so. His reply about being naked, and wanting to hide himself, revealed that his eyes had been opened, and he now had the experience of sin.

> He said, "Who told you that you were naked? Have you eaten of the tree of which I commanded you not to eat?" (Genesis 3:11)

Again, I cannot emphasize often enough that God knew the answer to this question. Today, there are people, who follow a line of theology called Open Theism. They believe that God does not know the future.

He does not know what decisions we will make. He is as much taken by surprise by events as we are. Such a God is not a God. It is not the God of the Bible, who is revealed as omnipotent, omnipresent, and omniscient. Therefore, the God of the Open Theists is, in fact, a false god.

The real God asks this question of Adam, to give Adam the opportunity to repent. We do not know why God decreed that these things should happen, but His Sovereign Decree does not diminish our responsibility for our sins. God reminded Adam, in His question, that there was a command involved. God did not suggest to Adam that it would have been a good idea not to eat the fruit. No, God issued a command, and Adam had directly disobeyed the command. The reminder to Adam of the command reminds the man that he is the Federal head, and holds the responsibility of the entire race. Adam was now to learn his responsibility, but, at the moment, he was not ready to repent. Instead, he makes one of the most feeble excuses of the Bible, blaming the event on his wife. Even worse, his answer contains a hint of criticism of God Himself.

> "The woman whom you gave to be with me, she gave me fruit of the tree, and I ate."

It is almost like Adam saying, "I couldn't help it. The women made me do it. And this is your fault, God, because you gave the woman to me."

God's Question to Eve

God's response to Adam's excuse will wait. For now, He turns to the woman, and questions her. But God's question to the woman is not as strong, because she was deceived. He simply asks "What is this that you have done?" But the woman's reply is not what it should be. Like her husband, she is not ready yet to repent, but offers the excuse that she had been deceived by the serpent. Now, Eve's answer is true, but is beside the point. She was indeed deceived, but she still had responsibility for her actions. We are reminded of the excuse offered by prominent German leaders after the Second World War - "I was only following orders". Then, as now, the truthfulness of an excuse does not diminish our personal responsibility.

Curse

God now turns to the serpent; to Satan. But we must notice that Satan is not asked a question. The questions asked of Adam and Eve are questions of hope, which we will see lead to the way of salvation. But there is no way of salvation for Satan. All angels and heavenly or spiritual beings – however Satan is to be classified – were separately created. If there were, theoretically, a way of salvation for them, then there would need to be an individual savior for each one. Of course, that would not have happened, because it is humans, not angelic beings, who were created *imago dei*. It is humans, not angels, who are in God's image. And all humans had a Federal head in the person of Adam, so it is possible for us to have a new representative, a new federal head, in the Last Adam, Jesus Christ. This is not possible for Satan and his angels.

So Satan gets no question at this point - only a curse.

> 14. The LORD God said to the serpent, "Because you have done this, cursed are you above all livestock and above all beasts of the field; on your belly you shall go, and dust you shall eat all the days of your life.
> 15. I will put enmity between you and the woman, and between your offspring and her offspring; he shall bruise your head, and you shall bruise his heel." (Genesis 3:14-15)

Sometimes people think that there is an intrinsic curse of all snakes. I do not think this is the case. Snakes are just animals, like any other. But some animals, and other objects, remind us of important truths. When we see a snake, slithering on its belly, it reminds us of that serpent in the garden, who was Satan. Henry Morris had this to say, about the symbolism of the situation, alluding to Romans 9:21:

> Lest anyone complain at God's injustice, since the serpent as an animal was not to blame for Satan's corrupt possession of its body, he should remember that the "potter hath power over the clay." Each animal had been made for a specific mode of life and with specific

> structures appropriate to such a mode. There were many other "creeping things", and God now made the serpent to join this group, for reason of the symbolism involved; but snakes, as animals, are no more capable of resentment at this lot than are moles and worms.[1]

God made clear, in this passage, that there was to be enmity between human descendants and Satan. Although there are people today who worship Satan, they are fooling themselves. Satan always seeks to destroy, and will seek to damage even those who think they are his friends. Satan could not have literal descendants, so his offspring refers to those who do his will – which is, of course, the whole of the human race, unless one has been born again.

The offspring of the woman, however, suggests a single person. The word translated offspring (or *seed* in the KJV) is *zera* (זֶרַע). Everywhere else in the Old Testament, *zera* refers to the descendant of a man. And biologically speaking, seed obviously refers to a man. So, the implication given here is that one day there will come a man, born of a woman, who does not have an earthly father. That can only refer to one person – Jesus. Moreover, it was the work of Jesus to bruise the head of Satan, which will destroy him, even though He Himself will suffer and die (his heel is bruised). This wonderful prophetic word is

1 Morris, H.M. (1976), *The Genesis Record,* (Grand Rapids, MI: Baker Book House), p. 119.

the very first giving of the Gospel. As far as I can make out, the Resurrection is not explicitly mentioned here, but that issue also comes up within a few chapters into Genesis. However, the final bruising of the serpent's head has not yet happened, so this implies that the dead Messiah has to be resurrected, in order to accomplish this future event. Because this verse refers to the way of salvation, by the Gospel, it is often referred to as the *protoevangelium* – the First Gospel.

It is particularly beautiful that this first statement of the Gospel comes so soon after the first sin. God has never left people without hope. There has always been a way of salvation. Not only that, but this judgment on Satan, and the giving of the Gospel, is being pronounced by the very same Person, who would, one day, take on that human form to fulfill this very prophecy, because, as we have suggested, the One speaking is the Second Person of the Trinity.

When God turns to the woman, to pronounce sentence on her, the punishment he gives, while severe, is temporal, and does not affect salvation. That aspect will be reserved for Adam, but Eve also inherits what Adam receives, because she was taken from his side. So the woman now gets pain in childbirth, and in child-rearing. While there was previously supposed to be an acknowledgment of Adam's primacy, this now becomes that Adam was to rule over his wife, with all that this stronger language implies.

Adam's curse is both temporal and spiritual, and, as I said, applies to Eve also, because she is a sort-of descendant of his, as far as the flesh is concerned.

In verse 17, God starts by reminding Adam that he had already previously known what the commandment was, and what the consequence for breaking the commandment would be. So, the process of death was now to begin.

The first clause of verse 17 can be misunderstood. God was not saying that a man should never listen to his wife. Far from it! What he was saying was that it was wrong to listen to his wife, and accept her word, when he had had a clear word from God to the contrary. The curse that God gave to Adam also affected the whole of creation, as Romans 8:20-21 reminds us. Now, even working the ground will be difficult for Adam, as the ground will produce thorns and thistles. And work, which was to be so important in a holy world, became toil. Adam was literally made from the dust, and our bodies literally return to the dust.

This relationship between the dying of Adam and the dying of the Creation is also important. It shows us that there was no death before the Fall. The idea, therefore, that fossils could be millions of years old does not hold water. This verse alone kicks the theory of evolution into touch, because there could not have been death before Adam's sin.

To summarize the last few paragraphs; God questioned Adam and Eve, to get them to consider their responsibility. God offered no such salvation to Satan. God pronounced the curse on Satan, on Eve, and on Adam. But He also gave us the true way of salvation, by the (then) future birth of the Messiah – the seed of the woman.

> The man called his wife's name Eve, because she was the mother of all living. Genesis 3:20.

Genesis 3:20 almost reads like a bunny trail – but it isn't. Because of Eve's unique creation, God emphasizes that all the rest of humanity was to be descended from Eve, and that is why she was the Mother of all Living – and the name Eve means exactly that.

In verse 21, we are back to salvation! God gave Adam and Eve clothes of skin. Adam and Eve had tried to cover their own nakedness, by means of fig leaves. Now, God gave them clothes of skin, because the shedding of blood was going to be necessary, for the remission of sins. These skins, and the animal or animals from which they came, are a type of Christ.

The conference within the Trinity of verse 22 is a little hard to grasp, at first sight. It is unsettling, though, to read God's comment about us now being "like one of us". Is it in some way admitting the truth of what Satan said in verse 5? By no means. It has been said that, where the English has the word "behold" or similar, from the Hebrew *hen* (הֵן), it is as if a little trumpet is being played. Certainly, this is the pronouncement of something that has to be seen – a spectacle. The spectacle is that of human beings, who had all the knowledge they needed of good and evil, but have now chosen to experience it. It is as if the statement is said ironically, as Calvin has suggested.[2] Bunyan speculates further on what the meaning is of this pronouncement of the council of the Trinity.

> Now Adam, you see what a god you are become: The serpent told you "you should be as gods," as one that was infinite in wisdom. But behold, your godhead is horrible wickedness, even pollution of body and soul by sin. A thing you little thought of when you pleased yourself with the thought of that high attainment; and now if you be not prevented, you will proceed from evil to evil; for notwithstanding I have made promise of sending a Saviour, you will, through the pollution of your mind, forget and set at nought my promise; and seek life and salvation by that tree of life which was never intended for the justification of sinners; therefore I will turn you out of the garden, 'to till the ground whence thou wast taken.'"[3]

2 Calvin, J., *The Book of Genesis*, (Edinburgh: Banner of Truth), p. 184.
3 Bunyan, J. (ed. Taylor, P.F. 2010), *Genesis: An Exposition of Chapters 1 to 11*, (Castle Rock, WA: J6D Publications), pp. 99-100.

We also note that the use of the First Person Plural is not a plural of majesty, as some have supposed, but a literal plural. As with comments we made on Genesis 1, while the doctrine of the Trinity is not explicitly stated at this point, verse 22 is consistent with the doctrine of the Trinity, and this is the best foundational starting point, with which to interpret the verse.

Finally, in verses 23 and 24, God drives the humans out of the Garden. N.T. Wright seems to think that Jewish readers would have read this passage, and assumed that it was their story; that is that the expulsion of Adam and Eve from the Garden was like the expulsion of the people from Israel, when they were carried away to Babylon.[4] This is one of his arguments for assuming that Adam and Eve were not real people, but simply act as archetypes. Wright's analysis assumes that Genesis was not written until the Exile. However, that point is highly disputable, and we would suggest that Genesis was compiled by Moses, long before the Exile. Not only that, but, as we have suggested, Moses's work on Genesis was probably as a sort of inspired editor, compiling the book from the previous Toledoth accounts.

Walton, meanwhile, believes that the expulsion from the Garden, with particular reference to being kept from the Tree of Life, proves that Adam and Eve had been created mortal, and that the fruit of the Tree

4 Wright, N.T. (2010), *Genesis with NT Wright*, < https://biologos.org/resources/genesis-with-n-t-wright >, accessed 4/17/2019.

of Life had properties that would extend life.[5] This is not the case. There was nothing magical about the fruit. However, the fruit was the pre-Fall equivalent of the Lord's Supper, and will be reinstated in the world to come (Revelation 22:2). God prevented Adam and Eve from taking fruit from the Tree of Life, not because it would have caused them to live forever, but because it was the sacrament of fellowship with Him, which was now broken.

What actually occurred is much simpler to understand. The Garden of Eden was symbolic of close, free fellowship with God. This sort of fellowship was no longer possible, so Adam and Eve were expelled from the Garden. This meant that they could not partake of the fellowship fruit with God. However, God chose, initially, to leave the Garden in place, with guards, as a reminder to humanity of what they had lost. From this point, up until the Flood, we can assume that the Garden had a real, physical, geographical location, and people could see the outside of it. The guards of the Garden were cherubim – among the fiercest of God's angelic host. Also, a flaming sword would keep people out of the Garden.

The Garden is no longer located on the surface of the Earth. It is likely to have been destroyed, along with the rest of the earth's surface, at the time of the Flood.

5 Walton, J.H. (2015), *The Lost World of Adam and Eve,* (Downers Grove, IL: InterVarsity Press), p.143.

Summary

So ends what is arguably one of the saddest chapters of the Bible, during which we see that death comes to the world as a result of sin, and that the whole universe is now cursed.

What a thrill it is, therefore, to read that these two features will be undone in the world to come, for those who have believed and trusted in the Gospel of Jesus Christ.

There will be no more death. (Revelation 21:4)

There will be no more curse. (Revelation 22:3)

And, best of all, complete fellowship with God will be restored.

> And I heard a loud voice from the throne saying, "Behold, the dwelling place of God is with man. He will dwell with them, and they will be his people, and God himself will be with them as their God. He will wipe away every tear from their eyes, and death shall be no more, neither shall there be mourning, nor crying, nor pain anymore, for the former things have passed away." (Revelation 21:3-4)

Genesis 4 Part 1 – Cain and Abel

(Genesis 4:1-16)

In many ways, the first three chapters of Genesis explain how the world got to where it is today. Genesis 4, therefore, can be taken as a historical account, set within the background of those first three chapters, and affected by the consequences of the same. It can be difficult for us, fully to understand the behavior and activities of people who are without sin, as Adam and Eve were before chapter three kicked off. From Genesis 4, we are in more familiar territory, dealing with human beings who, like us, were born with original sin – the first generation to be so affected.

"I Have Gotten a Man"

Fruchtenbaum has this to say about the way that the first two verses of chapter four are usually interpreted: "Few Bible translators really understand what Eve is saying here."[1] What he is saying is that we miss a good many of the important points of these two verses, by not looking at what the Hebrew says. Of course, Fruchtenbaum is an expert on the Hebrew, and I am not. I can only share with you what

1 Fruchtenbaum, A.G., (1998), *Messianic Christology*, (Tustin, CA: Ariel Ministries), p. 15.

Fruchtenbaum has given, and a graphical or tabular representation of the verses, obtained from the BibleHub website.[2]

[Table 4.1.1 - Hebrew Analysis of Genesis 4:1]

Strong's	Hebrew	English
120	וְהָֽאָדָ֕ם wə-hā-'ā-ḏām,	And Adam
3045	יָדַ֖ע yā-ḏa‘	knew
853	אֶת־ 'eṯ-	-
2332	חַוָּ֣ה ḥaw-wāh	Eve
802	אִשְׁתּ֑וֹ 'iš-tōw;	his wife
2029	וַתַּ֙הַר֙ wat-ta-har	and she conceived
3205	וַתֵּ֣לֶד wat-tê-leḏ	and bore
853	אֶת־ 'eṯ-	-
7014	קַ֔יִן qa-yin,	Cain
559	וַתֹּ֕אמֶר	and said

2 The table is taken from the BibleHub website, < https://biblehub.com/text/genesis/4-1.htm >, accessed 4/19/2019.

	wat-tō-mer	
7069	קָנִ֥יתִי qā-nî-ṯî	I have acquired
376	אִ֖ישׁ 'îš	a man
854	אֶת־ 'eṯ-	from
3068	יְהוָֽה׃ Yah-weh.	Yahweh
3254	וַתֹּ֣סֶף wat-tō-sep̄	And she again
3205	לָלֶ֔דֶת lā-le-ḏeṯ,	bore [this time]
853	אֶת־ 'eṯ-	-
251	אָחִ֖יו 'ā-ḥîw	his brother
853	אֶת־ 'eṯ-	-
1893	הָ֑בֶל hā-ḇel;	Abel

The first thing that we should note in these verses is the play on words. Names in the Old Testament usually mean something. Therefore, Cain was given his name, because it is related to the word for *gotten.* It is as if Eve had named her son Gotten. The name Abel, meanwhile, means *vapor*, and is used in the sense of something transitory. The word is found in Ecclesiastes, where it is variously translated as "vanity", or "meaningless".

More significant even than this, according to Fruchtenbaum, is the construction used to introduce people's names. Verse 1 starts with "Adam knew Eve, his wife..." The word "knew" is not just being used as a euphemism, though it certainly is that. It refers to the fact that Adam and Eve had sexual intercourse. The use of the word "knew" shows that sex is a means, by which partners should know each other fully, so, as I said, this is not just a "polite" euphemism, it is a statement of what the sexual act should be. That is also why the verse emphasizes that Eve was Adam's wife. Adam and Eve were the only two people on Earth at the time, but the verse is not just describing Eve as a partner, as I did above; the verse emphasizes that Eve was his wife. Therefore, we are reminded that the sexual act is only for use within marriage. And marriage, as we have seen, is intended to be between a man and a woman, for life. So, coupled with Genesis 2:24, we see that Genesis 4:1 cuts directly across modern uses, or rather abuses, of marriage, sex, and family.

In recent decades, many of the governments of the world have "redefined" marriage, or claimed that they are removing constitutional bans, so that marriage can be between a man and a man, or a woman and a woman. How long will it be before governments start to look at the number of people that can be involved in a marriage contract, therefore justifying polygamy? It cannot be emphasized too strongly – government is not competent to redefine marriage, because marriage has been defined by God. A Parliament could pass any law that it wanted, and this would have no effect on the legality of the institution of marriage in God's eyes. Right from the beginning of time, with the very first people, God has laid down that marriage is to be between a man and a woman, that marriage is normally to be sought, that it is supposed to be for life, and that the act of sex is instituted only within the institution of marriage, partly for the procreation of children, but also so that the married couple may know each other.

The next thing we note is that Eve's name is introduced with the Hebrew preposition *et* (אֶת־). In fact, most of the names in this section are so introduced. As I have emphasized, I am not a Hebrew expert, so I should quote Fruchtenbaum about the significance of the way these sentences are constructed. He suggests that Genesis 4:1 should read:

> וְהָֽאָדָ֕ם יָדַ֖ע אֶת־חַוָּ֣ה אִשְׁתּ֑וֹ וַתַּ֙הַר֙ וַתֵּ֣לֶד אֶת־קַ֔יִן וַתֹּ֕אמֶר קָנִ֥יתִי אִ֖ישׁ
> אֶת־יְהוָֽה׃

> *And the man knew Eve his wife, she conceived and bare Cain and said "I have gotten a man: Jehovah."*

Fruchtenbaum's justification is the next verse being constructed thus:

וַתֹּסֶף לָלֶדֶת אֶת־אָחִיו אֶת־הָבֶל וַיְהִי־הֶבֶל רֹעֵה צֹאן וְקַיִן הָיָה עֹבֵד אֲדָמָה׃

Again she bare his brother: Abel.

Below is the relevant extract from Fruchtenbaum's comments.

> Few Bible translators really understands what Eve is saying here, which is why our English translations do not read as given above. Eve has clearly understood from God's words in Genesis 3:15 that the serpent will be defeated by a God-Man. She obviously thinks that Cain *is* Jehovah. Her basic theology is correct: Messiah would be both man and God. Her mistake is her application of that theology. She has assumed that Cain, her first child, was the promised God-Man. That she quickly realized her mistake is evident at the birth of Cain's brother whom she names Abel, meaning "vanity."[3]

Fruchtenbaum goes on to show that the additional words used in many English translations have come from the Greek Septuagint. The Latin Vulgate also follows that pattern. However, some of the Targumim have interesting readings. Fruchtenbaum quotes the following Targumim:

3 This, and related adjacent comments, are from Fruchtenbaum, A.G., (1998), *Messianic Christology*, (Tustin, CA: Ariel Ministries), p. 15.

> I have gotten a man: the angel of Jehovah. (Jerusalem Targum)

> I have gotten for a man the angel of the Lord. (Targum Pseudo-Jonathan)

It would seem likely that the names given to these sons would not be Eve's idea alone, and therefore I suggest that these thoughts about mistaking Cain for the Messiah came from both Adam and Eve. If I am right, then this suggests that Adam and Eve had repented of their sins, and been forgiven. I think it very likely that we will meet this first man and woman in the world to come. However, even if I am right about this, we notice that forgiveness from this dreadful sin does not undo the temporal effects of the sin here on earth.

Offerings Accepted and Rejected

Growing up in a CoE[4] environment, I was sent to Sunday School as a child. In those days, Sunday School happened in the afternoon, so with morning and evening services, this meant that I attended church three times on a Sunday. Lessons followed familiar characters, with little to connect them in my childish mind. So there would be lessons on Adam and Eve, David and Goliath, Noah and the Ark, the Good Samaritan, Daniel in the Lions' Den, and, of course, Cain and Abel.

4 CoE is short for Church of England, the established Protestant denomination in England.

With the latter story – and it was definitely treated as a story, rather than an historical account, in my Sunday School – I always felt that God was being a bit unfair. I did not understand why God accepted Abel's offering, but rejected Cain. Wasn't God just showing favoritism? My Sunday School teacher could not help. She just suggested that Cain was not a nice person. But it does not make sense to presume something that the text does not say. If we take the text seriously, we can see that the text itself contains the reason why Abel's offering was accepted, while Cain's was rejected.

In order to understand what was going on, we should begin with their chosen professions.

Cain, we are told, was a "worker of the ground". Now this is an entirely honorable profession. It is not the work that Cain did, which caused him to be rejected. Adam, likewise, was set to work the Garden, even before his Fall. On a human level, therefore, one might understand Cain's desire to bring his best crops as an offering to God.

In the Church of England, there is a festival celebrated each Fall, called Harvest. The idea, from medieval times, was to bring in the best and first of the harvest of the land, to give thanks to God for His provision. By the time the 20th Century came around, most people in England were no longer on the land, but were mostly working in urban environments. So, when I was a child, and we had our Harvest

Festival at school, our parents usually bought food from the grocery store, such as tin canned food, and we gave that for our Harvest offering. This food was then distributed, usually to old people's homes. When I became a schoolteacher in a public school[5], I recall one Headteacher suggesting that students could give examples of their best schoolwork, as part of the offering. Though well meant, this headteacher had fallen into the same misunderstanding as Cain. Of course, it is a good thing, for those of us who know the Lord, to give of our best for Him. But the giving of our best gift, no matter how good, does not get us to be right with God. This was the lesson that Cain had not learned, whereas Abel had learned.

Abel, by contrast, was a "keeper of sheep". Why was he keeping sheep? Did he provide roast mutton for his family?

The answer to that would be "No!" Back in Genesis 1:29, we noted that God gave people plants to eat originally. This was to be amended in Genesis 9, but that change had not yet occurred. Therefore, Abel was not raising flocks for food, because that would have been contrary to what God had told them.

When we looked at Genesis 3:21, we saw that Adam and Eve were given clothes of skins to cover their nakedness, because the covering

5 In England and Wales, such schools are called Comprehensive Schools, or Government Schools. The term "Public School", in the UK, refers to a fee-paying independent school, which is not attached to the Church. I was a teacher in a Comprehensive School.

for guilt and sin could only be achieved by the shedding of blood. It therefore seems likely that Abel's job was the twin occupation of tailor and priest – providing clothes of skin for sin covering, and shedding the blood of the animals as atonement for sin.

Now we can see the difference in character between Cain and Abel. Abel knew that he could not be right with God by his own merit, and needed the atoning blood. Cain, in contrast, believed that he could be right with God, by his own efforts, bringing his best work to the Lord. But as we read in Isaiah "We have all become like one who is unclean, and all our righteous deeds are like a polluted garment". (Isaiah 64:6) Thus, the account of Abel and of Cain is an account of the contrast between the Gospel and all other forms of religiosity. Human religion tells us to strive to be better, whereas the Gospel shows us that the best we can do can never save us, because we need a Savior. This is the reason why Abel's offering was accepted. He offered a blood sacrifice, as an atonement for sin. And Cain's offering was rejected, because, however good it seemed, it was counted "like a polluted garment". The fact that Cain was angry shows that he did not understand this point, because he thought that reconciliation with God could be achieved by his own efforts.

God Asks Questions

Why does God ask questions? It is important to know the reason, because, in our own experience, we ask questions, in order to get information. But one of the most important attributes of God is His omniscience – God is all-knowing. As God is all-knowing, He does not need to get information from us. He already knows everything. Therefore, God already knows the answer to the question that He is asking. Yet, there must be a purpose in His asking the question. So, if the purpose of His question is not for His benefit, then it must be for our benefit – in this case, the answer to God's question to Cain must be for Cain's benefit.

God's question to Cain was "Why are you angry?" Although Cain would later take his anger out on his brother, presumably out of extreme jealousy, his anger was really against God. It was, after all, God, not Abel, who had rejected his offering. God says to Cain "If you do well, will you not be accepted? And if you do not do well, sin is crouching at the door." By doing "well", God is not referring simply to being good. Cain might argue that he had been good, as he had brought his best gift to God. But God's instruction is to do "well". Doing well refers to the conquest of sin. As we have seen, sin is only covered by the shedding of blood. There was, from Genesis 3 onward in the Old Testament, the typical shedding of blood, but in the

Messianic Covenant, this is superseded by the shedding of Christ's blood, once for all, upon the cross. In Hebrews 11:4, we read that Abel's offering was offered out of faith. Therefore, Cain's offering was not from faith, but from self. God's instruction to Cain to "do well" is an instruction to have faith. But Cain does not respond to God's admonition.

God told Cain that sin was crouching at the door. "Its desire is contrary to you, but you must rule over it." There is hope here. God has already given the proto-Gospel to Adam and Eve. So it is possible to rule over sin – not by our own merit, but by the atoning blood of Jesus.

Cain Kills Abel

So one man killed another. It happens all the time. The world keeps turning. It's no big deal, is it?

Well, the positioning of this chapter in the Bible tells us that this is a very big deal. The reason is that this is the first murder. This is the first time one man has ever killed another. This is the first time that human blood has been shed.

If you believe in evolution, then the murder in Genesis 4 is not a big deal. Cain and Abel, if they were real, were simply descendants of ape-like ancestors, who achieved the upward march of evolution by death, disease, and killing. The poet said that nature is "red in tooth and claw".[6] In fact, if evolution is true, or even if millions of years are true, then there is no significance to Abel's blood being shed. Commentaries on Genesis by theistic evolutionists cannot relate to the issue, which I will now approach. For example, Waltke – whose commentary on Genesis is pretty thorough – concentrates on the fratricidal nature of Cain's actions, but has nothing to say about Abel[7].

In one sense, it is not surprising that evolutionary commentators have nothing to say about Abel. At first glance, it appears that Abel himself has had nothing to say. Yet Jesus referred to Abel as a prophet[8]. Now a prophet is someone who speaks out God's words. Yet, where are the words of Abel's prophecies? We do not have any recorded. In fact, we do not have a record of anything Abel said at all. There are other prophets in the Bible, whose words are not recorded, but we can tell how their gifts of prophecy were exercised. For example, we can imagine how Obadiah's prophets in a cave exercised their gifts, in 1 Kings 18:13. And the daughters of Philip the Evangelist, in Acts 21:8-9, were clearly used in a church setting – probably in a similar manner to Agabus. But there seems, at first, no hint of Abel's prophecy, until we closely examine Genesis 4 again.

6 Tennyson, A. (1849), *In Memorium A.H.H.*, Canto 56, < http://www.online-literature.com/tennyson/718/ >, accessed 6/3/2019.
7 Waltke, B.K. (2001), *Genesis: A Commentary*, (Grand Rapids, MI: Zondervan), p.98.
8 Luke 11:50-51.

> "The voice of your brother's blood is crying to me from the ground" (Genesis 4:10).

Abel finds his voice through his shed blood. The Book of Hebrews confirms this aspect of Abel's prophecy.

> By faith Abel offered to God a more acceptable sacrifice than Cain, through which he was commended as righteous, God commending him by accepting his gifts. And through his faith, though he died, he still speaks. (Hebrews 11:4)

If Abel were just a product of a line of semi-evolved simians, or if he were just an allegorical figure, his blood would not have the same significance. But this is the first murder. This is the first death. This is the first human blood shed on the ground. It will forever have prophetic significance, because it points towards the death of the One who was to come. It is ironic that Eve had thought that Cain could be the promised Messiah, yet it is the blood of Abel, the Vapor, the Vanity, Cain's brother, whose blood is prophetic of the Messiah. Hebrews makes this link very clear in chapter 12.

> But you have come to Mount Zion and to the city of the living God, the heavenly Jerusalem, and to innumerable angels in festal gathering, and to the assembly of the firstborn who are enrolled in heaven, and to God, the judge of all, and to the spirits of the righteous made

> perfect, and to Jesus, the mediator of a new covenant, and to the sprinkled blood that speaks a better word than the blood of Abel. (Hebrews 12:22-24)

This prophetic typology makes no sense, unless these early chapters of Genesis are literally true. That is why a theistic evolutionary commentator misses the whole point of this narrative. The Genesis 4 account is a perfect example of why Christians need to believe all of Genesis to be true. If it were not true – just allegorical – then its prophetic significance is simply not there.

Cain's Relationship with God

The relationship that Cain had, or did not have, with God is instructive. I have already hinted that Cain did not really know God. Yet, a counter-argument to this would be that God spoke to him directly. But there are other people in Scripture, to whom God spoke directly, who were not followers of Him. One example that springs to mind is Balaam. This prophet and wandering sorcerer was available for hire, and was hired by Balak, King of Moab, to put a curse on the Children of Israel[9]. The Angel of the Lord met Balaam on the road, and spoke to him. Therefore, instead of curses, Balaam was forced to pronounce blessings. But Balaam's suggestions to Moab eventually led the Israelites into sin, and both Peter and Jude in their epistles, as well

9 See Numbers 22

as Jesus in his Revelation letter to the church in Pergamum, specifically criticize Balaam and his ways[10]. So, if God chooses to speak directly with an unbeliever, that does not indicate that the unbeliever in question has repented and trusted God, though, conversely, no one who feigns ignorance of God can expect God to speak to them, to satisfy their curiosity.

That Cain did not really know God can be seen in his answers to God's questions.

> Then the LORD said to Cain, "Where is Abel your brother?" He said, "I do not know; am I my brother's keeper?" (Genesis 4:9)

In Cain's reply, his first phrase shows that he had an inadequate view of God's omniscience. He lies to God. Why would he lie to God, unless he thought there was a chance he would get away with it?

Today, there is a school of thought, among many so-called evangelicals, called *Open Theism*. This idea seems to suggest that, although God is the most powerful being there is, He doesn't actually know the future – or at least does not know the decisions that His creatures might make. This line of thinking would suggest that God did indeed ask Cain questions in order to gain information. Scripture denies this form of reasoning, as expertly explained by Pink.

10 See 2 Peter 2:15, Jude 11, and Revelation 2:14.

> God is omniscient. He knows everything: everything possible, everything actual; all events and all creatures, of the past, the present, and the future. He is perfectly acquainted with every detail in the life of every being in heaven, in earth, and in hell. "He knoweth what is in the darkness" (Dan 2:22). Nothing escapes His notice, nothing can be hidden from Him, nothing is forgotten by Him. Well may we say with the Psalmist, "Such knowledge is too wonderful for me; it is high, I cannot attain unto it" (Psa 139:6). His knowledge is perfect. He never errs, never changes, never overlooks anything. "Neither is there any creature that is not manifest in His sight: but all things are naked and opened unto the eyes of him with whom we have to do" (Heb 4:13). Yes, such is the God "with whom we have to do"![11]

Cain's second phrase - "Am I my brother's keeper?" - is insolent. Having denied God's ability to know, Cain now denies God's right of authority. It is God, who has determined how we should behave, not mankind. Luther comments that Cain's very words are an admittance that he knew he ought to have been his brother's keeper.

> Cain thinks that he has made an effectual excuse for himself, by saying that he was not his brother's keeper; whereas, by the very mention of his brother's name, he at

11 Pink, A. W (2012), *The Attributes of God*, (Pensacola, FL: Chapel Library), Kindle Edition, location 245.

> once confesses that he ought to have been his younger brother's keeper. And then again does he not, by the same admitted confession, that he ought to have been his brother's keeper, accuse himself of being of a hostile mind towards his brother?[12]

Luther goes on to underline the eternal consequences of Cain's inability to confess his sin.

> Cain therefore by this very saying of his heavily accuses himself when he makes the excuse that the custody of his brother was no matter of his. Whereas if he had said to his father, "Alas, my father, I have slain Abel, my brother. I repent of the deed I have done. Return upon me what punishment thou wilt." Had he thus spoken, there might have been room for a remedy; but as he denied his sin and contrary to the will of God cast off the charge of his brother altogether, there was no place left for mercy or favor.[13]

Luther is right. There are murderers, who have repented of their sin. While they must still bear the temporal justice, meted out for such a crime, their eternal state can be one of reconciliation to God, and such repentant murderers are saved, and we will see them in glory.

12 Luther, M., *Commentary on Genesis*, < https://www.gutenberg.org/files/48193/48193-h/48193-h.htm#sect34 >, accessed 6/14/2019.

13 *ibid.*

But Cain was not repentant, and will not be among their number. John summarized the issue as follows:

> We should not be like Cain, who was of the evil one and murdered his brother. And why did he murder him? Because his own deeds were evil and his brother's righteous. (1 John 3:12)

The Consequences of Cain's Actions

Cain's actions were bound to have consequences. The outcomes were not the same as would or should be expected today, but this is not because God has changed. It is because the events of Genesis 4 were at an early stage in God's revelation of Himself. Following the Flood, God's covenant with the whole of humanity, often referred to as the Noahic Covenant, made clear that the appropriate punishment for murder is death.

> And for your lifeblood I will require a reckoning: from every beast I will require it and from man. From his fellow man I will require a reckoning for the life of man. Whoever sheds the blood of man, by man shall his blood be shed, for God made man in his own image. (Genesis 9:5-6)

God makes clear that the death penalty should be carried out by humans, just in case anyone was to think that only God could smite someone dead. Therefore, the judicial killing of a murderer is not the same as the sinful murder. And to emphasize the point, God states that the reason for this sanction is because man has been made in God's image. It is the *imago dei* which makes a human being valuable. We will discuss this further when we reach Genesis 9.

For now, we should note that our current subject matter precedes the Noahic Covenant. Therefore, the sanction for Abel's murder is assigned to Cain directly by God, who alone has the right to determine this sanction.

Cain's punishment was a curse. As a man who grew crops, the first part of his punishment seems to be that he would no longer be able to grow these crops. In verse 12, we read that the very *adamah*, which Cain had previously tilled, would "no longer yield to you its strength".

The second part of the curse is related. Since Cain cannot settle anywhere to till the ground, to produce crops, he must needs become a wanderer. Moreover, God banishes him from where he currently lives, which is probably a point close to the Garden of Eden, from where his parents were banished.

The fact that God did not immediately kill the world's first murderer demonstrates that Cain's sin was entirely his own responsibility. From a human point of view, we can see that even at this moment, Cain had the opportunity to repent. But Cain's words were not repentance. "My punishment is greater than I can bear". Instead of repentance, we have remorse, or regret. Cain is not sorry for his sin – he is sorry for the effect that his sin will now have upon him. Sarfati writes that Cain recognizes four ways that this punishment will affect him.

1. "You have driven me today away from the ground"--Cain knows he has now lost his profession of farming.

2. "From your face I shall be hidden"--loss of fellowship between God and Cain. Adam and Eve had certainly lost the direct fellowship they had in Eden, but Cain will now lose even the fellowship that had been possible at the place of sacrifice.

3. "I shall be a fugitive and a wanderer on the earth"--now Cain would have no permanent abode.

4. "Whoever finds me will kill me"--the one who so foully took his brother's life would be in fear of his own life.[14]

Cain's fear for his life must have been real. Therefore, Cain must have reached adulthood years before this event, and other sons and daughters of Adam and Eve must also have been around.

Bunyan insists (correctly, in my opinion) that Cain is an example of a reprobrate.

14 Sarfati, J.D. (2015), *The Genesis Account*, (Poweder Springs, GA: Creation Book Publishers), p.419.

> He that sins the sin unto death, is not to be prayed for (1 John 5:16), but contrariwise he is to be taken from God's altar that he may die (Exo 21:14). This was Cain's case, and now he knew it; therefore as one excluded of God from his mercy and all the means thereof, he breaks out with roaring under the intolerable burden of the judgment of God upon him, concluding his punishment at present "greater than he could bear," and that yet his sin should remain unpardonable for ever: As saith our Lord Jesus Christ, He hath neither forgiveness here nor in the world to come (Matt 12:32).[15]

In my earlier work on this book, I noted the following:

> Notice that Cain's journey did not just take him to the land of Nod. Clearly there was an earthly direction to his journey—eastward away from Eden. More significantly, however, Cain "went out from the presence of the LORD" (Genesis 4:16). The offer of salvation is now far from him.

This does not mean that God is not everywhere. God was and is certainly there, wherever Cain was. The verse is about Cain's spiritual state, which was out of God's presence.

Nevertheless, God was still merciful to Cain. He put two riders in place. First, that Cain would be protected by a severe deterrent – that

15 Bunyan, J. (ed. Taylor, P.F. 2010), *Genesis*, (Castle Rock, WA: J6D Publications), p.125.

if anyone were to kill Cain, the punishment on that murderer would be sevenfold. Obviously, no one can literally be killed seven times, so the use of the term sevenfold indicates the great severity of this sanction. Second, God put a mark on Cain, so that everyone would know who he was, and therefore not attack him. We have no idea what this mark might have been. There were white supremacist groups that claimed the Mark of Cain meant having black skin, whereas the Nation of Islam claim that the Mark of Cain means having white skin. Both are wrong. We can say two things very definitely about this mark. One, its meaning must have been obvious to all who saw it, without explanation, and two, we do not know what the Mark actually was.

Summary

In this section, we have seen the evidence for the nascent faith of Eve, and possibly of Adam. We have also seen how fundamentally important it is to accept that Genesis 4 speaks of real historical events. Without that acceptance, we cannot understand the significance of Abel's blood, nor understand why his offering was accepted, and Cain's was rejected. The whole account is soaked through with an early typology of the Gospel of Jesus Christ.

Genesis 4 Part 2 – Cain and his Descendants

(Genesis 4:17-26)

Just Who Was Cain's Wife?

Aha! Gotcha! Adam and Eve just had two children, so who were these other people supposed to be? And who was the woman that Cain married? See? It proves the Bible is wrong!

These sort of comments are common. Many evolutionists suppose they can catch us out, by referring to Cain's wife. Who was she? Bunyan's logic was impeccable.

> Cain's wife was his sister, or near kinswoman; for she sprang of the same loins with himself; because his mother was "the mother of all living" (Gen 3:20).[1]

Sarfati also points out that the Bible's teaching that all human beings are descended from Adam and Eve is very important. If this were not so, we would need more than one redeemer.[2] Biblically, one can only be redeemed by a relative. That is why it is so important to recognize that we are all descended from Adam. Jesus is related to each one of

1 *Ob cit*, p.134.
2 Sarfati (2015), p. 421.

us as the Last Adam, and can therefore fulfill the function of Kinsman-Redeemer for us.

A skeptic would clearly counter that we are therefore teaching that Cain broke God's law on incest. So we had better check God's law on this subject.

The law in question is found in Leviticus 18, which contains a list of relationships, where sexual relations are not permitted. These are summarized in verse 6, which says:

> You are not to come near any close relative for sexual intercourse; I am the LORD. (Leviticus 18:6 CSB)

The Christian Standard Bible, quoted above, is an accurate translation, but is giving the interpretation of the text – an interpretation which seems obviously correct. As I usually quote the ESV, let us look at that.

> None of you shall approach any one of his close relatives to uncover nakedness. I am the LORD. (Leviticus 18:6 ESV)

The word translated "nakedness" is associated with shame. Therefore, Leviticus 18 is referring to sinful behavior. While it might seem obvious to most readers that sexual intercourse with a close relative is sinful, we need to stop and ask, "why?". In the rules following verse 6, God makes it clear what definitions of "close relative" He is using.

However, the very detail being used suggests that these rules are very new for the people, and that, therefore, they had not previously applied.

In today's society, most people – even unbelievers – see the logic of these laws. Close sexual relations can produce offspring, who might have genetic defects. Every human being has genetic defects. But if the sexual partners are close relatives, it is highly likely that they will have the same genetic defects, so that these defects cannot be preferentially rejected as the genes passed on to the offspring.

In the case of Cain, he was of the second generation in the world. While Adam's sin might have started the whole business of genetic defects off, it is unlikely that there would be many defects in the second generation. It was completely genetically safe, therefore, for Cain to marry his sister. There would have been no moral problem with such close intermarriage from Cain's time, up to the giving of Leviticus 18. Other examples of non-sinful close-intermarriage, before Leviticus 18, include Sarah, being Abraham's half sister (Genesis 20:12), and Amram marrying his aunt (Exodus 6:20)[3]. This is not the only occasion when God made a law on a subject, prior to which there had been no law, and therefore no sin problem. Other examples

3 *Why did God allow incest in the Bible?*, < https://www.gotquestions.org/incest-in-the-Bible.html >, accessed 6/19/2019.

include the Mosaic dietary laws, which did not apply, before they were given through Moses.

As we will see, when we reach chapter five, Adam and Eve had other sons and daughters, and this was probably a large number, because, once again, problems associated with genetic mutations would still not have been very significant.

Cain's Descendants

If I had been a fiction writer, trying, perhaps like Tolkien, to write my own version or mythology on how the Earth came to be, I would not have called Cain's son Enoch. When we discuss Genesis chapter five, we will refer to a more well-known Enoch. The fact that we have two people mentioned here with the same name could be a little confusing! This confusion would not have been allowed to happen if the account were mythological fiction, whereas the matter is consistent with the account being true history. There is a similar confusion with two men called Lamech.

The etymology of the name Enoch (חנוך) has a great deal in common with the root of the word Hannukah (חנכה), and can mean to inaugurate, to train, or to dedicate. Hence, it is legitimate to translate the name Enoch as *Teacher*, but in Genesis 4:17, the name probably refers to dedication. After all, Cain's first city was named after this son, and it is possible that the city of Enoch was the first ever large scale urban settlement.

After the founding of the city of Enoch, we then read a short genealogy, of the descendants of Cain. These are listed to seven generations, including Cain. It is very likely that the genealogy is not complete. It seems unlikely to me that every character had just one son; with the pattern that we will observe in Genesis 5, I would suggest that the named son is just one of many sons and daughters. In the final generation, we are told of four children. Again, there may have been more, but the fact that the line ends at this point suggests that these four were of the last generation before the Flood.

The penultimate Cainite generation belongs to Lamech. This man took Cain's rebellion much further.

The first thing we notice about Lamech is that he took two wives. The pattern from the beginning was for marriage to be between one man and one woman, and we commented on this issue in chapter 2 part 2. In that comment, we showed that the pattern of monogamous, heterosexual marriage was endorsed by Jesus. Similarly, Paul comments "But because of the temptation to sexual immorality, each man should have his own wife and each woman her own husband." (1 Corinthians 7:2) The instructions about marriage, which Paul goes on to make, can only be understood in the light of biblical, heterosexual monogamy.

Yet, the objection can be made that there are many godly people in the Old Testament who were polygamous. Jacob, as we shall see later, had two wives, Leah and Rachel. David – that "man after God's own heart" - had many wives. In this latter case, it seems as if some of these wives were obtained by King David after prayer, or by God's approval.

We are familiar with the fact that the Mosaic Law allowed for divorce. Jesus said that this was because of "the hardness of your hearts" (Matthew 19:8). Bunyan suggests that the same is the case here.

> This man was the first that brake the first institution of God concerning marriage. "He took unto him two wives." The New Testament says, Let every man have his own wife. And so said the law in its first institution: therefore plurality of wives first came into practice by the seed of cursed Cain, and for a time was suffered in the world through the hardness of man's heart.[4]

Sarfati makes the same point.

> But whenever the Mosaic Law had provisions for polygamy, it was always the conditional, "**If** he takes

4 Bunyan, J. (ed, Taylor, P.F. 2010), *Genesis*, (Castle Rock, WA: J6D Publications), p.136.

> another wife to himself...” (Exodus 21:10), never an encouragement. God put a number of obligations of the husband towards the additional wives which would discourage polygamy. It is no wonder that polygamy was unknown among the Jews after the Babylonian exile, and monogamy was the rule even among the Greeks and Romans by New Testament times.[5]

Lamech’s two wives were called Adah (meaning *ornament*) and Zillah (meaning *shade*). Some have suggested that these pretty names, describing appearance, imply that Lamech was motivated by lust. Whether he was or not is, however, irrelevant, because his sin was not marrying good-looking girls, nor being sexually attracted to his wife, if he had had but one. His sin was marrying two women.

It will be remembered that God placed a curse on Cain, because of his actions, and yet also placed a protection that “If anyone kills Cain, vengeance shall be taken on him sevenfold” (Genesis 4:15). Lamech takes these words and turns them into a boast.

> Lamech said to his wives: “Adah and Zillah, hear my voice; you wives of Lamech, listen to what I say: I have killed a man for wounding me, a young man for striking me. If Cain's revenge is sevenfold, then Lamech's is seventy-sevenfold.” (Genesis 4:23-24)

5 Sarfati, J.D. (2015), *The Genesis Account*, (Powder Springs, GA: Creation Book Publishers), p. 432, emphasis original.

In the case of Cain, any sanction carried out to avenge his death would be undertaken by God. In Lamech's case, he usurps God's role, and threatens the action himself. Moreover, he maintains that he killed someone, not for killing someone else, but for wounding or striking him. This is an overreaction, and he had no mandate from God for such a plan. This next point is pure conjecture on my part, but could it be that the man that Lamech killed was Zillah's first husband? It is a thought I have often had, but as it is not in Scripture, it remains just a conjectural thought, and no theology can be made of it.

Lamech had three sons and one daughter. I wrote fictionalized accounts of these, in my book *Don't Miss the Boat.*[6] What we actually know, however, is very little.

Jabal was the father of those who dwell in tents and have livestock. This refers to husbandry – and, possibly, a nomadic husbandry at that. Jabal was not literally the father of such people – the word father is, in this context, referring to the founder.

Yet, we know that Abel had kept animals. However, we understood that Abel had done so for sacrificial reasons. So, Jabal must be the founder of a new type of husbandry. Given his descent from Cain, it is just possible that he was about to break God's commission, and use these animals for food. However, we cannot prove that Jabal was

6 Taylor, P.F. (2013), *Don't Miss the Boat*, (Green Forest, AR: Master Books).

breaking that Edenic command, because there appears to be no significant breaking of commandment by his brothers.

Jubal is the father of musical instruments. Different versions translate the Hebrew words *kinnor* (כִּנּוֹר) and *ugab* (עוּגָב) differently, but the former seems to refer to a stringed instrument, and the latter was a wind instrument. Most musical instruments are either string or wind.

Tubal-Cain worked metals. In particular, he worked three metals. Bronze is an alloy of tin and copper, so Tubal-Cain must have been able to extract both tin and copper from their ores, which is done by simple reduction with carbon, such as charcoal. Iron is a more complicated metal to extract, as it needs not only heat and carbon (charcoal), but also hot air being blasted on to the molten reactants. The technology required is not simple, and was clearly available before the Flood.

All three of these sons of Lamech indicate the antediluvian levels of industry – in agriculture, culture, and metallurgy.

Naamah, the only girl among three brothers, means *loveliness*. Was this just a comment about her appearance, or did it also imply something of her character? Once again, my next comment is conjecture, and cannot create a theology, but in my fictionalized account of Naamah, I had her marrying one of the sons of Noah (Ham). Although this was fictional, there are at least two other occasions when girls from outside the promised people put their faith in God, and even became ancestors of Jesus. The two that I am thinking of were Rahab, a Caananite, and Ruth, a Moabite. So if Naamah were a believer, this would not introduce an unbiblical theology.

Faith in the Darkness

Seth must have been born after the death of Abel, because of Eve's words: "God has appointed for me another offspring instead of Abel, for Cain killed him" (Genesis 4:25). Once again, we see a measure of Eve's faith. She had recognized Abel's importance, because, when he had become an adult, he had kept flocks as a priest, offering blood sacrifices to God. But, despite his bloodshed being prophetic of the Savior to come, in whom Eve had put her trust, Abel had no offspring. Now, she declared that there was a new appointment – and the name Seth means *appointment*, so that Eve is making another theological pun. God's purposes, as I suspect Eve had correctly surmised, was to bring the Messiah to the world, as a descendant of Seth. So Genesis 4 cannot end with the birth of Seth, but has to jump forward to Seth being a man, and fathering a child of his own – Enosh. The meaning of Enosh will be discussed in the next section. For now, we should note that the Moses tells us "At that time people began to call upon the name of the LORD" (Genesis 4:26) This would have been an important point to Moses. Remember that Lord, with small capitals, is the way most of our English translations render the word *YHWH* (יהוה), the Divine Name of God. It was to Moses that this Name was first explained (Exodus 3:14). This was in the context of Moses needing to know from where salvation for the Israelites was to come. The fact that at the end of Genesis 4, we read, "people began to call upon the name of the LORD," suggests that true worship was now happening. After all, the word LORD had already been used previously, so it was not new. It must be the worship of *YHWH* that is now considered to be new. This point will be of great importance, when we open up chapter six, because this worship was happening in a world, the majority of which was turning away from God.

Those who look for contradictions will find passages that they think are contradictory. In this case, we have just read that people were calling on the Divine Name, and we have assumed that this is genuine worship. Yet, three chapters after Moses's revelation of God as a burning bush, we read God saying: "I appeared to Abraham, to Isaac, and to Jacob, as God Almighty, but by my name the LORD I did not make myself known to them" (Exodus 6:3). Jamieson, Fausset, and Brown comment thus on that supposed contradiction.

> ...rather, interrogatively, by My name Jehovah was I not known to them? Amos not I, the Almighty God, who pledged My honor for the fulfilment of the covenant, also the self-existent God who lives to accomplish it? Rest

assured, therefore, that I shall bring it to pass. This passage has occasioned much discussion; and it has been thought by many to intimate that as the name Jehovah was not known to the patriarchs, at least in the full bearing or practical experience of it, the honor of the disclosure was reserved to Moses, who was the first sent with a message in the name of Jehovah, and enabled to attest it by a series of public miracles.[7]

Summary

In this section, we have seen the problems that the world was beginning to face, as a result of the Cainite line. We see Cain's own behavior after God cursed him, and we see that things got even worse under his descendant, Lamech. We also saw that technology and society were already developed, in just a few generations after creation.

In the midst of such difficult times, we also see that God preserved His promised line of descent, and that there was always a remnant, who would worship Him.

7 Jamieson, R., Fausset, A.R., and Brown, D. (1882), *A Commentary, Critical, Practical, and Explanatory on the Old and New Testaments*, note on Exodus 6:3, retrieved from the software *e-Sword* – www.e-sword.net

Genesis 5 - The Book of the Generations of Adam

(Genesis 5)

Don't Skip this Chapter!

I think that there is a temptation, when faced with Genesis 5, to consider that a list of names looks a bit dull, and to decide to skip to the next chapter. Please don't do that, when you are reading Genesis. God inspired Moses to include chapter 5 for a reason.

Most ancient cultures valued genealogies, and were quite happy for them to appear long and, by modern eyes, tedious. This is because such genealogies set the written accounts into history. They are a mark of the historical reliability of the document. We should see them in the same light. Moses, under the inspiration of the Holy Spirit, was not trying to bore his readers. He simply wants to underline that this first book of the Bible is a work of history.

The Book of the Generations

Genesis 5:1 is the beginning of a new *toledoth.* We discussed the division of Genesis into toledoths in chapter 2 part 2 (In the Garden). The Hebrew word *toledoth* is usually translated as *generations.*

This particular toledoth, beginning with Genesis 5:1 (and continuing until Genesis 6:9) is unique. There is an extra word in the designation - "This is the *book* of the generations of Adam" (emphasis added). The Hebrew word, translated as *book*, is *sepher* (ספר). This indicates something that is written down. Of course, all of Genesis was written down by Moses. But, as we have discussed, Moses was the divinely inspired editor of previously compiled accounts – some written, and some oral. Although other portions of Genesis may also have been written down, we can be almost certain that Genesis 5:1-6:8 was written down – most likely as a scroll, rather than what we think of as a book.

We get the same phrase in Matthew 1:1 "The book of the genealogy of Jesus Christ, the son of David, the son of Abraham". The Greek phrase used here is *biblos geneseōs* (βιβλος γενεσεως), and the same Greek phrase appears in LXX for Genesis 5:1. Just as Matthew 1:1 is indicating that the book is *about* Jesus, not *by* Him, in the same way Genesis 5:1 is emphasizing that Adam is being put in his historical context, and does not suggest that Adam wrote this document. It is not, therefore, a prophecy. It is a historical record.

In Adam's Image

The first two verses of chapter five are an important re-iteration of the account of the creation of Adam and Eve. The Hebrew word Adam appears several times. Even if (like myself) you cannot read Hebrew, you can look for the pattern of the word *adam* (אדם) in the text below.

(Genesis 5:1)

זה ספר תולדת **אדם** ביום ברא אלהים **אדם** בדמות אלהים עשׂה אתו׃

(Genesis 5:2)

זכר ונקבה בראם ויברך אתם ויקרא את־שמם **אדם** ביום הבראם׃

> This is the book of the generations of Adam (**אדם**). When God created man (**אדם**), he made him in the likeness of God. Male and female he created them, and he blessed them and named them Man (**אדם**) when they were created. (Genesis 5:1-2)

The reference to Adam in the phrase "the book of the generations of Adam" is using Adam as a personal name. This is also the case in Genesis 5:3. However, we then read in verse one that "God created man". This is the general use of the word *man*. And when God named *them Man*, this is the designation of mankind as a whole. So, the context suggests three different uses of the word *adam*. We are also reminded in verse one that Adam and Eve were created in the image, or likeness, of God. We have discussed this in our commentary on chapter 1.

We have also already discussed – in chapter 4 – that Seth was, in a sense, born in place of Abel, at least as far as Eve was concerned. It is likely that Eve's words were prophetic, because Abel was certainly a type of Christ, and we now see that a line of descent is to be created through Seth, which will eventually culminate in the Messiah – Jesus.

Other qualities ascribed to Seth could be ascribed to any of Adam and Eve's children. The accounts in Genesis 4 through 6 concentrate mostly on the Cainite line and the Sethite line. However, Genesis 5:5 makes clear that there were other sons and daughters born to Adam and Eve. There would need to be, for further generations, and, as we discussed when considering Cain's wife. There was, as yet, no divine objection to such close intermarriage, nor would there be any genetic risk posed by such close intermarriage.

So, then Moses tells us that Seth was "a son in his (Adam's) own likeness, after his image", this property applies to all the sons and daughters of Adam and Eve – including Cain and the martyred Abel. Adam was made in the image of God, so this means that all humans are in God's image, but the emphasis on the second and subsequent generations being in Adam's image shows that this *imago dei* property is now tarnished somewhat by sin. Although the *imago dei* is still there, all human beings are now born with original sin, which is inherited from our father Adam.

Numbers in the Genealogy

The genealogies of Genesis 5 and 11 are significantly different from other Jewish genealogies. These genealogies contain numbers. We can refer to them as the chrono-genealogies.

There is a wealth of information that we can glean from these numbers. The first and most important corollary is that these genealogies must be complete. There are no gaps in the genealogies.

This last statement is, of course, controversial. Long age advocates, such as the self-styled *progressive creationist* Dr. Hugh Ross, make much of the alleged gaps in the genealogies. Ross states:

> The words translated into English say this: "When X had lived Y years, he became the father of Z." Someone reading the same passage in Hebrew would see a second possibility: "When X had lived Y years, he became the father of a family line that included or culminated in Z."[1]

Ross's assertion that someone reading the Hebrew would understand the passage differently is incorrect. Indeed, Hebrew experts, who take a liberal position on the Bible, often explain this point better than so-called "conservatives", like Ross. For example, James Barr, a Professor of Hebrew at the University of Oxford, said this:

1 Ross, H.N. (1998), *The Genesis Question*, (Carol Stream, IL: NavPress), p.109.

> Probably, so far as I know, there is no professor of Hebrew or Old Testament at any world-class university who does not believe that the writer(s) of Genesis 1-11 intended to convey to their readers the ideas that: ...the figures contained in the Genesis genealogies provided by simple addition a chronology from the beginning of the world up to later stages in the biblical story.[2]

I have often said that I miss the old-fashioned liberals! These were theologians, who would honestly tell you what the Hebrew said, and explain why they could not accept it as true. So-called modern "conservatives" (I will refer to these as pseudo-conservatives) claim to believe exactly what the Bible says, but also believe evolution, so have to twist the meaning of Scripture to suggest that it does not mean what it appears to say. An example of this pseudo-conservative thought is the anonymous author of an article on the BioLogos website.

> So how old is the earth? Some people think the Bible says it was created about 6,000 years ago. While the Bible does include a number of genealogies, many conservative Bible scholars believe that these lists are not intended to be a complete method of dating the age of the earth. Instead God gave us another means to discover this kind of information: he created the natural world through

2 Barr., J., Letter to David C.C. Watson, 1984, cited in Sarfati, J.D. (2015), *The Genesis Account*, (Powder Springs, GA: Creation Book Publishers), p. 462.

> faithful, consistent processes. And as we observe these processes and their effects today, we can develop reliable conclusions about the past.[3]

The article's author suggests that the biblical lists "are not intended to be a complete method of dating the age of the earth", whereas the liberal scholar, James Barr, says that they are! Rather than being either a liberal or a pseudo-conservative, we take the genuinely conservative approach of accepting that the Bible means what it says, and that it is authoritative. Notice also that the author suggests that the extrapolation of modern, slow processes ("faithful, consistent") is described as something given to us by God. Yet the Bible specifically warns against that very backward extrapolation.

> They will say, "Where is the promise of his coming? For ever since the fathers fell asleep, all things are continuing as they were from the beginning of creation." For they deliberately overlook this fact, that the heavens existed long ago, and the earth was formed out of water and through water by the word of God, and that by means of these the world that then existed was deluged with water and perished. (2 Peter 3:4-6)

In 2 Peter, the apostle states that the scoffers are identified by their belief that processes have remained constant since the beginning, and

3 *How Old Is the Earth?*, May 16th 2015, < https://biologos.org/resources/how-old-is-the-earth >, accessed 7/8/2019.

then explains that this is not so, because the scoffers "deliberately overlook" the Creation and the Flood.

Another critic of the biblical timescale is Karl Giberson. He suggests that an acceptance of the literal timescale in Genesis is an aberration, introduced, not by evangelical Christians, but by Seventh Day Adventists. Looking at the works of biblical scholars, he suggests that:

> [The Fundamentalists] were not united in rejecting evolution as a mechanism of creation. And there was no rejection of the scientific research that indicated that the earth was far older than 10,000 years.[4]

This is easily checked, by reading what *The Fundamentals* says about the book of Genesis.

> The beginning of Genesis, therefore, is a divinely inspired narrative of the events deemed necessary by God to establish the foundations for the Divine Law in the sphere of human life, and to set forth the relation between the omnipotent Creator and the man who fell.[5]

The book continues, in a careful and very lengthy discussion of the early chapters of Genesis, to lay down the principle that, not only are

4 Giberson, K., *Adventist Origins of Young Earth Creationism*, < https://biologos.org/files/modules/giberson-scholarly-essay-1-1.pdf >, accessed 7/8/2019.

5 *The Fundamentals, volume 4*, (Grand Rapids, MI: Baker), p. 274

these early chapters literally, historically true, but that to deny this is to undermine the Gospel. There does not appear to be much room for equivocation there!

Biblical scholars like James Ussher, and Isaac Newton (yes, the Isaac Newton of gravity, light, and calculus fame) used these chrono-genealogies to calculate the age of the Earth. Neither suggested that one had to believe the exact age that they calculated, but their work was to build up a usable timeline of biblical history that would be self-consistent and make sense. Ussher, a former Archbishop of Armagh, at about the time of the Wars of the Three Kingdoms (which included the English Civil War), published his work *The Annals of the World* in 1664, and a version of this work is available, rendered into modern English.[6] I have produced my own humble contribution to the calculation of The Biblical Age of the Earth, in a little book, of that title.[7] My detailed explanations of the calculation are included in this book, while the present work contains just an abbreviated version.

Ussher's work shows that the analysis of the numbers in the chrono-genealogies does not require modern technology. However, the existence of spreadsheets is very useful, to help us see what the

6 Ussher, J. (1654, edited modern edition 2003), *The Annals of the World*, (Green Forest, AR: Master Books).

7 Taylor, P.F. (2013), *The Biblical Age of the Earth*, (Castle Rock, WA: J6D Publications).

numbers actually mean. I used the numbers in Genesis 5 and 11 to create the following spreadsheet[8].

Chrono-Genealogies							
Chapter	Name	Age when son born	Years after son	Age at death	Year of birth	Year of death	
5	Adam	130		930	0	930	
	Seth	105		912	130	1042	
	Enosh	90		905	235	1140	
	Kenan	70		910	325	1235	
	Mahalalel	65		895	395	1290	
	Jared	162		962	460	1422	
	Enoch	65		365	622	987	*
	Methuselah	187		969	687	1656	
	Lamech	182		777	874	1651	
	Noah	503		950	1056	2006	
11	Shem	100	500	600	1559	2159	*
	Arpachshad	35	403	438	1659	2097	
	Shelah	30	403	433	1694	2127	
	Eber	34	430	464	1724	2188	
	Peleg	30	209	239	1758	1997	
	Reu	32	207	239	1788	2027	
	Serug	30	200	230	1820	2050	
	Nahor	29	119	148	1850	1998	
	Terah	130		205	1879	2084	
	Abram	100	75	175	2009	2184	*

8 This spreadsheet, and the charts created from it, is based on figures from the Masoretic text, as used in most of the major English translations. For a discussion of the differences caused by the figures in the LXX, see the discussion towards the end of section 11 02 – the Generations of Shem.

From these figures, it is easy to produce a bar chart.

This chart shows a considerable amount of generational overlap. I will shortly use these charts to illustrate an argument that there are no gaps in the genealogies, but, if for the moment, you will allow me that assumption, then we can draw some interesting information from the charts.

First, we notice that Adam's life overlapped with every Genesis 5 patriarch, up to Lamech. Noah could not have conversed directly with Adam, but his grandfather Methuselah could have done so, and perhaps even Noah's father Lamech. This illustrates that their historical accounts did not require many voices, in order to transfer them to Moses.

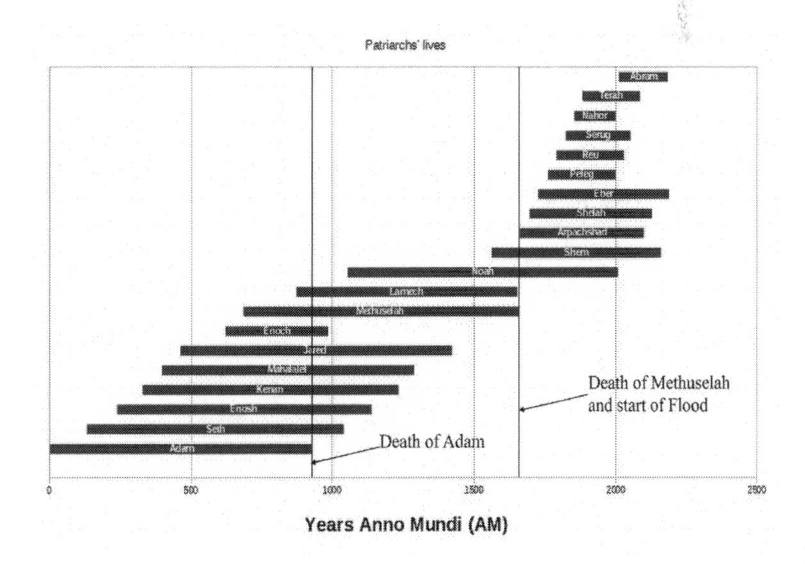

Second, we should notice that Methuselah – the longest-lived patriarch – died the same year that the Flood came. This is a very significant point, and we will examine this later.

Third, we see a decrease in the ages of the patriarchs after the Flood, with some startling overlaps, showing that, for example, Shem, who had been on the Ark, died only 25 years before Abraham, and therefore his life must have overlapped with that of Isaac.

Using data from Genesis 5 and 11, and including data from Genesis 12:4, 12:10, Exodus 12:40, Galatians 3:127, 1 Kings 6:1, 11:42, and Ezekiel 4:4-6, I calculated the year of Creation to be 4003 BC, and the full calculation can be found in my book, referenced above. I also suggested that there are margins for error. For example, every one of the patriarchal births could be out by a year. If Seth's son Enosh was born when Seth was 130, was Enosh born on Seth's 130th birthday, or was he born the day before Seth's 131st birthday? Also, the time I have given to the Israelite captivity in Egypt could be out by 215 years, depending on when you wish to date the start of Israel's 430-year sojourn. So, we could stretch the date of creation back to about 4,300 BC. At the time of writing, that gives an age for the Earth of about 6,320 years. But you will see that it is not possible to extend the age of the Earth even to 7,000 years without doing damage to the text. Those so-called Young Earth Creationists, who state that they believe the

Earth to have been created about 10,000 years ago, have not got that figure from the Bible.

The Age of the Patriarchs

We need to say something about the great ages, to which the pre-Flood patriarchs lived.

It is likely that the aging process would have sped up, as more mutations became present in subsequent generations. However, the Flood came after ten generations, and caused a significant genetic bottleneck. It follows that the number of mutations after the Flood would have increased, and we will discuss this when we reach chapter 11. For now, we can observe that the smallness of the number of mutations would allow for greater ages before the Flood.

In previous times, supporters of the Canopy Theory suggested that greater pressures of oxygen before the Flood would have caused longer life. Such creationists also used to point to air pockets in amber fossils, which contained a greater percentage of oxygen than today's air. However, this can easily be explained by the differences in diffusion rates of nitrogen and oxygen. In any case, increased oxygen concentration, while beneficial temporarily for patients with breathing difficulties, is actually deleterious to the lifespans of most vertebrates. As we have seen, the postulation of climatic differences is not necessary to explain the differences in longevity, which is better explained by mutations and the genetic bottleneck.

Names of the Genesis 5 Patriarchs

Names in the Old Testament are almost always significant. An extra significance to the names of the Genesis 5 patriarchs is due to the fact that the list is repeated, as an unexplained and abrupt list, in 1 Chronicles 1:1-3. The Chronicler's intention is to fix the accounts of the Kings of Israel and Judah into the account of God's purposes throughout history. One commentator has suggested that the Chronicler is preaching a sermon, and his text is the history of the people of Israel.[9]

Seth, as we have seen, means "appointed". Eve refers to Seth's birth with a Hebrew pun, as she did with both Cain and Abel. As an aside, the use of such Hebrew puns suggests – but does not absolutely prove – that the single, primordial language, prior to Babel, could have been Hebrew, or something similar to it.

The chosen line from Adam did not pass through his eldest son, who was Cain. Also, Genesis 5 refers to other sons and daughters, of which there must have been many, in order for Cain to get himself a wife, before the birth of Seth. There is no reason to suppose that any of the

9 Wilcock, M., *The Message of Chronicles*, (Leicester, UK: IVP).

sons listed in the Genesis 5 and 11 genealogies are the first sons. The chosen line could easily have varied in each generation.

Seth's son was Enosh. This name means "mortal". He was the third generation and it is being emphasized that human mortality will not cease naturally, but the problem of mortality is due to sin, and can therefore only be removed by God's actions, for which He was preparing this line of descent.

Enosh's son is Kenan. This name means "sorrow". Kenan's son was Mahalalel. This means "the God who is to be praised". After all, it was probably those of the Sethite line, who began to be those calling on the Name of the Lord in Genesis 4:26.

Mahalalel's son was Jared, which implies descent, or "coming down". Then comes Enoch, whose name means "teacher". His son, Methuselah, means "his death shall bring it about". Lamech means "weary", and Noah means "rest". Lamech pre-deceased his father, dying at the age of 777. In an era, when life expectancy appeared to be about 900 years, and given Lamech's name, perhaps Lamech's comparatively early death was due to a lack of faithfulness on his part. As we will see, there was no guarantee that everyone in the Sethite line would be saved, and indeed most were not.

Therefore, the names of the first ten patriarchs are:

- Man

- Appointed
- Mortal
- Sorrow
- The God who is to be praised
- Coming down
- Teaching
- His death shall bring it
- Weary
- Rest

It is not too far a stretch to suggest that 1 Chronicles 1:1-3 could be rendered in English as "Man is appointed mortal sorrow, but the God who is to be praised shall come down, teaching that His death shall bring the weary rest". Could it be that the names of these patriarchs spell out the Gospel of Jesus Christ? After all, He is the God who is to be praised, who came down, and died to bring us salvation.[10]

The Strange Case of Enoch

At the end of each entry, concerning one of the patriarchs, we read something like "Thus all the days of X were Y years, and he died" -

10 For a fuller breakdown of these names, see McIntosh, A. (2014, 5th edition), *Genesis for Today*, (Leominster, UK: Day One Publications), p.154.

except one. The account of Enoch is very different, so we ought to quote it in full.

> When Enoch had lived 65 years, he fathered Methuselah. Enoch walked with God after he fathered Methuselah 300 years and had other sons and daughters. Thus all the days of Enoch were 365 years. Enoch walked with God, and he was not, for God took him. (Genesis 5:21-24)

The phrase "he was not" is very unusual, but its contrast with the other patriarchs suggests that Enoch did not actually die. In other words, he was translated directly by God - "God took him". We do not know why, or how this happened, but we can make a few surmises, by comparing with other passages.

There is one other character in the Old Testament, who did not die. This was Elijah.

> When they had crossed, Elijah said to Elisha, "Ask what I shall do for you, before I am taken from you." And Elisha said, "Please let there be a double portion of your spirit on me." And he said, "You have asked a hard thing; yet, if you see me as I am being taken from you, it shall be so for you, but if you do not see me, it shall not be so." And as they still went on and talked, behold, chariots of fire and horses of fire separated the two of them. And Elijah went up by a whirlwind into heaven. And Elisha saw it and he cried,

> "My father, my father! The chariots of Israel and its horsemen!" And he saw him no more. Then he took hold of his own clothes and tore them in two pieces. (2 Kings 2:9-12)

Elijah and Enoch were both prophets, and both godly men. However, this is not an explanation as to why they were translated without death. After all, Elisha was a prophet equally as godly, and equally as much used by God as Elijah, yet he grew old and died (2 Kings 13:14-21).

So we have two men, who have been taken bodily into heaven, and who have not died. This next point is a conjecture on my part, and I am not going to hold to it very strongly; perhaps these two could be the two witnesses of Revelation 11, so that they will in fact see death, before Jesus returns. However, this is just a conjecture, and I will not build a theology on this suggestion!

More pertinent is the fact that Enoch was a prophet. Indeed, we have some words of prophecy of Enoch in the Bible. They are found in the epistle of Jude.

> It was also about these that Enoch, the seventh from Adam, prophesied, saying, "Behold, the Lord comes with ten thousands of his holy ones, to execute judgment on all and to convict all the ungodly of all their deeds of ungodliness that they have committed in such an ungodly

> way, and of all the harsh things that ungodly sinners have spoken against him." (Jude 1:14-15)

Jude is referring to blasphemous unbelievers, and is sounding a warning to those who take spiritual issues lightly. Jude has already described such people as following "the way of Cain", so Enoch's prophecy, which seems to foretell the coming of the Flood, after his time, is very pertinent.

It is at this point that we need to exercise a little caution. The same words of Enoch are found in the pseudepigraphal work 1 Enoch. The reference is 1 Enoch 1:9.[11] There are some who see this as justifying the whole of 1 Enoch, and perhaps 2 and 3 Enoch as well. This point will be of great importance, when we discuss Genesis 6. However, Jude's quotation of the words of Enoch could just as easily have come from oral tradition, as Gill suggests.[12] Even if Jude did quote from 1 Enoch, this no more endorses the rest of the unbiblical book than Paul's quotations from Epimenides are an endorsement of the Greek poet's work. What Jude is, in fact, doing, however, is making clear that the particular words of Enoch that he has quoted are genuine, and,

11 Lumpkin, J.B. (editor: 2nd edn 2011), *The Books of Enoch*, (Blountsville, AL: Fifth Estate), p.28.

12 Gill, J. *Exposition of the Old and New Testaments*, < https://www.biblestudytools.com/commentaries/gills-exposition-of-the-bible/jude-1-14.html >, accessed 7/9/2019.

indeed, inspired, because Jude has quoted them under the inspiration of the Holy Spirit.

We have at least established that Enoch was a prophet. This is apt, given the name he gave his son – Methuselah. Methuselah means "his death shall bring it". Since it is likely that the coming of the great Global Judgment known as the Flood was Enoch's theme, his own son's name seems prophetic of the same. If there are no time gaps in Genesis 5, then Methuselah died the very same year that the Flood came. Methuselah's long life ensured that, upon his death, there were no more ancestors of Noah and his sons still alive. That family would have seen their grandfather's death as a fulfillment of prophecy and a warning sign of the impending judgment.

Birth of Shem

Note that in Genesis 5:32 we read "After Noah was 500 years old, Noah fathered Shem, Ham, and Japheth." Although Shem is listed first, he was not the first to be born chronologically, nor were these three boys twins. One of them must have been born when Noah was 500 (1556 AM) – probably Ham – but the other two would be born later. Shem is listed first simply because he is the one we are interested in, because he was in the godly line that would lead to the Messiah. Shem's son Arpachshad was born two years after the Flood[13]. As the

13 Genesis 11:10.

Flood lasted just over a year, Arpachshad was born in 1659 AM, and Shem was 100 years old. Therefore, Shem was born in 1559 AM, when Noah was 503 years old.

Conclusion

Genesis 5 was a written document, available for Moses to include in his work. The genealogy confirms the historical truth of the whole account in Genesis. It shows that God was working His purposes out, as He prepared history ahead of time for the coming of the Messiah.

Genesis 6 - Prelude to the Flood

(Genesis 6)

Why Did the Flood Happen?

As creationists, we understandably, and rightly, spend a lot of time explaining the mechanism and results of the Flood. The worldwide Flood would have had a great many scientific implications, and our acceptance of the fact that the Flood happened causes us to interpret many scientific phenomena in ways very differently from mainstream, evolutionary science. However, this does lead to a danger that we might not concentrate enough on the reasons that the Flood happened. Genesis 6 gives us the clear reasons why the Flood happened, and the arguments are theological.

We must not forget that the reason why the Flood happened was that "The LORD saw that the wickedness of man was great in the earth, and that every intention of the thoughts of his heart was only evil continually." (Genesis 6:5) The Flood was a judgment upon sin; it was a punishment for sin.

This sin was not a new phenomenon. It had begun with the original sin of Adam, but had progressed into worse sin in the actions of Cain and of his descendants. Genesis 6:5 suggests that this sin was not limited to Cain's descendants only, but must have included descendants of Adam and Eve's other children – even descendants of Seth, who were not in the godly Messianic line.

Jesus made clear that the Flood was analogous to the judgment due at His return.

> For as were the days of Noah, so will be the coming of the Son of Man. For as in those days before the flood they were eating and drinking, marrying and giving in marriage, until the day when Noah entered the ark, and they were unaware until the flood came and swept them all away, so will be the coming of the Son of Man. (Matthew 24:37-39)

Life for most people, before the Flood, went on as normal. Jesus said that the people were "unaware". Why were they unaware? Had there been no warning? Indeed, there had been plenty of warning, as we shall see. And there has been plenty of warning about the judgment to come, at Jesus' return. But people were still unaware, because they paid no heed to the warnings. And that is what will happen at Jesus' return – people will pay no heed to the warnings that have been clearly given. That, incidentally, is why the apostle Paul can say that the day of the Lord will be like "a thief in the night", whereas for those of us watching, it should not take us unaware.

> For you yourselves are fully aware that the day of the Lord will come like a thief in the night. While people are saying,

> "There is peace and security," then sudden destruction will come upon them as labor pains come upon a pregnant woman, and they will not escape. But you are not in darkness, brothers, for that day to surprise you like a thief. (1 Thessalonians 5:2-4)

In the time of Noah, the Flood should not have taken people unaware, but it did. And those, who were unaware, were all swept away, while those who trusted God remained and were saved.

So, as we read through the first section of Genesis 6, we need to flesh these thoughts out.

Genesis 6 Follows Genesis 4

The most important exegetical comment we should make at this point is that Genesis 6 follows Genesis 4. Genesis 5 has been an excursus. It has been an important excursus, but that is, nevertheless, what it was. The Genesis 5 genealogy was there to put this whole account into a historical context, and to underline how God was working out His purposes, by producing the Messianic line of descent, even giving a Gospel account through their names.

Genesis 4 showed a generational descent into more and more sin. Even the murderer Cain married only one wife; Lamech needed two, to satisfy his sexual needs. God promised to avenge any harm that might befall Cain, but Lamech threatened and executed his own punishment on those, who he believed had "wronged" him. So the context, prior to Genesis 5, is one of increasing sin. But the context also suggests spiritual awakening among some. After referring to the birth of Seth, we read about people calling upon the Name of the Lord. That narrative is picked up again, at the beginning of Genesis 6, and many of the errors that occur in the exegesis of Genesis 6 happen because of a failure to see that continuation of narrative.

This background is needed, as we tackle the issue raised in Genesis 6:1-2 of the "sons of God" and the "daughters of men", and their problematic marriage unions. Although Adam and Eve had many sons and daughters, Genesis 4 has concentrated first on the contrast between Cain and Abel, and then, following Abel's murder, the contrast is between the descendants of Cain and the descendants of Abel's replacement, Seth. It therefore follows that Genesis 6 is continuing the contrast between the Cainites and the Sethites.

On this basis, the "sons of God" must be the Sethites. We have already seen that Genesis 4 alludes to those who call on the Name of the Lord being Sethites. On the other hand, the Cainites are representative of fallen humanity, so the "daughters of men" are Cainites. The sin being reported in Genesis 6:2 is that of those purporting to be followers of God intermarrying with those who oppose God. This is reminiscent of Paul's words in 2 Corinthians 6:14-15:

> Do not be unequally yoked with unbelievers. For what partnership has righteousness with lawlessness? Or what fellowship has light with darkness? What accord has Christ with Belial? Or what portion does a believer share with an unbeliever?

There will be many objections to the interpretation that I have given, and there are those who hold to a mature and godly view of Genesis who will disagree with me. I will answer these objections in due course. A more common view is that the "sons of God" are fallen angels. They are said to be followers of Satan, who fell at the same time that he did. In that case, the "daughters of men" would simply be any human females. In support of this view, the question could be asked, why does the narrative not refer to "daughters of God" intermarrying with "sons of men"? Surely, Seth had daughters as well as sons? This would, however, be a fallacious question. The pattern would be for men to be marrying women, and therefore, while it would not matter which way around the phrases were given, it makes more sense to be concentrating on the family leaders of the so-called worshipers of God.

Supporters of the "fallen angel" interpretation include many very learned creationists, with whom I agree on almost everything else. The late Henry Morris suggested that "this naturalistic interpretation is so forced and awkward that it seems to do disservice to the doctrine of divine inspiration to suppose that this is really what the writer meant to say".[1]

Jonathan Sarfati has a great deal to say in support of the angelic view, and, to get a balanced view, the reader should study his reasoning. One of his arguments involves referring to King Nebuchadnezzar looking in on the three men, who had been thrown into the fiery furnace.

> But he looked in, and saw that the three men were unharmed, and there was a fourth man "like a son of the gods". This was clearly supernatural, whether this 'man' was an angel or the pre-incarnate Christ. So, the OT and cognate languages use 'sons of God' to mean 'angels' everywhere else. It looks like special pleading to treat Genesis 6 as one exception to this general rule. This should not be done without very good reason.[2]

To this I would point out that we do indeed have very good reason.

There is no doubt that the phrase *bene elohim* (בני־האלהים) refers to angels in some other parts of Scripture. For example, the phrase occurs in Job 1:6 and 2:1. In those two verses, it does seem clear that the context refers to angelic beings, even though Satan is specifically

1 Morris, H.M. (1976), *The Genesis Record*, (Grand Rapids, MI: Baker Book House), p.168.

2 Sarfati, J.D. (2015), *The Genesis Account*, (Powder Springs, GA: Creation Book Publishers), p. 476.

differentiated from them. However, context can often require different meanings for phrases in different places. I would respectfully suggest that the context in Genesis 6 does not require us to believe that "sons of God" means angels, and therefore I would suggest that the Sethite interpretation is more natural. We have already had a precedent for this. The phrase "without form and void" clearly does not mean the same in Genesis 1:2 as it does in Jeremiah 4:23 – the only other place that the phrase appears.

There are pseudepigraphal sources that refer to the angelic interpretation, and these sources would explain why the angelic view was common among many Jewish scholars. For example, in 1 Enoch, we have the following recorded.

> And it came to pass when the children of men had multiplied that in those days were born to them beautiful and fair daughters. And the angels, the sons of heaven, saw and lusted after them, and said to one another: 'Come let us choose us wives from among the children of men and have children with them.'[3]

Similarly, the Book of Jubilees has the following, in Jubilees 5:1-2.

> And it came to pass when the children of men began to multiply on the face of the earth and daughters were born

3 1 Enoch 6:1-3; Lumpkin, J.B. (ed. 2011), *The Books of Enoch*, (Bluntsville, AL: Fifth Estate Publishers), p.30.

> unto them, that the angels of God saw them on a certain year of this jubilee, that they were beautiful to look upon; and they took themselves wives of all whom they chose, and they bare unto them sons and they were giants. And lawlessness increased on the earth and all flesh corrupted its way, alike men and cattle and beasts and birds and everything that walks on the earth - all of them corrupted their ways and their orders, and they began to devour each other, and lawlessness increased on the earth and every imagination of the thoughts of all men was thus evil continually.[4]

We surely do not need to rehearse how one cannot base a theology on writings such as these, however interesting they may be. For example, just a few verses further in 1 Enoch, we read the following.

> And all of them together went and took wives for themselves, each choosing one for himself, and they began to go in to them and to defile themselves with sex with them. (1 Enoch 7:1)

> And the women became pregnant, and they bare large giants, whose height was three thousand cubits. (1 Enoch 7:3)

4 *The Complete Apocrypha, with Enoch, Jasher, and Jubilees*, (2018: Covenant Press), p.244.

If the “sons of God” were angels, then they were already defiled, as followers of Satan. It would have been they who defiled the women, not the other way around. This point is pertinent, because there is no evidence in the book of Job that the “sons of God” were Satanic, because they are clearly differentiated from Satan. And notice also the height of the giants. Three thousand cubits is a clearly unrealistic height for these giants, and most people who accept the angelic theory would suggest that the giants were more the sort of height of Goliath (1 Samuel 17:4), rather than the thousands of cubits mentioned here. If one is going to base a theology on 1 Enoch, then it seems odd to want to pick and choose which elements to accept.

The angelic view is very widespread, and it possible that you have not come across an argument before for the Sethite interpretation of “sons of God”. It will come as a shock, therefore, to find that I am not alone in my opinion.

Bunyan compared Genesis 6:1-2 with the way that Balaam had the children of Israel seduced.

> A snare that was often used in the hand of the devil, to intangle withal the church of God; yea, and doth so usually speed, that it hath often been counted by him as infallible; so that this is the doctrine of his prophet Balaam, and it prevailed, when all the engines of hell beside were prevented. “The people began to commit whoredom with

> the daughters of Moab" (Num 25:1, 2). It may be this child of hell, in this his advice to Balak looked back to the daughters of Cain, and calling to remembrance how of old they intangled the church, advertised him to put the same into practice again (Rev 2:14).[5]

Luther had this to say.

> The true meaning is that Moses calls those men the sons of God, who had the promise of the blessed seed. This is a New Testament phrase and signifies the believers who call God, Father, and whom, God in turn, calls sons. The flood came not because the generation of Cain was corrupt, but because the generation of the righteous who had believed God, had obeyed his Word, and had possessed the true worship, now had lapsed into idolatry, disobedience to parents, sensuality, oppression. Even so the last day shall be hastened, not by the profligacy of Gentile, Turk and Jew, but by the filling of the Church with errors through the pope and fanatical spirits, so that those very ones who occupy the highest place in the Church exercise themselves in sensuality, lust and oppression.[6]

Calvin agrees with this position.

5 Bunyan, J. (ed. Taylor, P.F. 2010), *Commentary on Genesis*, (Castle Rock, WA: J6D Publications), p.161.

6 Luther, M., *Commentary on Genesis, Vol. 2*, Project Gutenberg eBook edition, Kindle location 2437-2442.

> It was, therefore, base ingratitude in the posterity of Seth, to mingle themselves with the children of Cain.[7]

Calvin has this to say about the angelic view:

> That ancient figment, concerning the intercourse of angels with women, is abundantly refuted by its own absurdity; and it is surprising that learned men should formerly have been fascinated by ravings so gross and prodigious.[8]

John Gill, who was the predecessor of Charles Spurgeon at London's Metropolitan Tabernacle, had the following pertinent comments:

> Those "sons of God" were not angels either good or bad, as many have thought, since they are incorporeal beings, and cannot be affected with fleshly lusts, or marry and be given in marriage, or generate and be generated.[9]

This is an important point. Angels are not the same beings as humans, even if they might look similar, even if angels visit the earth in human form. We discussed the impossibility of breeding across *baramins* earlier, and yet these marriages were supposed to produce offspring, an eventuality that would be as impossible as a wolf-lion hybrid.

7 Calvin, J. (ed. 1965), *Geneva Commentary: The Book of Genesis*, (Edinburgh: Banner of Truth), p.238.
8 *ibid.*
9 Gill, J., *Commentary on the Whole Bible*, (text from e-Sword Bible software at Genesis 6:2).

Moreover, Jesus told us that angels "neither marry nor are given in marriage" (Matthew 22:30). Some object that this only refers to angels in heaven, but that is not a relevant distinction, and does not imply that the angels of Matthew 22 are of an altogether different kind to those alleged to be in Genesis 6:2.

So, for the reasons given above, it seems that the most obvious, contextual interpretation of the "sons of God" and "daughters of men" is that these refer to people of the Sethite and Cainite lines.

Nephilim

Commenting on Genesis 6:4 will continue our controversy for a while. It will be worth quoting the verse in full.

> The Nephilim were on the earth in those days, and also afterward, when the sons of God came in to the daughters of man and they bore children to them. These were the mighty men who were of old, the men of renown.

Most versions transliterate the Hebrew word *nephiyl* (נְפִיל), but the KJV and NKJV translate the word as "giants". This is probably because of the LXX, which has γίγαντες (*gigantes*). It is possible, as described below, that the term refers to giantism, but this is not necessarily the case. It certainly could not imply giant humans thousands of cubits tall.

Under the angelic theory of the "sons of God", the Giants are assumed to be the offspring of the angels and women. Now, Genesis 6:4 does indeed refer to the offspring of the "sons of God" and the "daughters of men", and it is certainly theoretically possible that some or all of these could be large, but there is no reason, from the verse, to suggest that the Nephilim and the aforementioned offspring are the same. Indeed, it is probable that the verse is referring to different things, because it states that there were Nephilim "on the earth in those days, *and also afterward*" (emphasis added). Nephilim are mentioned again in Numbers 13:3 by the spies, who went into Canaan. Now, these spies gave a bad report, so it is possible that they were lying, but notice this information regarding the spies, from earlier in Numbers 13.

> And they came to the Valley of Eshcol and cut down from there a branch with a single cluster of grapes, and they carried it on a pole between two of them; they also brought some pomegranates and figs. (Numbers 13:23)

How many clusters of grapes did they cut? Just one. How many men did it take to carry this cluster of grapes? Two. That is one giant cluster of grapes. This is, indeed, a clue as to what the word *Nephilim* refers. It is talking about giantism in general. Here we have evidence of giantism after the Flood, and, of course, Goliath would be in the same category. But, before the Flood it is likely that giantism was more common. This is why, I would suggest, we find fossils, which are often much bigger than their modern counterparts. Here are some examples.

1. A fossil *meganeura* (a type of dragonfly), discovered in Derbyshire, England, in 1975 has a wingspan of over 2 feet! Modern dragonflies can be big – but not that big![10]

2. Fossil horsetails – normally growing about 2 feet tall in your back yard – could be over 60 feet tall.[11]

3. An anecdotal account, from the area near Pennlyn Castle, in Glamorgan, Wales. Marie Trevelyan was told (in 1903) by an elderly woman about the winged serpents that used to fly around the local woods. These winged serpents, which to our ears sound a bit like pterasaurs, were only about the size of large foxes.[12] If this second-hand account is true, then it is consistent with the concept of pre-Flood giantism.

Regardless of whether or not the term *Nephilim* refers to the offspring of the "sons of God" and the "daughters of men", Genesis 6:4 tells us that the actual offspring were "the mighty men who were of old, the

10 Taylor, Paul D.; Lewis, David N. (2007). *Fossil Invertebrates* (repeated ed.). Harvard University Press. p. 160.

11 Encyclopaedia Britannica, < https://www.britannica.com/plant/Calamites >, accessed 7/12/2019.

12 Trevelyan, M. (1909, facsimile 2007), *Folk-lore and Folk Stories of Wales*, (Whitefish, MT: Kessinger).

men of renown". Perhaps some of the characters of legend were these very antediluvian people.

Before leaving this topic, I should comment on the strength of the argument. If you inform me that you believe in the Gap Theory, for example, I will give you strong biblical reasons why you are wrong. However, if you tell me that you belief the "sons of God" were fallen angels, I am not going to come on so strong. While I do not agree with that position, for the reasons given above, there are a lot of very godly, biblical creationists who will differ with me, and argue strongly for the fallen angel position. In the interests of balance, therefore, having read my reasonings above, the fallen angel position is argued impressively by my friend Tim Chaffey, in his book *Fallen.*[13]

Additionally, I have given the Sethite argument, which suggests that the "sons of God" were human. Do not therefore presume that I do not believe anything spiritual was going on. The widespread presence of evil before the Flood strongly suggests that demonic activity was rife. There are some people who take a middle view, suggesting that the "sons of God" were humans, possessed by demons. While I do not think there is general evidence for this position, I am nevertheless quite sure that there were many people dabbling in the occult,

13 Chaffey, T. (2019), *Fallen*, (Risen Books). See < http://midwestapologetics.org/ >, accessed 8/10/2019.

playing with fire and the doctrines of demons (1 Timothy 4:1), just as I am convinced they were in Genesis 11.

Judgment and Grace

It is always the case that God, in His judgment, provides mercy also. So, when He announced that there would be a coming judgment, there is mercy in the fact of the announcement, because it gave time for people to repent. The warning in verse 3 is, however, very pertinent today; "My Spirit shall not abide in man forever". There is a limit to God's patience, with regard to sin, and therefore there will be a limit to the time that this world is here, before the LORD chooses to bring it to an end.

The time that God set, from this prophetic word being given, was to be 120 years. There are some who think that this refers to a new lifespan for human beings, after an era in which a typical lifespan was over 900 years. I think not – the context suggests that this is God's indication to humanity that the antediluvian world was coming to an end, and He gave it 120 years. We do not know how this word from God was delivered. It could have been delivered through a prophet – perhaps the warning was delivered through Methuselah. It is also possible that an audible voice from God could be heard worldwide. But one way or the other, this is a warning to humanity.

In view of this, verses five through seven are sobering.

> The LORD saw that the wickedness of man was great in the earth, and that every intention of the thoughts of his heart was only evil continually. And the LORD regretted that he had made man on the earth, and it grieved him to his heart. So the LORD said, "I will blot out man whom I have created from the face of the land, man and animals and creeping things and birds of the heavens, for I am sorry that I have made them."

It is difficult to get our heads around these verses. How can it be that the Lord had regret? Gill suggests that the Lord's regret is a statement "after the manner of men". This does not change God's plans, or the fat that His outworking of His plans is for the purpose of His Glory. The Hebrew word *nâcham* (נָחַם) suggests a deep sigh, rather than a repentance or regret. This is akin to Jesus weeping at the tomb of Lazarus, even though He knew He was about to raise Lazarus from the dead.

The language of these dreadful verses gives us a measure of the seriousness and the dreadful extent of sin before the Flood. It is difficult for us to imagine how depraved the world had gotten. In our own day, the world is getting worse all the time. In my earlier commentary on Genesis, originally published in 2003, then republished in 2007, I wrote "our own world is probably nearly as bad".[14] In the 16 years since I wrote that sentence, even more dreadful sins have not only become commonplace, but governments have legislated to celebrate those very sins. We are reminded of Paul's words at the end of Romans 1.

> They were filled with all manner of unrighteousness, evil, covetousness, malice. They are full of envy, murder, strife, deceit, maliciousness. They are gossips, slanderers, haters of God, insolent, haughty, boastful, inventors of evil, disobedient to parents, foolish, faithless, heartless, ruthless. Though they know God's righteous decree that those who practice such things deserve to die, they not only do them but give approval to those who practice them. (Romans 1:29-32)

I find the phrase "inventors of evil" a particularly frightening phrase. The New Living Translation renders this phrase as "They invent new ways of sinning". After such a catalog of sins, that people should invent new ways to sin is telling. So is that final phrase – they not only do the things that they know will lead to God's punishment of death upon them, but they "give approval to those who practice them".

Jesus said that the days leading up to His return would be like the days of Noah (Matthew 24:37). I could have looked around the world

14 Taylor, P.F. (2007), *The Six Days of Genesis*, (Green Forest, AR: Master Books), p. 141.

in 2003, and thought that those days were days of great sin. Yet new ways of sinning have been invented since then. In 2003, homosexuality was legal, but in 2019 two men or two women can legally be married, in ceremonies recognized by national governments. In 2003, there were a small number of people, who were known to want to dress as members of the opposite sex. Now, many legislatures have made it illegal to refer to people by pronouns which refer to their biological gender, if they have chosen personally to identify as a member of the opposite sex. Some of the situations we have today we could never have dreamed of in 2003, and they would have been thought of as nonsense in 1977, the year when I became a Christian. Yet I wondered if we were in days like the days of Noah in 2003. It is possible that the Lord may yet tarry, and there may yet be even more grotesque ways in which people invent new ways of sinning.

Following these three painful verses, we come to one of the most beautiful verses in the Old Testament.

> But Noah found favor in the eyes of the LORD. (Genesis 6:8)

Noah, like anyone else, had flaws, as we will see when we discuss the time just after the Flood. But Noah was not saved, because of his innate righteousness. Noah was saved by favor, and favor means grace. Noah was saved by the grace of God.

In that wonderful "hall of faith" passage, in Hebrews 11, we read:

> By faith Noah, being warned by God concerning events as yet unseen, in reverent fear constructed an ark for the saving of his household. By this he condemned the world and became an heir of the righteousness that comes by faith. (Hebrews 11:7)

Noah was indeed a righteous man, but not by his own efforts. His righteousness was that which comes by faith. So Noah was saved by grace, through faith, and this was not his own doing, but rather from God. And that is the way that we are saved today, as we read in Ephesians 2:8-9.

> For by grace you have been saved through faith. And this is not your own doing; it is the gift of God, not a result of works, so that no one may boast.

Genesis 6:8 is so precious to me that, when I am asked to sign books, I will usually quote Genesis 6:8 in my signature.

And with that word, about the efficacy of the Gospel in the antediluvian world, the toledoth of Adam comes to an end.

Noah's Preparations

In this new toledoth, we start to get some detail about Noah, as God prepares him for the catastrophe to come. Noah, we learn, was "a righteous man". We have already seen that this righteousness was the righteousness that comes by faith. Genesis 6:9 further describes Noah as "blameless in his generation". This is an interesting description. It is clearly not possible to describe any human being, after the sin of Adam – except, of course, Jesus Christ – as sinless. But there are some who can be described as blameless, because, despite imperfections, their lives are not characterized by major sins. Blamelessness, therefore, appears to be a realistically possible condition, and is one to which we should aspire. Abraham was commanded to be blameless (Genesis 17:1), and the children of Israel (and, by implication, we also) were commanded to be blameless in Deuteronomy 18:13. The psalms are full of words of longing for blamelessness, though, clearly, David was not always blameless in his actions.

Three men in the Old Testament are described as blameless. The first is Noah. The second is Job (Job 1:8), and the third is Daniel (Daniel 6:22). Indeed, these three men are collectively praised by God, through the prophet Ezekiel.

> "Or if I send a pestilence into that land and pour out my wrath upon it with blood, to cut off from it man and beast, even if Noah, Daniel, and Job were in it, as I live, declares

> the Lord GOD, they would deliver neither son nor daughter. They would deliver but their own lives by their righteousness." (Ezekiel 14:19-20)

This comment shows that no human righteousness can make up for other people's sin. It is only Christ who has that right. But the verse is also commending these three men, as those who were well known for their blamelessness.

Not only was Noah righteous, and blameless, we also read that he "walked with God". This implies a close fellowship with God, as Adam used to have at the beginning in the Garden. Another who was said to walk with God was Enoch, mentioned in Genesis 5. So, we can see that Enoch's translation was not an inevitable reward for godliness, because, although Enoch clearly was a godly man, it is certain that Noah was at least equally as godly, if not more so. God had His own reasons of His Sovereign Will for translating Enoch, while giving Noah a boat-building Messiah-like task here on Earth.

As mentioned in the previous chapter, Noah had three sons. All of these were saved in the Ark. It does not, however, tell us that these sons were righteous, blameless, or that they walked with God. Nor does it say anything about Noah's wife, or the wives of the sons. Yet all eight were saved from the Flood. It is my conjecture that all of these at least assented to faithfulness in God, but others have made a case for one or more of the sons and / or wives being apostate. Some legends suggest, for example, that Naamah – the daughter of the Cainite Lamech – was Noah's wife, or possibly Ham's wife. Some of these then go on to suggest that everything bad in the post-Flood world proceeded from Naamah. I think this is unfair, and does not take into account that the original sin, into which all human beings are born, renders all post-Flood people, as pre-Flood people, capable of the most grotesque evil. In my book, *Don't Miss the Boat*, I included four fictional short stories, one each about Naamah and her three brothers. These were designed to give an impression of what life was like before the Flood. In Naamah's story, I imagined her marrying Ham, but that she did this, after repenting and trusting in the Lord. I did this deliberately, in spite of what I have written about the sons of God not marrying the daughters of men. If Naamah was truly saved, then she ceased to be a daughter of man. A biblical example of this would be that the Israelites had been forbidden from marrying Moabites. In Deuteronomy 7:2-5, the Israelites are forbidden from intermarrying with any of the cursed people groups, whom they were displacing in the Promised Land. Then, in Deuteronomy 23:3, we find there is a special injunction against the Ammonites and the Moabites. And yet, Ruth the Moabitess marries an Israelite. Indeed, Boaz was part of the Messianic line of descent, and therefore Ruth was an ancestor of Jesus! The key to the seeming contradiction, of course, is found in Ruth 1:16-17:

> But Ruth said, "Do not urge me to leave you or to return from following you. For where you go I will go, and where you lodge I will lodge. Your people shall be my people, and your God my God. Where you die I will die, and there will I be buried. May the LORD do so to me and more also if anything but death parts me from you."

If Naamah were a convert, and married Ham, there would be no theological problem. Note that I am getting my theology here from the book of Ruth, which is in the Bible, not from my conjecture about Naamah, which is not, and which was only meant to be a fun short story. If you have a problem with my conjecture on a daughter of Cain being saved, you should note that most of the sons of God – the Sethites – were also destroyed in the Flood, so were not considered righteous people of faith. And that latter point is clearly taught in the Bible; Genesis 5:7: "Seth lived after he fathered Enosh 807 years **and had other sons and daughters**." (emphasis added).

Genesis 6:11-13 is a recapitulation of Genesis 6:5-7. Remember that the chapter divisions are not inspired, although they are helpful, and were added to Bible editions much later. The real division of text is that found at Genesis 6:9, with the beginning of the new toledoth. It might be worth pausing to make a comment aside at this particular recapitulation, however. We discussed in chapter 2 part 2 ("In the Garden") about the JEPD theory, which suggests that these early portions of Genesis are compiled from two documents – J, the Yahwist writer, and E, the Elohist writer. So advocates of that theory see this recapitulation as support for their idea, since Genesis 6:5-7 uses the word LORD (*yahweh*), while Genesis 6:11-13 uses God (*Elohim*). As we explained before, there is no substance to this idea, because LORD and God are used interchangeably, but it is likely that discussions on this passage may bring that error to the fore.

So God tells Noah about the destruction to come. He does not give Noah the opportunity to discuss the issue, and nor does Noah seek this. However, God does now reveal to Noah the work of salvation, which He is going to bring about, through Noah and the Ark, which He was to commission from him.

Blueprint for the Ark

In Genesis 6:14-17, God gives Noah some instructions on how to make the Ark. We sometimes wish that we had more information about the Ark, but we can also comment that it would have been possible to have considerably less!

The first point to consider here might well be the meaning of the word Ark. The Hebrew word is *têbâh* (תבה), and it seems to refer to a box or vessel, in which to store something. There is one other object in the Old Testament, to which the word *têbâh* is applied. The basket, into which the baby Moses was placed by his mother was also a *têbâh.* The Ark of the Covenant, on the other hand, is a different word in Hebrew (*ârôn* (אָרֹן)), though the word used in the LXX is the same for Noah's Ark, Moses's basket and the Ark of the Covenant – namely *kibōtos* (κιβωτός), which means box.

There now follows a brief outline of the design of the Ark. However, a more detailed article on the design of the Ark can be found in my book *Don't Miss the Boat*[15] – or, better still, John Woodmorappe has written a whole book on the subject, called *Noah's Ark: A Feasibility Study*[16].

We are told that the Ark was to be made of gopher wood. Unfortunately, we are not told what gopher wood is. Some traditions suggest it could be cedar. It is also quite possible that it is a kind of wood, from a kind of tree that does not exist today. We are told, however, that there were to be rooms on the Ark. The word used can also be translated as "nests". It is likely that we are referring to pens for the animals. One objection to the truthfulness of the account of the Ark is the idea that the lions would have eaten the antelopes. We do not know whether or not animals such as big cats had yet

15 Taylor, P.F. (2013), *Don't Miss the Boat*, (Green Forest, AR: Master Books), pp.115-124.
16 Woodmorappe, J. (2003), *Noah's Ark: A Feasibility Study*, (Dallas: ICR).

degenerated into being full carnivores, but even if they had, it is clear that they would have been kept separate from one another.

It is also interesting that Noah was instructed to cover the Ark inside and outside with pitch. What would this pitch have been? We will see, in a moment, that there is no reason to equate the Ark's pitch with the modern bituminous substance of that name. However, it is likely that the pitch covering was designed to waterproof the Ark, which is what a bituminous covering would do.

Today's pitch is a heavy oil fraction – a by-product of refining petroleum oil. Petroleum oil is classified as a fossil fuel, and it would seem, therefore, that its formation would have required the decomposition and pressurization of dead organic material, during the Flood. This pitch, however, was applied to the Ark before the Flood, and the Hebrew word implies it had to be waterproof, but not necessarily an oil fraction.

The word translated here as "pitch" is *kâphar* (רפכ). The literal meaning of this word is "covering". That is why this material could be any sort of waterproof covering. The interesting fact to note here is that the word *kâphar* appears many times in the Old Testament, but it is never again translated as "pitch". In most other occurrences, it is translated as "atonement"! We see this in Leviticus 17:11.

> For the life of the flesh is in the blood, and I have given it for you on the altar to make atonement for your souls, for it is the blood that makes atonement (*kâphar*) by the life. (Leviticus 17:11)

Noah and his family were protected against the watery judgment of God, by the atonement of pitch. We are protected against the fiery judgment of God to come, if we are under the covering of the atoning blood of Jesus Christ.

The dimensions of the Ark were to be 300 cubits by 50 cubits by 30 cubits. Now a cubit is literally the distance from your elbow to the tip of your middle finger. However, everyone has a different size arm. There were a number of different standard cubits in the ancient world. Answers in Genesis have researched a number of sizes, ranging from the Hebrew short cubit of 17.5 inches to the Egyptian long cubit of 20.6 inches.[17] Using these two extremes, the Ark would have been a minimum of 440 x 74 x 44 feet, and a maximum of 515 x 86 x 51.5 feet. Even with the minimum measurements, this was clearly a very big boat – between 1¼ and 1½ x the length of a football pitch. A football (soccer) pitch is pretty much the same length as an American football field.

17 Hodge, B. (2007), *How Long Was the Original Cubit?*, < https://answersingenesis.org/noahs-ark/how-long-was-the-original-cubit/ >, accessed 7/15/2019.

The size of the Ark leads to a number of controversies, which we must briefly address – though Woodmorappe's book addresses these in detail, as does a newer book, by Tim Chaffey and Laura Welch.[18] To look at just two problems: first, how could such a large ship be built entirely of wood? Chaffey and Welch quote work by Tim Lovett, which shows that early shipbuilders (who must have been post-Flood) could build ships of a similar size, using wooden joints and overlaps. The floor space would have been considerable. Given that there were three decks, the floor space must have been around 4 million cubic feet.

Having hinted that the Ark was too large, other critics suggest that it was too small. They do not understand how Noah could have fitted all the millions of species on the ark. The answer to this issue is that he didn't. As we discussed earlier, the basic animal units here were the created kinds (baramins). Chaffey and Welch, utilizing research led by Dr. Jean Lightner, suggest that there could have been fewer than 7,000 animals on boar the Ark.[19] (Woodmorappe had previously suggested 16,000 – a figure which also works). This would lead to us estimating that each animal would have had a space of 14' x 14', even if they were all restricted to just one of the three decks, leaving another deck for food, and another as plenty of space for the eight humans. Morris and

18 Chaffey, T. and Welch, L. (2016), *Inside the Ark: Why It Worked*, (Green Forest, AR: Master Books).
19 *ibid, p.20.*

Whitcomb had, at one time, suggested that the average size of the animals on the Ark was about that of a sheep. Newer figures from Woodmorappe, and from Chaffey and Welch, suggest that this is, if anything, an over-estimate of size, even if all animals aboard the Ark were adults. In practice, it is likely that many of the animals would have been smaller, young animals, to maximize the chance of them breeding after the Flood.

We then read that Noah was to make a *window*. Some versions, such as the ESV, refer to a roof, instead of a window. In fact, the passage does not use the usual word for "window". Instead, it uses a word usually translated as "noon". In other words, this was a noon light, rather than a window, and this term refers to a protected opening along the roof of the Ark. It is also worth noting at this point that there was only one door on the Ark. We will comment again on this door in our next section.

After reminding Noah that He was going to "destroy all flesh" in the Flood, God promised to make a covenant with Noah after the Flood, and that Noah, his wife, his three sons, and their wives would be saved. This is such an important development, because there is no previous mention of God making a covenant with anyone (other than the eternal covenant made in Eternity Past among the persons of the Trinity). We will discuss this covenant with Noah, when we comment on Genesis 9.

God's final command in this chapter were that Noah would be taking representatives of every kind of land animal and bird. This is explained in more detail in chapter seven. Noah was also required to stock the Ark with "every sort of food that is eaten" for his family, and for the animals. So what an important verse we have at the end of Genesis 6.

> Noah did this; he did all that God commanded him. (Genesis 6:22)

Noah – a man, who was saved by grace, through faith, was obedient to God.

Conclusion

In this section, we have discussed the reason why the Flood happened; it was God's judgment on a wholly wicked world of people. We recorded the strange case of the "sons of God" and the "daughters of men", noting that most evangelical commentators through the ages have suggested that these were the Sethites and the Cainites, rather than representing intermarriage between humans and angels.

> We also saw that Noah was commissioned to be a savior (small s) for the world, and we discussed God's instructions to Noah about the building of the Ark.

Genesis 7 - The Flood Begins

(Genesis 7)

Was there Really a Flood?

It will not have escaped your notice that I treat the events of Genesis as actual historical events. I commented generally on my reasons for this in Chapter 1 Part 1 (Approaching Genesis), but it might be appropriate to make some specific points about the historicity of the Flood. These will be brief comments, because I have written a whole book, previously, on the exegesis, historicity, and science of the worldwide flood, called *Don't Miss the Boat*.[1] If there are further details that you need on the subject, then I would recommend your reading that book. It would also be useful, at this point, to give you a brief mini-bibliography of books specifically about the Flood. All these titles are included in the bibliography at the end of the book, but it will be useful to have a brief reference list now.

- **Grappling with the Chronology of the Genesis Flood,** Steven Boyd and Andrew Snelling (editors)
- **Inside Noah's Ark**, Tim Chaffey and Laura Welch (editors)
- **Global Flood Pocket Guide**, Ken Ham et al

1 Taylor, P.F. (2013), *Don't Miss the Boat*, (Green Forest, AR: Master Books).

- **A Flood of Evidence**, Ken Ham and Bodie Hodge (editors)
- **The Genesis Flood (50th Anniversary Edn)**, John Whitcomb and Henry Morris
- **How Noah's Flood Shaped our World**, Michael Oard and John K Reed
- **Earth's Catastrophic Past**, Andrew Snelling
- **Don't Miss the Boat**, Paul Taylor
- **Noah's Ark: A Feasibility Study**, John Woodmorappe

A worldwide Flood would leave a great deal of evidence behind, in the form of fossils in sedimentary rock. But theistic evolutionary commentators, believing evolution as they do, have already adopted a different explanation for how they believe fossils came about. Therefore, they have to suggest that the Flood was not global in extent, even if they acknowledge that there really was such an event.

For example, John Walton and Tremper Longman III, whose works are often cited by BioLogos (the "evangelical" evolutionary organization) have written a book, *The Lost World of the Flood*, which typifies the way that neo-conservative theologians misuse the Bible.[2] Notice how they wriggle from presenting the obvious, plain reading of the text, and

2 Longman III, T, and Walton, J.H. (2018), *The Lost World of the Flood*, (Downers Grove, IL: IVP Academic).

their reasons for doing so. For example, on page 49, after a discussion about the key points concerning the nature of the Flood, they conclude:

> Thus, it is our conclusion that Genesis 6– 8 describes a worldwide, not a local flood. This conclusion leaves us with what at first read, at least from our twenty-first-century Western perspective, is an error or at least a contradiction. The Bible describes a worldwide flood, yet absolutely no geological evidence supports a worldwide flood. While some people believe that this means that science must be wrong if the Bible is right, we believe that if science is right, then it leads us to a better interpretation of the biblical material, the interpretation that gets us to the original intent of the biblical author.[3]

The authors can do nothing better than conclude that Genesis 6-8 is meant to describe a worldwide Flood. But they cannot accept that this is correct, because this leads to the conclusion that "science must be wrong". Their error is to conflate evolutionary timescales with actual science. Nothing about the biblical account of the Flood opposes what we study in science about hydrodynamics, or about meteorology. It is true that the biblical account is not compatible with an evolutionary timescale, but the authors are incorrect in assuming that these timescales are definitively proven. In fact, as we know from numerous

3 *ibid*, p.49.

other studies, there are many subjective assumptions used in the calculation of age, not the least of which is the assumption that the rates of processes used in age calculations have remained constant. For a refutation of that fallacious position, one can consult the book *Thousands... Not Billions*, especially the first chapter.[4] The uniformitarian assumption is also refuted in the Bible.

> [Know] this first of all, that scoffers will come in the last days with scoffing, following their own sinful desires. They will say, "Where is the promise of his coming? For ever since the fathers fell asleep, all things are continuing as they were from the beginning of creation." For they deliberately overlook this fact, that the heavens existed long ago, and the earth was formed out of water and through water by the word of God, and that by means of these the world that then existed was deluged with water and perished. But by the same word the heavens and earth that now exist are stored up for fire, being kept until the day of judgment and destruction of the ungodly. (2 Peter 3:3-7)

To summarize the apostle – the reason people think that rates of processes have remained unchanged since the beginning is because such scoffers deliberately forget the Creation and the Flood. When those are factored into the equation, everything becomes clear.

4 DeYoung, D. (2005), *Thousands... Not Billions*, (Green Forest, AR: Master Books).

An application of this to Longman and Walton is this. In the passage quoted above, they opine "The Bible describes a worldwide flood, yet absolutely no geological evidence supports a worldwide flood." In fact, there is massive geological evidence for the Flood. Almost every fossil that exists is evidence for the Flood. Of course, evidence means little by itself. Evidence is always interpreted according to one's worldview. Longman and Walton see no evidence of the Flood, because they have placed evolutionary theory as superior to the Bible. They say that they have not done so. They claim that the Bible is their supreme authority. Yet this very statement proves otherwise. There was, after all, a time when historians would not believe there was a real people group called the Hittites, even though they were mentioned in the Bible, because there was no "independent" evidence. We need to stop thinking that external "evidence" trumps biblical evidence. It did not do so in the case of the existence of the Hittites, and it should not do so in our acceptance of the fact of the Flood.

This impasse between what one thinks one knows about science and what the Bible says is of great importance. We should emphasize it again, with another quote, from an uncredited writer on the BioLogos website. This writer emphatically states:

> The scientific and historical evidence is now clear: there has never been a global flood that covered the entire

> earth, nor do all modern animals and humans descend from the passengers of a single vessel.[5]

The article's author requires us to accept that, if we believe Scripture to be inspired, we must adjust our interpretation of Scripture to conform to what this "book of nature" has revealed. In fact, the correct approach is to adjust our understanding of science to the truthful objective fact of Scripture. Science means knowledge, but it is not perfect, or without error. The Bible **is** without error.

Seven Days until the Flood

At the beginning of chapter seven, we find that God waited another seven days, after Noah was aboard the Ark. This was not because God was waiting to see if anyone else turned up. We need to remember that the Flood was not an accident, nor was it a fit of Divine pique. The Flood, like the cross, was planned in eternity past. Again, God did not suddenly look on the world one day, and think "This has turned out worse than I thought; I had better start again". Our belief in the Sovereignty of God leads us to see that He was working His purposes out through the destruction of the Flood, and the salvation achieved by Noah and the Ark.

5 *How should we interpret the Genesis flood account?*, < https://biologos.org/common-questions/how-should-we-interpret-the-genesis-flood-account >, accessed 7/19/2019.

So Genesis 7 starts with Noah and his family being ordered on to the Ark. God again reminds us that Noah was righteous, and, as we have discussed, this righteousness was by faith.

Then we get clarification of the sort of animals that are to go on the Ark. In Genesis 6:19, we have been reminded that the animals will be taken on the Ark according to their "kind" - this is the *created kind*, or *baramin*, discussed earlier. Noah does not need to take examples of every kind. He is given a number of criteria. The kinds are to include all kinds of birds, or, in fact, fowl (*oph*), as discussed earlier. *Oph* includes other flying creatures, such as bats, and, probably, pterosaurs. He was also to include animals (cattle) and creeping things. This suggests various land vertebrates. The animals should be in pairs – one male and one female.

In Genesis 7, God further requires that there should be seven pairs of clean animals. The number seven pairs is probably to be preferred to seven, though the numbering is unclear, because it is already suggested that we are considering the animals in pairs. That these animals should be clean is an interesting concept. The cleanness or otherwise of animals is a Levitical concept. Is it possible that God had given Noah advance knowledge of which animals were to be considered clean and unclean under the Mosaic covenant? It is impossible to tell, but I would suggest that it is likely, especially given that the extra animals were to be reserved for sacrifice after the

Flood. There were also to be seven each of the *oph* or "birds". Of other land vertebrates there was to be just one pair. The fact that the animals would be vertebrates is seen by another restriction, placed in Genesis 7:15, that these animals were to have the "breath of life". As we saw in the last section, this would amount to a total of less than 7,000 animals, who average size was quite a bit less than that of a sheep.[6]

Again, we are reminded that Noah did as he was commanded, because he was a righteous man. We are also reminded that Noah's family as with him – wife, three sons, and their wives.

So, with everything ready, why did God wait seven days? God is patient and longsuffering. And He is perfect in His judgments. There was to be no excuse, from those who were taken away by the Flood – no excuse that they did not know what was about to happen, or that they had insufficient time to prepare.

The Initiation of the Flood

I have described in detail how most creationists believe the Flood began in my book *Don't Miss the Boat*. That book outlines a flood model known as Catastrophic Plate Tectonics (CPT). CPT has been defined over many years by a number of leading creationist geologists, and all

6 Chaffey, T. and Welch, L. (2016), *Inside the Ark: Why It Worked*, (Green Forest, AR: Master Books), p.20.

their views were distilled into one major work by Dr. Andrew Snelling (who was one of the designers of CPT) in his monumental work *Earth's Catastrophic Past*. Although this appears to me to be the best model available, it is not the only one. In recent years, Michael Oard and John K Reed have been working on a model called Vertical Impact Tectonics, and some of this is outlined in their book *How Noah's Flood Shaped our World*. Perhaps a future edition of this book will contain more information on VIT, but, at the moment, CPT is the only working model more thoroughly explained. We should, at this point, note that we hold to Scripture firmly, but to our models much less firmly. Scripture will not change, but our models do. For example, we explained in chapter 1 part 6 why we do not hold to the Vapor Canopy model, which used to be the main way of explaining the initiation of the Flood. Additionally, other models, such as the hydroplate model[7], have proven less than robust under peer review. So, at the time of writing, CPT is by far the most successful model.

The initiation of the Flood is described in Genesis 7:11-12.

> In the six hundredth year of Noah's life, in the second month, on the seventeenth day of the month, on that day all the **fountains of the great deep** burst forth, and the

7 If you wish to read Dr. Brown's hydroplate model, he described it in Brown, W. (2008, 8th edition), *In the Beginning: Compelling Evidence for Creation and the Flood*, Center for Scientific Creation. To read a number of peer-reviewed critiques of his model, search for "hydroplate" at answersingenesis.org.

> **windows of the heavens** were opened. And **rain fell upon the earth** forty days and forty nights. (Emphasis added)

We can highlight three initiation events; the fountains of the great deep, the windows of heaven, and the rain for forty days and forty nights.

We can imagine that the word fountains implies water being thrown into the atmosphere. However, the great deep suggests the bottom of the pre-Flood ocean. The bursting forth suggests cracks opening in the crust. The heat of the magma would flash some water, and there would be more highly pressurized water coming up from the Earth's mantle. This superheated water would all have been thrown high into the air at supersonic speed. When it came down, it would be a deluge – as if the windows of the heavens were opened! Obviously, the water would fall in the form of rain. As discussed before, we do not know whether or not this was the first time the Earth had experienced rain, but I suspect not.

In terms of chronology, we have two statements. First, Noah was 600 years old when the Flood began, and second, the flood began on the 17th day of the second month. This calendar date of 2-17 is probably calculated against the calendar of the time, not with respect to Noah's date of birth.

Today, the first month in the Jewish calendar is in the Spring, because it relates to the date of the Passover. However, at the Passover, it would appear that God changed which month was to be the first month of the year (Exodus 12:2). It is likely, therefore, that the start of the Flood was to be in the Fall, and would be related to the old civil year, which began with the Fall Equinox – about September 21st.

If the Flood began on 2-17, then Noah and his family entered the Ark on 2-10. And God closed the door on them. There was only one door, and it was not for Noah to close the door. God did this, because it is God who saves. This event reminds us that Jesus said "I am the door. If anyone enters by me, he will be saved and will go in and out and find pasture." (John 10:9)

The duration of the Flood appears, at first, to be easy to calculate. I created the following table in a spreadsheet, by adding and subtracting the relevant quantities, and assuming that every month in this Hebrew calendar was exactly 30 days long.

Flood Chronology			
Event	**Time (days)**	**Progress**	**Reference**
Entering the Ark	0	0	7:1
Flood starts, fountains of the great deep, windows of heaven, rain	7	7	7:11
Rain stopped	40	47	7:12
Flood prevailed – Ark rests in Ararat	110	157	8:3
Mountain tops	74	231	8:5
Noah opens window, sends raven, then dove	40	271	8:6
Dove sent second time	7	278	8:10
Dove sent third time	7	285	8:12
Noah removes covering	36	321	8:13
Disembark	56	377	8:14
Total – not including initial 7 days	**370**		

However, it is important to note that there are possible variations in this chronology, based on varying interpretations of the Hebrew letters used for numbers (as Hebrew does not actually have numerals), and a number of other factors. My table is therefore likely to be simplistic, and one should refer to the book *Grappling with the Chronology of the Genesis Flood* to research these points better.[8]

8 Boyd, S. and Snelling, A.A. (2014), *Grappling with the Chronology of the Genesis Flood*, (Green Forest, AR: Master Books).

The Waters Prevailed

If there is a repetition of something in Scripture, we can assume that there is an emphasis being placed on it. As Moses was writing this account, under the inspiration of the Holy Spirit, he did not have bold emphasis fonts at his disposal, nor could he underline sentences. Repetition achieves the same end.

So, from Genesis 7:17-24, the phrase “the waters prevailed” appears four times. The very repetition of the phrase gives the lie to the idea that this was a local flood. If it had been a local flood, then there would have been little need to rescue animals, and definitely no need to rescue the birds, who could have flown away to a dryer area.

In verse 17, we read that the waters rose, and the Ark was carried high. Then we have the repeated phrase that the waters prevailed. This tells us that the Flood was a deliberate act by God, which He sustained, and it tells us that the Flood would have had an enormous effect on the topography of the land below the waters.

During this period, there would have been great movement of continents. The splitting open of the fountains of the great deep would be the beginning of the separation of the Earth’s crust into tectonic plates, which, today, are sliding around very, very slowly indeed. During the early days of the Flood, however, we assume that they must have been moving fast. Some plates would have slid under others, in a process known as subduction. The CPT model suggests that this subduction would have happened at a runaway rate. Waters rising, receding, and rising further on Rodinia (the pre-Flood super-continent) would have laid down beds of marine fossils, and the collision of tectonic plates, under the prevailing waters, would have thrown up mountain ranges. Creation geologists have done a great deal of work, tracking where these fossils and mountains were made, and then split up again, and even suggest that there must have been another temporary submerged super-continent called Pangaea during the Flood, as plates crashed together, then split apart again. My brief, and simplistic, explanation of CPT might, wrongly, lead you to believe that this is a simple mechanism. However, CPT has been worked on over a couple of decades, by very qualified and brilliant scientists, and the published detail of explanations is remarkable. Suffice to say here that CPT is a much better, and more detailed explanation of geological features around the world than long-age evolutionary geology.

Let me just give you one case study, based on something I talk about at the Mount St Helens Creation Center. Mount St Helens is part of the

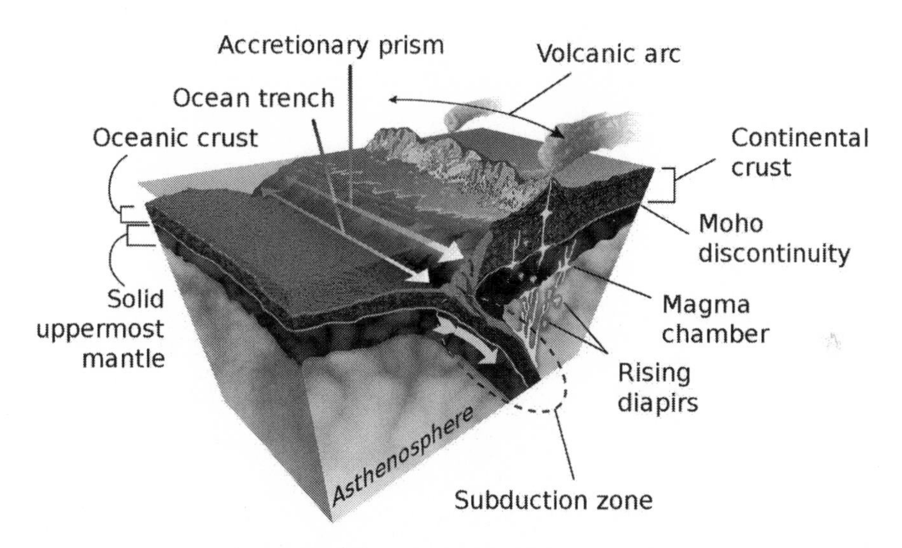

Cascade Range of mountains, which includes a number of other active volcanoes. This range, in turn, is part of the famous "Ring of Fire" around the Pacific Ocean. Off the coast of the states of Washington and Oregon, there is a small tectonic plate, called the Juan de Fuca plate. This is being subducted under the North American plate. The friction melts rock at the base of the North American plate, and the resulting magma, and superheated water, can make its way upwards, thrusting up the Cascade Range, and occasionally causing new eruptions. If this subduction had taken millions of years, the magma would have cooled and solidified by now. CPT suggests that the subduction was originally at a runaway rate, generating lots of heat, and this happened only about 4,400 years ago, at the time of the Flood. The deep-time explanations do not make as much sense.

Another fascinating local feature in the Pacific Northwest is the

Columbia Gorge. There is a great deal I could say about this, but the only issue I will raise here is the fact that the Columbia River bisects the Cascade Range of mountains, in what is known as a water gap. Water gaps make little sense for evolutionary geologists. Why would a river attempt to erode through mountains? Surely, the path of least resistance would take its flow around the range. Deep-time geologists have a number of explanations. One of their major explanations is that the river existed before the range was thrown up, and that the rising of the range was at the same rate as the river eroded the new land height. This sounds far too convenient an explanation! As creationists, we can see that such water gaps are easy to explain by rapid erosion, caused by large volumes of water draining off the continent at the end of the Flood. The river was then able to make its way through this new point of least resistance.

Some evolutionists might point to the Missoula Flood (or, as they believe, a range of Missoula Floods) rushing through the range. However, even most evolutionists would accept that the Columbia River water gap was there before the Missoula Flood, which simply carved the existing valley into a gorge.

Having mentioned the Missoula Flood, that event had huge implications for Eastern Washington state. Water from the worldwide Flood was retained by post-Flood glaciation in the area of Missoula, Montana. As the glaciers retreated, eventually the water broke through, flooding West through Idaho, and into Washington, where it washed southwards, forming the huge flat-bottomed gorges known as coulees. In the Grand Coulee, there is a huge receding waterfall, about four times the size of Niagara, but which has no water going over it today. Hence it is called the Dry Falls. It is likely that this feature was carved in just a few days. Eventually, the Missoula floodwater funneled into the Columbia Valley, and carved out the Columbia Gorge.

These are features seen in just one region of one country. The detail that we can describe, of features caused by the worldwide Flood, is immense – I have not even scratched the surface of what I could tell you about the Pacific Northwest! The Genesis Flood affected everything in the world, and, wherever you live, there is almost always something nearby, which is best explained by the account of that global event.

In verses 19 and 20, we read that all the mountains and hills were covered by the water. There are those who object that the Floodwater could not have been high enough to cover Everest. Of course, Everest did not exist before the Flood. The pre-Flood mountains were lower and the pre-Flood ocean trenches less deep than after the Flood. These features were altered by the conclusion of the Flood.

> The mountains rose, the valleys sank down to the place that you appointed for them. You set a boundary that they may not pass, so that they might not again cover the earth. (Psalms 104:8-9)

It is a completely biblical exercise to look at the scientific implications of what the Scripture says, but to include much more here would take away from the exegetical message, on which we must concentrate. That is that God achieved what He set out to do with the Flood. Everything died. Only Noah and his family were left.

Conclusion

In this section on Genesis 7, we looked at a range of books, that can help with detail about the Flood. Then we looked at reasons why we accept that the Flood was a worldwide event. We discussed details about the animals taken on to the Ark, and the details of how the Flood began. After a brief look at the Flood Chronology, we introduced Catastrophic Plate Tectonics (CPT), and saw some of the implications of that model to the Pacific Northwest of the United States – the area where I live and work.

Genesis 8 - The Flood Abates

(Genesis 8)

God Remembered Noah

How easy it is to read our failings into what we learn about God. I remember our Religious Education teacher explaining to us that God now changed His mind again, and took away the waters of the Flood.

God had never forgotten Noah. The fact that we read that God remembered Noah is simply a word for our encouragement. God is in control, because He is Sovereign. He planned that He would bring the Flood, and He planned that He would remove it again. He promised Noah that He would save Him through the Flood, and now, in His good time, He chose to fulfill that promise. It is also noteworthy that God was not just remembering Noah. He was also remembering all the animals, which were on board the Ark. It was His plan to repopulate the Earth, and make it a place of life again.

As with the events that began the Flood, we see a combination of processes, bringing the Flood to an end. Some of these are scientifically understandable. Others, though still understandable scientifically, required God's direct, as opposed to indirect, intervention. Thus, we see that God sent a wind across the surface of the Earth, and this wind was probably substantial, because it had enough power to make the waters subside. However, the mechanisms of the "Fountains of the Great Deep" and "the Windows of Heaven" were stopped directly by God. Therefore, there was no new water flooding the Earth, and therefore the rain was restrained, but there are many scientifically understandable ways in which the waters could have subsided.

The Pattern of the Flood

Genesis 8:3 informs us that the waters began to abate "at the end of 150 days". The chronological pattern of the events of the Flood is not easy to map out. But we have a certain number of clues, which help us to make an initial draft of the timescale. We can tie this together with the various stages of the Flood. Creation Geologist Dr. Tas Walker has put this all together in his Biblical Geologic Model. The model simply provides a framework for understanding what must have been happening at different stages during the Flood.

Walker's model recognizes that most of the world's sedimentary rocks, and hence most of the world's fossils, were formed during the Flood. Genesis 8:1-3 neatly points out the division between the Inundatory and Recessive stages of the Flood. These stages are further subdvided as follows:

- Inundatory
    - Eruptive

    - Ascending
    - Zenithic
- Recessive
    - Abative
    - Dispersive

Walker illustrates the model with these two diagrams and a table, all of which are reproduced from his Biblical Geology website.[1]

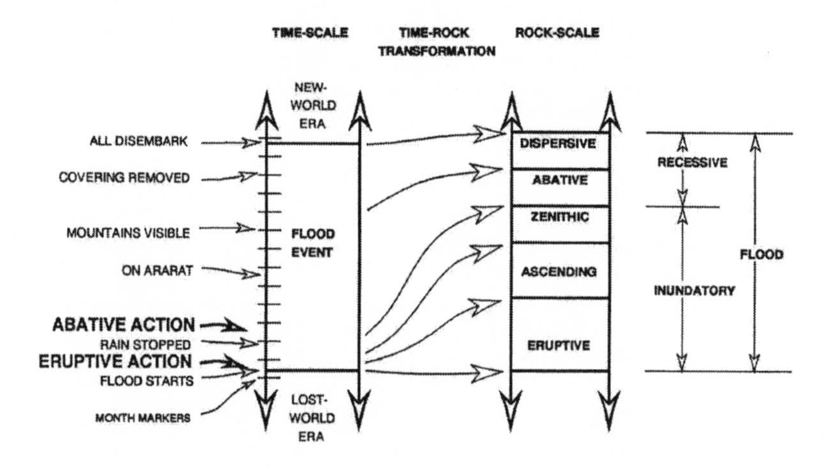

1 Walker, T. (1994), *A Biblical Geology Model*, < http://biblicalgeology.net/Model/A-biblical-geological-model-ICC-paper.html >, accessed 8/6/2019.

Yr	Mth	Day	Event	Duration Days	Genesis Reference
600	2	10	Noah entered the ark		7:7,10,11
600	2	17	Heavens and earth opened		7:11
600	3	27	Rain stopped	40	7:12
600	7	17	Ark rested on Ararat	110	8:3,4
600	10	1	Tops of mountains seen	74	8:5
600	11	10	Raven - did not return	40	8:6,7
600	11	18	Dove - returned	7	8:8
600	11	25	Dove - returned with leaf	7	8:10,11
600	12	2	Dove - did not return	7	8:12
601	1	1	Covering removed - ground dry	29	8:13
601	2	27	Everyone disembarked	56	8:14-16
			Total Duration of the Flood	370	

Chronology of the Flood Event

Eruptive, ascending, and zenithic phases are what must have occurred in Genesis 7. So the abative and dispersive phases occurred in Genesis 8. The abatement of the waters is at once a supernatural and a natural act. The fountains of the great deep and the windows of heaven close, because of God's actions, but He chose not to simply remove all the water from the earth, but to allow it to abate in its own time. It is likely that the abative phases was coming to an end, as the Ark touched down and came to rest "in the mountains of Ararat".

We can assume that this mass of water, and the events which had triggered and produced it, had great geologic effects. Most notable to us would be the onset of catastrophic plate tectonics, as the fractured crustal plates began to move around, relative to each other. We discussed this briefly in the previous section, and I covered it in more detail in my book *Don't Miss the Boat.*[2] The results of this rapid and catastrophic geologic activity is also reflected in Psalm 104:

> You covered it with the deep as with a garment; the waters stood above the mountains. At your rebuke they fled; at the sound of your thunder they took to flight. The mountains rose, the valleys sank down to the place that you appointed for them. You set a boundary that they may not pass, so that they might not again cover the earth. (Psalms 104:6-9)

2 Taylor, P.F. (2013), *Don't Miss the Boat*, (Green Forest, AR: Master Books).

The KJV has "[The waters] go up by the mountains; they go down by the valleys", but most study Bibles list the idea given in the ESV above as the norm. So it is the mountains and valleys that moved, not the waters. Indeed, the "valleys" probably refer to the deep parts of the sea – the ocean trenches. Therefore, these geologic movements of mountains and land being thrust up, and ocean trenches being deepened, explains where the water from the Flood went. The truth is that it did not go anywhere at all! All the water of the Flood is still with us, but post-Flood land is higher, and ocean basin lower, than those of the pre-Flood world. During this final dispersive phase of the Flood, it is likely that large scale scouring of the earth took place. It was at this point that so much of the Earth's topography and physical geology was formed. Perhaps spectacular locations like the Grand Canyon were formed at this time, though it is also possible (and, indeed, likely) that large lakes of water were retained at the end of the Flood, which then breached their dams, and the resulting secondary floodwaters carved out the Canyon. Either way, the best mechanisms for the formation of the Grand Canyon, and so many other features, are as direct or indirect results of the dispersive phase of the Flood.

The Ark Rested

It should be noted that Genesis 8:4 tells us that the Ark rested "upon the mountains of Ararat". The word for "mountains" is plural. It is not necessary to suppose that the Ark actually landed on Mount Ararat itself. Indeed, Mount Ararat is a dormant volcano, which was almost certainly formed in the years following the Flood, so may not have been there when the Flood ended. Ararat is described as a locality in the Bible. For example, in 2 Kings 19:37, we read "And as he was worshiping in the house of Nisroch his god, Adrammelech and Sharezer, his sons, struck him down with the sword and escaped into the land of Ararat". This region is in the east of the area known today as Turkey, though the region also extends into Armenia and Iran.

Given that there is some indication of the geography of the landing site in Scripture, one might suppose that it would be possible to find evidence of the Ark. A number of people claim to have found the Ark, and have produced books or documentaries on the subject. For my part, I am personally skeptical that the Ark will ever be found – though I would love to see it! I suspect that we cannot find pieces of the Ark, just as we cannot find pieces of the cross, on which Jesus was crucified. But, whether we find it or we don't, the proof that the Ark existed, and was used for the salvation of those eight people, is that it is recorded in Scripture. And that is all the evidence that we really need.

The Raven and the Dove

It is notable that the water dispersed slowly. Because we think that the floodwater was accommodated by the land rising and the ocean trenches lowering, we expect that this would not have been a gentle process, and this would explain why god caused the Ark to settle among high mountains, as the water levels swirled below. It was to be 40 days, before Noah felt confident enough to take any action. He opened the window at that point, and we have already discussed the fact that the Hebrew word, which is here translated as window, really means noon light, and refers to the opening on the roof of the Ark.

Many commentators have noted that the first bird released by Noah – a raven – is a scavenger. John Bunyan had this to say:

> But what did the raven then do? Why, certainly she made a banquet of the carcasses of the giants that were drowned by the flood; it fed upon the flesh of the men that had sinned against the Lord.
>
> The raven therefore was a type of those messengers that God sends out of his temple against Antichrist; that is, for "eating the flesh of kings, and the flesh of captains, and the flesh of mighty men, and the flesh of horses." He was, I say, a type of those professors that God saith he hath a great sacrifice to sacrifice unto, a sort of professors in his

> church; as the raven was one that had his being in the ark.[3]

While others have also commented on the raven being a scavenger, and, therefore, finding easy food in this new post-Flood world, Bunyan seems alone in pointing out a parallel with the angels coming out of the Temple in Revelation 15:5-6.

One notable issue, however, is the translation of the actions of the raven. Bunyan quotes from the 1611 edition of the King James Version, which seems to suggest that the raven just flew to and fro. The ESV reads in a similar manner.

> And he sent forth a raven, which went forth to and fro, until the waters were dried up from off the earth. (Genesis 8:7 KJV)

> ...and sent forth a raven. It went to and fro until the waters were dried up from the earth. (Genesis 8:7 ESV)

From this, Bunyan surmises that the raven did not return to the Ark. Calvin, on the other hand, suggests that the raven kept coming back to the Ark, and then flying off again.[4] Unlike Bunyan, Calvin suggests that Noah was looking for a bird not to come back, so that he would

3 Bunyan, J. (ed. Taylor, P.F. 2010), *Commentary on Genesis*, (Castle Rock, WA: J6D Publications), pp. 222-223.

4 Calvin, J. (Banner edn, 1965), *Commentary on Genesis*, (Edinburgh: Banner of Truth Trust), p. 279.

know the floodwaters had abated. Following Calvin's lead, the translators of the Geneva Bible rendered the verse thus:

> And sent forth a rauen, which went out going forth and returning, vntill the waters were dried vp vpon the earth. (Genesis 8:7 Geneva)

There would seem to be a strong argument for this latter view. In the Hebrew, we have a repeated word, *yâtsâ'* (ויצא), meaning "to go out". This sort of construction we have seen before, when God told Adam that the day he ate of the fruit of the tree of knowledge of good and evil, on that day he would "surely die" - *mûth mûth* or "die die". In Genesis 8:7, we have "go out go out", suggesting again that the action is a continuous action. This suggests that the raven repeatedly left the Ark, but kept on returning – *shûb* (ושוב). The repetition of the word can be seen in the Hebrew.

וישלח את־הערב ויצא יצוא ושוב עד־יבשת המים מעל הארץ

So, Noah releases a dove. The dove is not a scavenger, and therefore wants to find fresh food. On its first release, the dove found no resting place. On its second release, the dove returned with an olive leaf. Olives do not grow on the top of mountains, so this suggested that the new sprouting was at a lower level, suggesting that the Ark's inhabitants would soon be able to disembark. So, on the dove's third outing, it did not return, suggesting that there was now sufficient land, and this was the sign, for which Noah had been watching.

On the first day of the next year (40 days later), Noah could remove the cover, but he still had to wait another 57 days, to the 27th day of the second month, until God commanded Noah, and all the occupants of the Ark, to disembark. Presumably, these animals immediately began moving away from the Ark, though we read that Noah retained some of every clean animal, in order to make sacrifice.

Worship and Response

Noah's first act in this new world was to worship God. It is difficult to picture the scene of devastation that Noah and his family would have witnessed – though those who saw the immediate aftermath of disasters like the 1980 eruption of Mount St Helens might have some idea. None of us could realistically put ourselves totally into this family's shoes, however. Noah, his wife, his three sons, and their wives now looked upon a land that had been destroyed. Perhaps some new shoots were appearing. There must have been sufficient dry wood, for example, for Noah to light a fire on the altar that he made. But much of the land would have been bare.

Noah's act was not just one of worship. He was offering sacrifices. These sacrifices were therefore for his own sins, and the sins of his family, who now constituted the entire human race. This was an important cleansing act. It should also be noted that Noah was not doing this from his own resources. The resources had been given to him by God. It was God who determined that there should be more pairs of clean animals on the Ark, in order that some could be sacrificed. God Himself provides the sacrifice, and it is simply Noah's job to accept this, and worship Him. This is a theme, to which we shall need to return with Genesis 22.

Who was supposed to offer sacrifices to the LORD? Under the Mosaic Covenant, there were priests anointed and set aside for that purpose. But, although God was about to make a covenant with Noah and his family, He had not yet done so, so there was no provision for who could act on behalf of the people, to make propitiation. It was appropriate, on this occasion, for Noah to carry out the sacrifice, since he was the one, to whom God had given the instructions for the Ark, and the Ark was a type of Christ, covered, as we have seen, with the atonement of pitch. But Noah did not perform the sacrifice because he was better than the other members of his family. Perhaps there was an element of suggesting that he was the head of the household, and therefore head representative of the human race, at the moment. But someone had to do the sacrifice, because sins had to be atoned for in this New World. So Noah stepped up to the plate. Therefore, we read that "the LORD smelled the pleasing aroma". Our worship is a pleasing aroma – a “sweet savor”, as the KJV puts it – to God.

God’s words in Genesis 8:21 are a little hard to follow.

> I will never again curse the ground because of man, for the intention of man's heart is evil from his youth. Neither will I ever again strike down every living creature as I have done.

Before the Flood, God had said He would send the Flood *because* of the sinful nature of man’s heart. Perhaps we could now understand if God had said that He would not send another Flood *despite* the sinful nature of man’s heart. But what God actually said was that He would not send another flood *because* of the sinful nature of man’s heart. I would suggest that the reason for this is that, with the first Flood, God demonstrated His holiness, and His anger with sin, and He had demonstrated His mercy by saving Noah and his family. A second flood would be capricious of God. The Flood pointed the way towards the Messiah – Noah’s distant descendant. There could not be a second Ark, because that means of salvation was temporary. The next Ark of Salvation was to be a man – THE Man – Christ Jesus. The next destruction of the world was to be the final destruction, at the end of all things. It might seem repetitive for God to mention this again in Genesis 9, but in that next section, we will see how God phrased these issues into a covenant with Noah. For the moment, God is simply responding to the worship by, and atonement for, this tiny human population, to set His seal on what was to come.

The World, Climate, and Change

Calvin had little to say on the subject of Genesis 8:22, simply noting that God had restored the pre-Flood weather patterns. Luther has no comment on the verse at all. There is no reason why there should be much comment, as the issue, which I will now briefly address, had no currency at the time of the Reformation.

God prefaced his remarks in verse 22, with the qualification that the statements about climate would last only "while the earth remains". Bunyan points out that this reminds us that the Earth will not always remain.[5] There will come a time, when God will bring the world to a complete end. This will not be as a second Flood, or any similar temporary disaster. This will be by the winding up of history, the destruction of the present heavens and earth, and the creation of the New Heavens and New Earth.

The idea that the seasons will continue, much as they are, is not a popular one today. I could easily be led into a long bunny trail on the subject of climate change, which would not be appropriate for a

5 Bunyan, J. (ed. Taylor, P.F. 2010), *Commentary on Genesis*, (Castle Rock, WA: J6D Publications), p. 249.

commentary on Genesis. However, Genesis 8:22 is clearly on the subject of climate, so it is not in order to say nothing. My comments will therefore be brief, and I will refer readers to some other places for information.

No one really denies that Climate Change has occurred. There have indeed been periods in history when the Earth has been, on average, warmer or cooler than today. The phrase "on average" is a key phrase, because average conditions always allow for the fact that there will be areas which are not average. So, despite the modern, politically correct name, the argument is not over Climate Change. The argument is over Catastrophic Anthropogenic (caused by people) Global Warming, or CAGW for short. That such warming has occurred is an article of faith today, taught to our children in high school. One science textbook from England says this:

> Global temperatures changed very little, only about a quarter of one degree, over the thousand years to 1850. Since then temperatures have gone up by nearly 1°C, and by 2100 they are likely to be between 1.5°C and nearly 6°C hotter.

> Scientists are predicting devastating changes to weather patterns and raising sea levels. How can we change our lifestyles to reduce the level of greenhouse gases?[6]

Yet the science of Climate Change is a long way from being settled. There are a lot of modern climate scientists, who do not accept the concept of CAGW. We could discuss the science of carbon dioxide concentrations in the atmosphere at this point, but that would be to detract from the point of this commentary. If you want to research the science and the theology of CAGW further, then there are two websites, whose articles and publications you should read.

1. The Global Warming Policy Foundation. This is a British based political and scientific think tank, founded by Nigel Lawson, a former UK Chancellor of the Exchequer. www.thegwpf.org
2. The Cornwall Alliance for the Stewardship of Creation. This is an evangelical Christian organization in the US, comprised of theologians and scientists. www.cornwallalliance.org

The one Scriptural comment it is important to make is this. There may be changes in climate, and there may be extreme weather. But all weather is under God's control, even up to the end of this present age.

6 Honeysett, I. *Et al*, (2006), *OCR Additional Science for GCSE*, (Oxford: Heinemann), p. 211.

Therefore, this one verse of Scripture, Genesis 8:22, is the refutation of CAGW.

The Ice Age

The worldwide, global Flood recorded in Genesis would have resulted in some major climate changes, which could have lasted perhaps 300 years or so. Perhaps God's reminder that there would always be "cold and heat, summer and winter" was partly a reassurance to Noah, his family, and their immediate descendants, who would all be enduring the coming Ice Age. The Flood began with volcanic activity, causing the post-Flood oceans to be warmer than they are today. Also, the volcanic sols in the atmosphere would have partially blocked sunlight, causing the atmosphere to be colder than it is today. Warmer oceans means more evaporation, and cooler air means more precipitation of that evaporated water vapor, probably as snow in areas where not so much snow happens today. Therefore, there would, very quickly, have formed ice sheets over much of northern North America, northern Eurasia, as well as Greenland and Antarctica. The evidence of massive glaciation by ice sheets can be seen on the ground in all these places.

Evolutionary climatologists believe there were several ice ages. Some of these can simply be explained as cyclic advances and retreats of the ice sheets in the one Ice Age. Other alleged ice age formations can be explained as debris flows occurring under water. Creation researcher Michael Oard has written extensively on this post-Flood single Ice Age and its effects, and further information is best obtained from his work.[7]

Conclusion

In this chapter, we have seen how the Flood was always part of God's plan, not a sort of divine Plan B. We have seen how the Flood formed a definite pattern with a definite chronology, and we have looked at a simplified overview of how geology was caused by the actions of the Flood and its water. The nature of Noah's act of worship and propitiatory sacrifice was discussed. Finally, we saw how Genesis 8:22 refutes modern ideas of Catastrophic Anthropogenic Global Warming, and also explains the origin of the Ice Age as a post-Flood phenomenon, lasting a couple of centuries, not thousands of years.

7 Oard, M. (1990), *An Ice Age Caused by the Genesis Flood*, (ElCajon, CA: ICR).

Genesis 9 - God's Covenant with Humanity

(Genesis 9)

Commission and Command

God does not change His opinions, or change His methods of working or salvation. We do not believe that early revelation is abrogated by later revelation, as Muslims believe of the Quran. However, we do believe in progressive revelation. God did not tell everything at once to Adam and Eve. If He had, there would have been no need for all the Scriptural record that we have subsequently, in 66 books. So, in Genesis 9 we have reached a point where God is about to reveal more of His nature to His creatures – not abrogating what had been said to Adam and Eve, but revealing more of the truth. In passing, we should note that this process of Progressive Revelation is now complete – since the closing of the New Testament, god's revelation to us is complete, and He will not be adding a 67th book.

In the beginning, Adam had been given a Commission and a Command.

Adam's Commission was "Be fruitful and multiply and fill the earth and subdue it, and have dominion over the fish of the sea and over the birds of the heavens and over every living thing that moves on the earth." (Genesis 1:28). Noah's Commission was a restatement of this, but with some subtle changes.

> And God blessed Noah and his sons and said to them, "Be fruitful and multiply and fill the earth. The fear of you and the dread of you shall be upon every beast of the earth and upon every bird of the heavens, upon everything that creeps on the ground and all the fish of the sea. Into your hand they are delivered. (Genesis 9:1-2)

Noah was still to have dominion over all the creatures, because this was not abrogated. However, those creatures in this sin-affected, and flood-devastated world would now have a fear and dread of human beings. This fear and dread is the normal reaction of animals today. Wild animals will usually be affected by this fear and dread, by fleeing humans, or by attacking them. Partnership with animals, though desirable, is not the natural state. Domestication of animals takes time, and sometimes takes generations of breeding and care. I am well aware that everyone will have an anecdote, which "refutes" this point, about the wild animal that came out of the forest and ate food straight from your hand. But such events are the exception, and do not invalidate the general rule.

Adam was given a single commandment.

> You may surely eat of every tree of the garden, but of the tree of the knowledge of good and evil you shall not eat,

> for in the day that you eat of it you shall surely die. (Genesis 2:16-17)

After the Flood, the Garden of Eden no longer existed, and, in any case, no one had had access to the tree of the knowledge of good and evil since Adam and Eve were expelled from the Garden. So what standards were Noah and his family to follow? The standards were many-fold. Noah's family still retained that knowledge of good and evil that Adam and Eve had, and their consciences could tell them, as they do for us today, what is according to God's law and what is against it.

> For when Gentiles, who do not have the law, by nature do what the law requires, they are a law to themselves, even though they do not have the law. They show that the work of the law is written on their hearts, while their conscience also bears witness, and their conflicting thoughts accuse or even excuse them on that day when, according to my gospel, God judges the secrets of men by Christ Jesus. (Romans 2:14-16)

God's law is accompanied by a covenant, based on that law, and here in Genesis 9, we have the first explicit covenant that God made. This covenant, made with Noah, applies to the whole human race. Unlike the Mosaic Covenant, this covenant has not been updated or superseded. It still applies to the whole human race, even if a large proportion of humanity refuse to accept it. As this covenant was first spoken to Noah, we can refer to it as the Noahic Covenant, so long as it is understood that it was not a covenant just for Noah and his family, nor was it restricted in time to this early post-flood era.

There is considerable discussion over how many covenants there are in the Bible. Some say just one (only one way of salvation); some say two (Old and New); some say seven (seven dispensations); some say five. Elements of all these answers are true. I certainly think there has only ever been one method of salvation – repentance and faith in the Messiah. History itself is divided in two, by those who looked forward to the coming Messiah, and those of us who now look back to the messiah, who visited this planet, and who will come again. Those who see seven covenants do so, because they believe there was a covenant with Adam, though many of us would see this simply as a command. Therefore, in practice, I accept five covenants. These are Noahic, Abrahamic, Mosaic, Davidic, and Messianic. All five covenants are mentioned in the Old Testament, and also in the New. Four of the five covenants are still in operation – the sole exception being the Mosaic Covenant – the only one we can really call "Old", which has been fulfilled by the Messianic Covenant.[1]

1 For more information on the nature of these covenants, see Pawson, D. (2013), *By God I will: The Biblical Covenants*, (Ashford, UK: Anchor Recordings).

The Noahic Covenant itself concerns how humanity is to govern itself in a godly society.

> Every moving thing that lives shall be food for you. And as I gave you the green plants, I give you everything. But you shall not eat flesh with its life, that is, its blood. And for your lifeblood I will require a reckoning: from every beast I will require it and from man. From his fellow man I will require a reckoning for the life of man. "Whoever sheds the blood of man, by man shall his blood be shed, for God made man in his own image. And you, be fruitful and multiply, increase greatly on the earth and multiply in it." (Genesis 9:3-7)

The first element is that God lifts a restriction He made in Genesis 2, so that people can now eat animals, as well as plants. This is a permissive regulation, recognizing that the Fall of Adam has resulted in some animals eating other animals. It is also possible that mutations in people now made it much more difficult for them to ingest the right quality of protein to stay healthy. Animal protein contains all amino acids necessary for our bodies, whereas most plant protein does not, requiring balanced vegetarian meals to contain a balance of different food groups. We should note that this verse does not make it mandatory to eat meat. It is completely in order for people to choose to be vegetarian, or vegan. It should also be noted that it is no longer possible, in this changed post-Flood world, to mandate either vegetarianism or veganism, so it is also completely in order for people to eat meat. If a Christian chooses to be vegetarian, then God bless you, but please check that your vegetarianism is not based on a false, evolutionary view of the relationship between animals and humans.

This lifting of the restriction on meat eating also helped to emphasize the care, with which we need to consider the importance of blood. Leviticus 17:11 reminds us that "the life of the flesh is in the blood" - the word "life" being *nephesh* – a concept that we discussed at length earlier. Genesis 9:4 contains these elements; life, flesh, and blood. There are some, who consider that this means we should not consume products containing blood. Some suggest we should not eat red meat; others that red meat is okay, if the animal was killed according to kosher practices. Yet, we remember that Peter was told not to call anything unclean that God had declared clean (Acts 10). I suggest that the verse is simply referring to not eating animals alive. They should be killed humanely before eating. This is part of our responsibility towards, and stewardship of, creation. Some of you may think I am simply making an excuse, so that I can go on eating one of my favorite foods; black pudding. However, I think this is what the text is saying, and the purpose of the text is to enable us to show respect towards the shedding of blood, without which there is no remission of sins. Some might object further, and ask if I am forbidding the eating of certain shellfish, which are usually eaten alive. Not at all. I believe that the Mosaic restriction on eating shellfish is lifted, by the events of Acts 10, and, in any case, I have already made the distinction between nephesh animals and non-nephesh animals. Shellfish are definitely non-nephesh, so I see nothing unbiblical in eating oysters alive. My personal view is that I see good common sense reasons for not eating oysters alive! So, when you are suffering from food poisoning, just remember that you have done nothing unbiblical, though I doubt that thought will remove the symptoms!

God proceeds from referring to animal blood to referring to the death of humans, at the hand of fellow humans. We are now seeing a new biblical law, which covers the "Cain and Abel" situation. Once again, let us remind ourselves that God was not changing His mind – it is simply that revelation is progressive. The fact that revelation is progressive does not mean that earlier verses are abrogated. The Bible contains no "Satanic verses".

Here I will become a little more controversial. It seems clear to me that God is initiating the death penalty for murder. This deterrent was not in place, in the time of Cain. But now, in this new post-Flood world, God puts the death penalty in place for murder. We have already stated that the Noahic Covenant has not been superseded. It therefore follows that the appropriate penalty for murder, in human societies today, is still the death penalty. The Mosaic Law defined a large number of crimes or sins, for which the death penalty was appropriate. Theonomists will state that these, too, should still be in operation, while Dispensationalists usually tend to suggest that the penalties applied to breaking the Mosaic Laws do not apply, under the Messianic Covenant, even if the sin still holds. This is not the place to discuss the relative merits of theonomic and dispensatational theologies. I will simply point out that, even if you hold to the dispensational view of Mosaic Law, you have to note that the death penalty for murder is not part of the Mosaic Covenant. It predates the Mosaic Covenant. It is part of the Noahic Covenant, which is still in force, and applies, not just to God's people, but to the whole of humanity. Therefore, the death penalty for murder is the only correct justice for such cases, and societies that have abolished the death penalty for murder have done so in opposition to the teaching of Scripture.

One might wonder why there were no other laws stated at this point. I do not know why God did not give all His revelation to Noah – or why He didn't give a totality of revelation to Adam. But, in His Sovereignty, this is how He chose to operate. This overarching commitment to human society makes one requirement – that human beings respect blood, and apply the death penalty for murder.

The Sign and Extent of the Covenant

In verses 8 through 10, God shows that the covenant is made to Noah, his sons, and all their offspring, which means all humanity forever. The covenant also extends to the animals. The whole of life in this new world were placed under this covenant, which applied to all nephesh life.

God's promise under this covenant was that He would never again destroy all flesh, or flood the Earth in its entirety. This does not mean that our current world will last forever. One day God will bring it all to a close, and make a perfect New Heavens and New Earth. What it does is leave the worldwide Flood as a permanent type of the judgment to come, and the Ark as a permanent type of the salvation which is available. As the engine driving the onset of the Flood involved rain, it is appropriate that the sign of the Noahic Covenant is a rainbow. A rainbow is a universal symbol, available to be seen everywhere. A rainbow involves the refraction of light by raindrops, so it can occur when there is rain. Therefore, it reminds us that God's judgment will not come again by the same method, but it also reminds us that there will indeed be a judgment, in God's timing.

There are some who suggest that there would have been no rain before the Flood, and therefore there could be no rainbow before the Flood. We have already discussed that we do not know if there was no rain before the Flood – only that there was no rain during the creation week. It is possible, therefore, that God was simply using a phenomenon that He had already made, as the sign of this new covenant. Calvin says:

> From these words certain eminent theologians have been induced to deny, that there was any rainbow before the deluge: which is frivolous. For the words of Moses do not signify, that a bow was then formed which did not previously exist; but that a mark was engraven upon it, which should give a sign of the divine favor towards men.[2]

The sign was for our benefit, but the keeping of the remembrance was for God alone. It is He who remembers His covenant, when He sees the bow in the clouds.

In a possible allusion to the Flood, Habakkuk refers to God unsheathing His bow (Habakkuk 3:9). At the end of the Flood, God re-sheathed His bow, and the striving against humanity from before the Flood (Genesis 6:3, see KJV) had now ceased, to be replaced with judgment, covenant, and salvation. Hamilton says "A common motif in ancient Near Eastern iconography is that of a bow-wielding deity.... [The bow's] placement in the clouds points to the cessation of God's hostilities against mankind."[3]

2 Calvin, J. (Banner edn, 1965), *Commentary on Genesis*, (Edinburgh: Banner of Truth Trust), p. 299.

3 Hamilton, V.P. (1990), *The Book of Genesis, chapters 1-17*, (Grand Rapids, MI: Eerdmans), p.314.

Not a Perfect New World

It is very easy to misunderstand the purpose that God had for the Flood, even among those of us who acknowledge that it was a real, historical event. We addressed earlier the fact that the Flood was planned by God. It was not a reaction to unexpectedly sinful events. It was certainly divine judgment on sinful people, but it was not unexpected. The Flood was not a failed attempt by God to reset the world to what He had in the Garden of Eden. When we read "The LORD saw that the wickedness of man was great in the earth, and that every intention of the thoughts of his heart was only evil continually" (Genesis 6:5), God is not saying that man shall now be perfect after the Flood. And so, with the surface of the Earth barely dry, we see problems begin to arise.

I say that the surface of the Earth was barely dry, as a sort of hyperbole. In fact, the events of the second half of Genesis 9 may have been a while later, because there had to be time for Noah to plant his vineyard, and then for him to make wine.

Verses 18 and 19 tell us that the whole population of the world today is descended from Noah's three sons, Shem, Ham, and Japheth. The whole of Genesis 10 will be an expansion of that issue, and there are important descendants of each of the three brothers to note. So, it seems a little odd that the only grandson of Noah mentioned in these verses is Ham's son Canaan. Indeed, Canaan is mentioned more than once. There is clearly something critically important to the emphasis of this name right here. Is it possible that Canaan was already born, and even grown up, by the time of the events of Genesis 9:18-29? It is impossible to tell, though I suspect it may well be the case. Therefore, the incident with the vines and the wine may have been several years after the landing of the Ark.

The raw facts are these. Noah plants a vineyard. Noah makes wine. Noah gets drunk, and lies naked in his tent. Ham sees Noah's nakedness and tells his brothers, who cover him, without looking at him. So far, so easy to understand. How far was Noah to blame for his part in this account? Some commentators suggest that Noah was naïve, and was not aware of how strong the wine would be. Others suggest that this was a sinful act. The commentators who make most sense to me accept both points of view. It is in order to accept Noah's naïveté, yet still hold him responsible. The Scripture holds that Noah was "righteous" and "blameless". However, neither of these terms suggests sinless perfection, which is not possible in this world. Noah had the righteousness obtained by faith, and his actions were normally exemplary. Yet, here in Genesis 9, I believe we see an imperfection in Noah, and that imperfection, this sin of drunkenness, remains forever associated with Noah. Calvin says "Noah, by the judgment of God, has been set forth as a spectacle to be a warning to others, that they should not become intoxicated by excessive drinking."[4] Note that his sin was getting drunk, not fermenting wine. The Bible commends wine in many places, and the fermentation of juices was an important way of preserving them.

Noah is not responsible, however, for the incident being made worse by his son, Ham. It would appear that Ham dealt disrespectfully with his father. Noticing his father's nakedness, he could then have looked aside, and placed the covering over him himself. No one else needed to know. Instead, Ham looks on his father, then goes to tell his brothers. Shem and Japheth, by contrast, dealt respectfully with their father, covering him, without dwelling on his nakedness.

It is when Noah wakes up that the account takes an unusual turn. We could imagine Noah waking, repenting, finding out what had happened, and then dealing with Ham. What is odd about the story is that instead of a rebuke, Noah hands out a curse, and instead of cursing Ham, he curses Ham's son Canaan. How do we make sense of this?

Sarfati suggests that Noah was speaking prophetically. The subsequent history of the Canaanites shows them to have been a particularly degraded people. It was appropriate that their land was to be removed from them in later generations, and given to God's people, the Israelites. The Canaanites, for example, worshiped Molech

4 *ob cit*, p. 301.

– and part of their worship was to burn their own children as sacrifices to this false god. (Leviticus 18:21) Yet we note that even some of God's people followed the same practice, copying the Canaanites (Jeremiah 7:31), while God was able to provide mercy to Canaanites, who trusted in Him, such as Rahab in Jericho (Hebrews 11:31) and the Canaanite woman with the demon-possessed daughter (Matthew 15:22). John Bunyan also holds that Noah's curse is prophetic.

> By these words one would think that Canaan, the grand-child of Noah, was the first that discovered his nakedness; but of this I am uncertain: I rather think that Noah, in a spirit of prophecy, determined the destruction of Ham's posterity, from the prodigiousness of his wicked action, and of his name, which signifieth indignation, or heat; for names of old were ofttimes given according to the nature and destiny of the persons concerned. "Is not he rightly called Jacob?" (Gen 27:36). And again, "As his name is, so is he" (1 Sam 25:25). Besides, by this act did Ham declare himself void of the grace of God; for he that rejoiceth in iniquity, or that maketh a mock, as being secretly pleased with or at the infirmities of the godly, he is declared already, by the Spirit of God, to be nothing (1 Cor 13).[5]

5 Bunyan, J. (ed. Taylor, P.F. 2010), *Commentary on Genesis*, (Castle Rock, WA: J6D Publications), p. 279.

The fact that not all of Ham's descendants were cursed is certainly a mercy from God. Again, wee should emphasize that even those who were cursed (the Canaanites) had as much opportunity of salvation as everyone else – God had His elect among this cursed people, at least one of whom (Rahab) had the honor of being one of Jesus' direct ancestors.

Canaan was described as a "servant of servants". We have already noted how this repetition of words is a method of emphasis, or underlining the text. In their cursed state, they would eventually be ejected from the Promised Land – yet, not completely, because of the disobedience of the Israelites themselves, and, of course, because of God's mercy. However, some have suggested that the phrase justifies the enslavement of black African people, who, it is stated, are descendants of Ham, and therefore under the Hamitic curse. We should make a number of points on this issue, even though there are far fewer people who hold to the view than there used to be. Nonetheless, there the view holds a residual sway among "British Israelites" and followers of the Identity movements in the US South.

Our first point should be to note that there never was a Hamitic curse. Though Ham had sinned, the curse was specifically placed prophetically on his son Canaan. Second, black Africans, though almost certainly descended from Ham, are not descended from Canaan. They are probably descended from Canaan's brother Cush. So there is no curse on black African people, any more than any other people group – because, as we have repeated several times, God has the Sovereignty even to undo His own curse, and redeem His people from among the cursed Canaanites. Third, Canaanites were *described* as "servant of servants". This was a description of prophetic fact. It was not a command for Japhethites (some of whom would become white Europeans) that it was their duty to enslave Canaanites. In fact, the Bible nowhere suggests that such an industry in human trafficking should be started. While it gives rules for slaves who become Christians, on how they are to behave, it does not commend the state, in which these slaves find themselves. Pioneering evangelicals in the 18th and 19th centuries recognized the unbiblical nature of slavery, and were instrumental in having the practice abolished; of particular note, in this context, was the British Christian politician and statesman, William Wilberforce, who worked tirelessly, through much of his life, to have the slave trade abolished throughout the British Empire.[6]

The enslavement of black African people by white European people was a particularly pernicious and historically significant form of slavery. It was not, however, unique. Indeed, the word *slavery* is derived from the word Slav, indicating that there were times when

6 Taylor, P.F. (2006), *William Wilberforce: A Leader for Biblical Equality*, < https://answersingenesis.org/ministry-news/ministry/william-wilberforce/ >, accessed 8/15/2019.

white Europeans (such as Slavs) were forcibly enslaved also. Of course, I do not include that point as any sort of justification of the evil practice.

One further error that people make in their racist association of black African people with slavery is that there are some who suggest that blackness is the "mark of Cain", and that, therefore, black people must in some way be descended from Cain – a view often referred to as *Serpent Seed theory*. Such people are even more muddled in their thinking than those who hold to a Hamitic Curse. The Serpent Seed theory holds that Adam was not Cain's father – that this was Satan, in the form of the serpent. Yet Scripture makes fully clear that Cain was Adam's son, and, in any case, all Cainites were destroyed during the Flood.[7]

As a last comment, to the account of the Flood, we are reminded of its historicity, by these two short and succinct verses:

> After the flood Noah lived 350 years. All the days of Noah were 950 years, and he died. (Genesis 9:28-29)

7 I have toyed with the idea, fictionally, that Naamah – a descendant of Cain – might have been Ham's wife. As I do not accept that Ham was cursed, this would not have exacerbated the Canaanitic curse, nor would it have implied that Canaan was the "seed of the serpent", because, with the sole exception of the Messiah as prophesied in Genesis 3:15, all people are reckoned as the seed of the **fathers**, not their mothers. And, in any case, this was just fiction, and does not constitute any sort of factual basis for anything. The fictional story of Naamah is found in Taylor, P.F. (2013), *Don't Miss the Boat*, (Green Forest, AR: Master Books), pp. 171-174.

Summary

In this section, we have contrasted God’s commission and command to Adam, with His commission and covenant with Noah. Additionally, we looked at how the new world began imperfectly, and have scotched some of the ugliest rumors, abounding from faulty exegesis of this chapter.

Rounding Up Volume 1

This is obviously not really the end of the commentary. It is simply a fairly arbitrary place to finish. But there is some method to choosing the end of Genesis 9 as the end of this first volume.

Genesis 1 began with the creation of the world. The rest of this commentary deals with what we might call the *Old World* – that is to say, the world that God destroyed with the Flood. The aftermath of the Flood was very much a new world. So, Genesis 9 just gives us a glimpse of the beginning of the colonization of this new world.

Chapter 10 will take us somewhere altogether new. Genesis 10 is often named the *Table of the Nations*, and is a record of the migration of people post-Babel. Clearly, this is the start of a very new era. So it makes sense to place that information at the beginning of Volume II.

As I stated in the Preface, I do not know yet, as I write, how many volumes there will be in this commentary – two o three. At the time of writing this end piece, I have already written comment up to the end of Genesis 17.

Where Do We Go from Here?

Indexing a work like this will be a major undertaking. So it is my plan to proceed as follows.

- Volume 1 is being released *as is*, without indexing. Volume II, and possibly a Volume III, will be released in a similar manner.
- At that point, I will undertake to combine all the volumes, and provide subject, Scripture, and illustration indexing.
- Any new material required at that point will be inserted ninto the text, and noted in Appendices. There may also be appendices with other information in.

Please continue to pray for this major undertaking. This is a big work, but not a technical one. It is my objective that the commentary should be reasonably easy to understand. I hope I have achieved that end.

May God bless you, and thank you for reading this work.

Just Six Days Publications

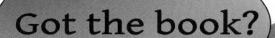

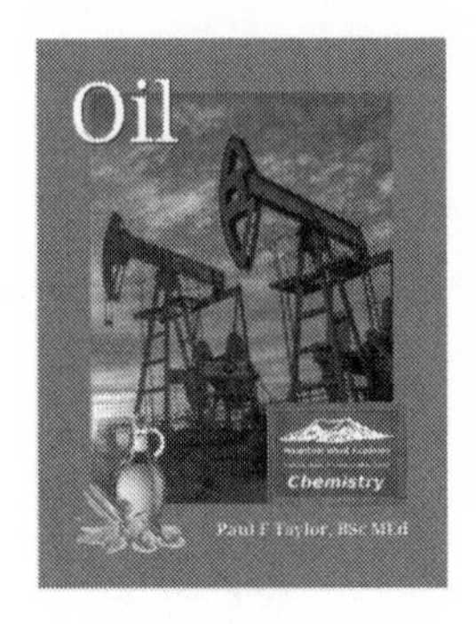

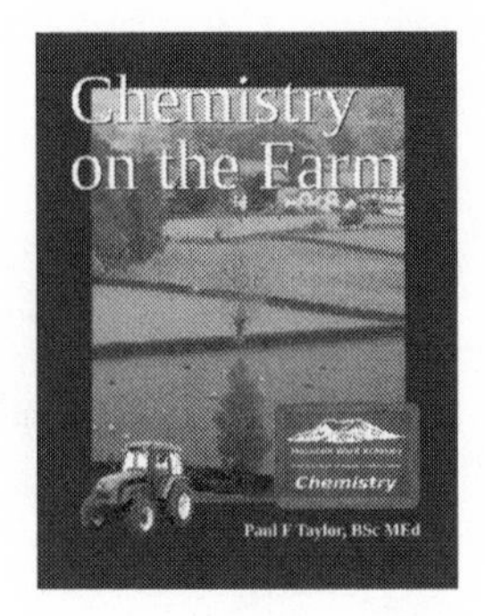

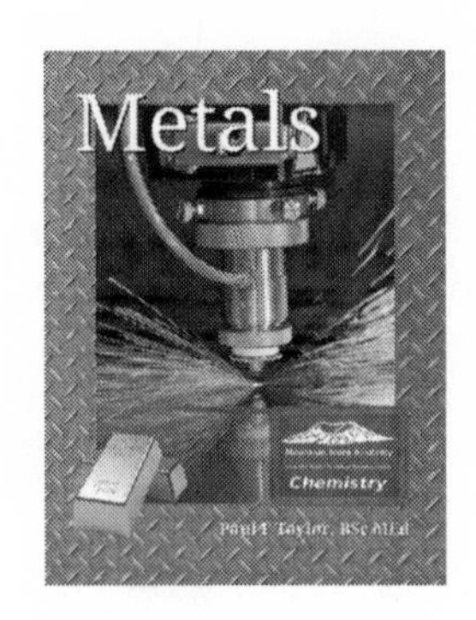

Mountain Word Science is an exciting new science curriculum for older teenagers, based on a classical model. The course is designed to train young people to think scientifically, not just amass a lot of scientific “facts”.

Mountain Word Academy
from the Mount St Helens Creation Center
Physics

Available from:

justsixdays.com

mshcreationcenter.org

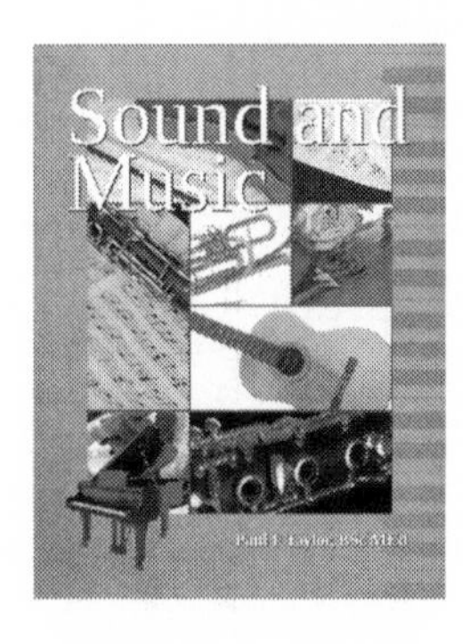

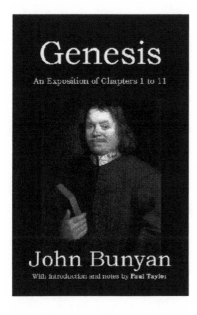

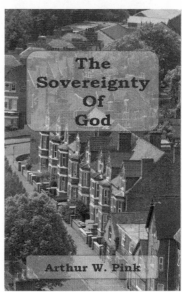

Made in the USA
Monee, IL
04 February 2020

21310027R00247